T0340363

Airport Finance and Investment in the Global Economy

While there are a multitude of publications on corporate finance and financial management, only a few address the complexity of air transport industry finance and scant attention has been given to airport financial management. This book deals exclusively with airport issues to rectify this. It does this with an analysis of the theoretical concepts relevant to the subject area combined with a detailed investigation of current practice within the industry.

Airport Finance and Investment in the Global Economy bridges the gap between much academic research on airports published in recent years – lacking much managerial relevance – and real-world airport financial management. This is achieved by featuring expert analysis of contemporary issues specific to airport finance and funding strategies, illustrated by worked examples from a wide range of different countries to enhance understanding and create a global perspective.

The book is designed to appeal to both practitioners and academics. Airport-specific topics include: performance measurement and benchmarking, valuation, tools for financial control and management, alternatives of financing, privatisation, competition and implications of economic regulation.

Anne Graham is Reader in Air Transport and Tourism at the University of Westminster. Her research interests include airport management, economics and regulation, and the relationship between the tourism and aviation industries. Her recent books include *Managing Airports* (4th edition, 2014), *Aviation Economics* (ed. with Peter Morrell, 2015), *Airport Marketing* (with Nigel Halpern, 2013) and *Aviation and Tourism* (ed. with Andreas Papatheodorou and Peter Forsyth, 2008). Between 2013 and 2015 she was Editor-in-Chief of the *Journal of Air Transport Management*.

Peter Morrell joined Cranfield's Department of Air Transport in 1991 where, until his recent retirement, he held a chair in air transport economics and finance. He has been involved in airport projects around the world, including in Argentina, Mongolia, Hannover, Berlin, Luton and Barcelona. He also directed a number of major studies for the European Commission. His books include *Aviation Economics* (ed. with Anne Graham, 2015), *Airline Finance* (4th edition, 2014) and *Moving Boxes by Air* (2011). He has continuing links with Cranfield as a visiting professor and serves on the editorial boards of the *Journal of Air Transport Management* and *Tourism Economics*.

Airport Finance and Investment in the Global Economy

Anne Graham and
Peter Morrell

LONDON AND NEW YORK

First published 2017
by Routledge

2 Park Square, Milton Park, Abingdon, Oxfordshire OX14 4RN
52 Vanderbilt Avenue, New York, NY 10017

Routledge is an imprint of the Taylor & Francis Group, an informa business

First issued in paperback 2020

British Library Cataloguing in Publication Data
A catalogue record for this book is available from the British Library

Library of Congress Cataloging in Publication Data
Names: Graham, Anne, 1958- author. | Morrell, Peter S., 1946-
Title: Airport finance and investment in the global economy/Anne Graham and Peter Morrell.
Description: Abingdon, Oxon; New York, NY: Routledge, 2017. | Includes bibliographical references.
Identifiers: LCCN 2016016284 | ISBN 9781472440204 (hardback) | ISBN 9781315566498 (ebook)
Subjects: LCSH: Airports—Finance. | Airlines—Finance.
Classification: LCC HE9797.4.F5 G73 2017 | DDC 387.7/36—dc23
LC record available at https://lccn.loc.gov/2016016284

ISBN: 978-1-4724-4020-4 (hbk)
ISBN: 978-0-367-51215-6 (pbk)

Typeset in Bembo
by Keystroke, Neville Lodge, Tettenhall, Wolverhampton

Contents

Figures

Tables

Preface

The purpose of the book is to provide a broad understanding of all areas of airport finance. The aim is to satisfy a growing number of those involved in the airport business whether as airline users, airport managers, together with other on-airport suppliers, financiers, investors or students. To do this, it has been necessary to sacrifice some detail, for example in terms of accounting and economic concepts, but references will be given to allow readers to explore more complex topics further. A wealth of additional material is also available in general textbooks on economics and finance. These provide a basic understanding of areas such as risk management, corporate finance and competition theory.

It is hoped that each area of airport finance and financial management will be discussed in sufficient depth to satisfy both those in the industry without any financial or economic background, and newcomers to the industry, perhaps with some knowledge of finance. No prior knowledge is required of accounting, economics or statistics to gain considerable benefit from the book. In a few cases, notably in the chapters on investment appraisal and the determination of the weighted average cost of capital, mathematical formulae have been used, but in such cases they are based on relatively simple compound interest concepts.

The opening chapter describes the financial trends for airports as a whole, with developments for the major regions and airports of varying sizes contrasted. The second chapter examines airport costs and revenues, a key to many of the discussions in later chapters. This is followed by an analysis of an airport's financial statements, focusing on the major items in each statement and relating these to those of London Heathrow Airport Ltd. These also provide the inputs to the main financial ratios that are widely used by airports themselves, investment analysts, commercial banks (as targets in loan and bond covenants) and investors in support of their decisions to buy or sell airport assets.

Next, Chapter 5 considers airport benchmarking which offers a number of ways of evaluating airport efficiency and productivity, developing and comparing the data found in Chapter 2, and complementing the more financially oriented ratios presented in Chapter 3. Various ways of valuing airports as a whole or in parts are the subject of Chapter 6, using a number of ratios that the reader will be familiar with from Chapter 3. This fits in with the later chapter on airport privatisation, where the government owner of one or more airport(s) will need a valuation as will a number of potential buyers. To do so they will choose one or more of the techniques developed in this chapter.

The growing importance of first financing and investing in airports is recognised in Chapter 7 which looks at short- and long-term finance, equity and other securities. Privatisation is described in Chapter 8, with governments worldwide seeking private sector finance and management for their airports as they prioritise areas that must remain in the public sector such as health, defence and social services. The move to the private sector has led to more emphasis on examining competition in the industry and how this may have to be remedied through economic regulation, and these two topics are addressed in the final two chapters of the book.

It would be impossible to mention all those who have contributed, knowingly or otherwise, to the book. Over the past years, MSc students of air transport management at both the University of Westminster and Cranfield University have made numerous valuable comments, pointed out errors, and generally provided the motivation for the development of much of the material presented here. Over the same period, air transport industry executives attending short courses at Westminster and Cranfield have done the same, often from a more industry-centric perspective. Special thanks must also be extended to senior airport industry experts who have given up their precious time over the past years to contribute to those courses (and our understanding of the industry), in particular Andrew Lobbenberg, a former colleague at Cranfield University now with HSBC, and Rafael Echervarne, former Director of Economics at ACI and now Chief Executive at Montego Bay airport.

We are also grateful to all our former colleagues at our respective universities for their help in discussing both industry trends and the more specific concepts included in this book. A very special thanks must go to Hans-Arthur Vogel who provided some of the original impetus to write this book and was initially a joint author, and Guy Loft at Routledge for his never-ending support and encouragement. Last but not least, we would like to thank Ian and Ruth for their patience and understanding with putting up with the disruption to their lives while we have been writing this book.

1 Introduction

1.1 Introduction

This chapter provides an introduction to this book and the subject of airport finance. It begins by considering the broader environment within which airports operate, focusing very much on political, economic and technological developments. This is followed by an overview of airport traffic volumes and patterns around the world and the prospects for the future. Drawing on these general industry trends, an overview of airport investment, airport financial characteristics and airport business models is then provided in the next three sections. Much of this discussion is used as a basis for setting the scene for the other chapters which explore various aspects of airport finance in greater detail.

1.2 The airport operating environment

The airport industry is a very important economic activity which typically operates 24 hours a day, 365 days a year. In 2014, 6.7 billion passengers travelled through world airports and 102 million tonnes of cargo were handled. In total there were 84.4 million aircraft movements (Airports Council International (ACI), 2015a). Moreover it is estimated that globally 470,000 people work for airport operators with a further 4.6 million working in retail, car hire, government agencies, freight forwarders and catering jobs at airports (Air Transport Action Group (ATAG), 2014). This does not include the large number of airline and ground handling jobs at airports.

Airports have often evolved over many years from their original air force and defence role to their current commercial usage. Although nowadays airport operators are responsible for a common set of activities (some of which may be outsourced) to satisfy the needs of airlines, passengers and cargo shippers, the external environment in which airports function can have a significant impact on the nature of individual operations, and the financial characteristics of airports. In particular, any consideration of airport finance needs to be undertaken against a backdrop of key developments related to political, economic, environmental and technological developments.

One of the most significant of these is the deregulation of air services (International Transport Forum (ITF), 2015). Beginning in the US with the domestic market in 1978 and then a number of international US routes, deregulation has now spread to many parts of the world. Europe has a single aviation market, and likewise a single aviation area is being established with the ten Association of Southeast Asian Nations (ASEAN) countries (although not at so liberal a level). A number of other domestic markets, including the large ones of Canada, India, Brazil, Australia and Malaysia, have been deregulated. Moreover, numerous Open Skies agreements have been signed, most commonly with the US or a European country (including the 2008 US–EU agreement) but also in other areas such as Asia, the Middle East and South America. More deregulation will undoubtedly follow but the resulting high growth rates experienced by some airlines, especially the Gulf carriers, have ignited debates as to whether totally free markets are always best and the playing fields are necessarily level (De Wit, 2013).

A major consequence of deregulation has meant that airlines are now freer to choose where they fly to and from, and many now set fares, frequencies, capacities and routes solely according to commercial considerations. This has encouraged growth and opened up many markets to much greater competition (Doganis, 2010). This in turn has had a very significant impact on the air services at each individual airport, increasing the amount of competition between airports and giving rise to new opportunities for airports to market themselves to airlines. Another significant development due to deregulation has been the emergence of new or modified airline business models, most notably the low-cost carriers (LCCs), which have also brought new challenges for airports and given them a strong reason to deviate from past practice. Therefore such changes to the airline industry have had a significant impact on the financial situation of airports, providing them with a greater incentive to be more innovative and proactive with their airline customers.

In addition there have been some major changes in the ownership of the airline industry (Morrell, 2007). Historically almost all the world's major airlines were state-owned, primarily for reasons of prestige, defence and/or to fulfil wider objectives such as economic development and the growth of tourism. However, attitudes have changed considerably in many countries and many formerly state-owned airlines have been totally or partially privatised. This in turn has had a major impact on the airport–airline relationship, particularly in the area of pricing or so-called aeronautical charging.

Concurrently with this evolution of the airline industry, the way in which airports are owned and operated has changed. In many countries, the sector has moved from an industry characterised by public sector ownership and national requirements, into a new era of airport management where larger airports have become major international companies that tend to be owned and operated by the private sector. The first major airport privatisation of the British Airports Authority (BAA) in the UK took place in 1987 and the trend for airport privatisation has continued since then. This has had many consequences for airport finances, with private airports abiding by commercial and fiscal disciplines just like any other business. Even when airports have not been privatised, more and more are being corporatised, and/or viewed as dynamic commercially oriented businesses with all the opportunities and challenges that this new paradigm brings. New sources of funding are available and far greater consideration is being given to the non-aeronautical aspects of airports, such as the generation of revenues from shops, food and beverage and other commercial facilities. Moreover, one of the most visible consequences of privatisation has been the emergence of international airport companies. These include the traditional operators at airports such as Frankfurt, Zurich and Singapore, and newer airport companies or subsidiaries, such as Vinci Airports and TAV Airports. Without privatisation (which is discussed in further detail in Chapter 8), this internationalisation of the airport industry could not have happened.

In addition to these important developments related to aviation regulation and ownership, there are other key factors which are having a major impact on the financial situation of modern-day airports. One such influence concerns the environment where there are pressures on the whole of the aviation industry to reduce its harmful noise and emission effects, and generally to become more sustainable in areas such as energy/water use and recycling. This can have various financial implications, for example on the airport operator's charging policy where it may choose to differentiate between airlines according to the environmental performance of their aircraft. Airport costs may also be reduced with the pressure to make more efficient use of resources. However, there may also be negative financial impacts due to mitigation measures that an airport has to introduce to reduce the harmful effects of its operations or due to environmental restrictions being placed on the airport. This may include night closures or a limitation on night flights, which could affect the airport's attractiveness in the eyes of its airline customers and also limit its ability to maximise its use of its assets.

Undoubtedly in some parts of the world, the most challenging result of such environmental concerns is that it is becoming progressively more difficult to expand airport operations or build new airports. This is particularly the case in a number of European countries and North America, but also in other countries such as Japan and Australia. As a result there are various airports that remain congested and apparently unable to grow because of the strong opposition from local communities and other environmental groups who fiercely oppose airport expansion. However in other regions, for example, the Middle East and China, the environmental impacts of airport expansion tend to play a less dominant role in decisions concerning capacity expansion.

Another high-profile issue is security. Since 9/11 and more recent terrorist threats and events, airports have become subject to more rigid security procedures. This includes restrictions on liquids, aerosols and gels (LAGs), the inspection of shoes and the use of full body scans. This has been costly for airport operators, particularly if they have the sole responsibility for providing security services themselves. Indeed in Europe security costs have risen from less than 8 per cent of operating costs before 9/11 to over double this now (ACI-Europe, 2013). These developments have also negatively affected the passengers' airport experience, and their ability and preference to fully take advantage of the commercial facilities at the airport, especially if the security measures have restricted their shopping time or the products which they are allowed to purchase.

A major influence on the financial performance of many companies is associated with technological developments and the airport industry is no different here. Typically this will require short-term investment but, if successful, can often result in long-term cost reductions. In addition, there can be considerable revenue and marketing implications associated with various types of technology, ranging from the use of social media to the analysis of Big Data. There are many areas where the airport industry has benefited from increased technology, both in the airfield and in the terminal, which are too numerous to discuss in much detail. These can range from accommodating new initiatives such as airport-collaborative decision making (A-CDM) which aims to improve airport operations and streamline traffic flows through improved technology that allows the sharing of information in real time, or the tracking of vehicles and other movable assets using GPS-based maps, to terminal information technology (IT) developments such as self-service check-in and automated e-gates for checkpoints and boarding gates, sensor technologies using beacons, and real-time 'day of travel' information services sent directly to passenger apps. Spending on IT alone in 2014 was estimated to account for around US$8 billion, representing close to 6 per cent of total revenues (SITA, 2015). Some of these developments in turn may influence the airport's non-aeronautical revenues if they affect the dwell time of passengers at airports. Technological enhancements in other aviation sectors will also be influential. For example, new aircraft technology may be costly for airports to handle, with the most notable case being the Airbus A380 aircraft which has required changes to airport infrastructure (such as reinforcing airfield pavements, extending runway and taxiway widths, and enlarging gaterooms and airbridges) and modifications to other processes (such as check-in, immigration, customs, security and baggage handling) to cope with the larger passenger volumes.

Finally it is noteworthy to mention that the travelling public is becoming more experienced and less loyal and are generally placing greater demands on airports to deliver a quality product or a 'good passenger experience'. The more stringent security controls discussed previously may adversely affect the overall passenger experience, whereas technology innovations may have either a positive or negative impact depending on the effectiveness of the technology and the passenger's attitude towards the new technology. Whilst it can be argued that the passenger experience will have limited actual influence on their choice of airport (this being influenced primarily by airline and locational factors), an unsatisfied passenger may well not spend so much on the airport's commercial facilities, which may have a significant impact on its non-aeronautical revenues. Thus a constant challenge for modern airports is handling the trade-off between lower airport costs that will filter through to lower aeronautical charges, and maximising non-aeronautical revenues and satisfying customers.

1.3 Airport traffic

Having identified some of the key influences of the airport's external operating environment, the focus now shifts to considering traffic trends at airports. Passenger traffic has grown substantially in the last few decades, reflecting trends within the overall air transport industry. Throughout the history of the industry, growth has always been dampened by economic downturns and occasional external 'shocks', but since the turn of the century there has been a more volatile situation as a result of an increased occurrence of natural disasters, socio-political upheaval and other shock events such as 9/11, SARS, swine flu, the Eyjafjallajökull ash cloud, the Japanese earthquake, the Arab Spring uprisings and the Ebola outbreak. Moreover, the recent global economic recession had a very major impact on traffic levels in 2008 and 2009, as have government austerity measures which have followed. Fuel prices have also been more volatile.

In spite of this more uncertain environment, passenger numbers grew on average by more than 4.2 per cent per year during the last ten years with the highest growth rates being experienced in the Middle East and Asia. Cargo traffic has been more stagnant in recent years but grew in 2014. Aircraft movements have recently grown very little, reflecting trends towards the curbing of airline capacity and consolidated operations to improve airline financial performance coupled with airport capacity constraints. As a result the average passengers per movement or aircraft size has been increasing (Figures 1.1 and 1.2).

Traditionally the two most important regions for airport traffic were North America and Europe, but slower economic growth and more mature demand mean that emerging economies have been taking an increasingly large share of the traffic. For example the Asia-Pacific passenger market share now represents 34 per cent of the total (Figure 1.3). This compares to only 21 per cent in 2004. The market share for cargo is even greater for this region (Figure 1.4). The latest published ACI forecasts show that passenger numbers are expected to increase by 4.1 per cent per annum to exceed 12 billion by 2031, whilst cargo operations are expected to grow by 4.5 per cent and reach around 225 million tonnes (Airport World, 2012). The slightly more up-to-date Boeing and IATA forecasts have similar, although marginally less optimistic, annual passenger growth rates to 2034 of 4 per cent and 3.8 per cent, respectively (Boeing, 2015; IATA, 2015a). The ACI forecasts show that by 2031 around three-quarters of the passengers will be

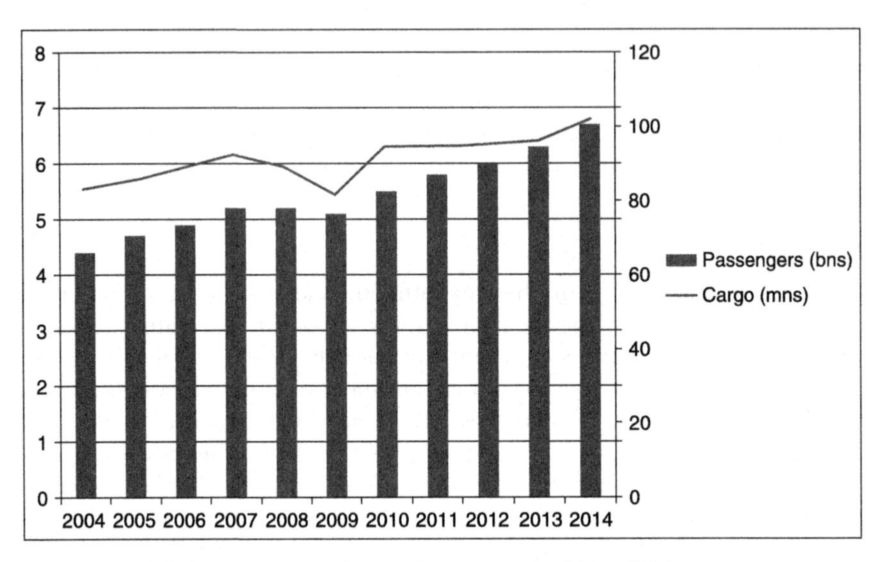

Figure 1.1 Global passenger numbers and cargo tonnes 2004–2014

Source: ACI (2015a).

Note: Left hand axis relates to passengers, right hand axis relates to cargo.

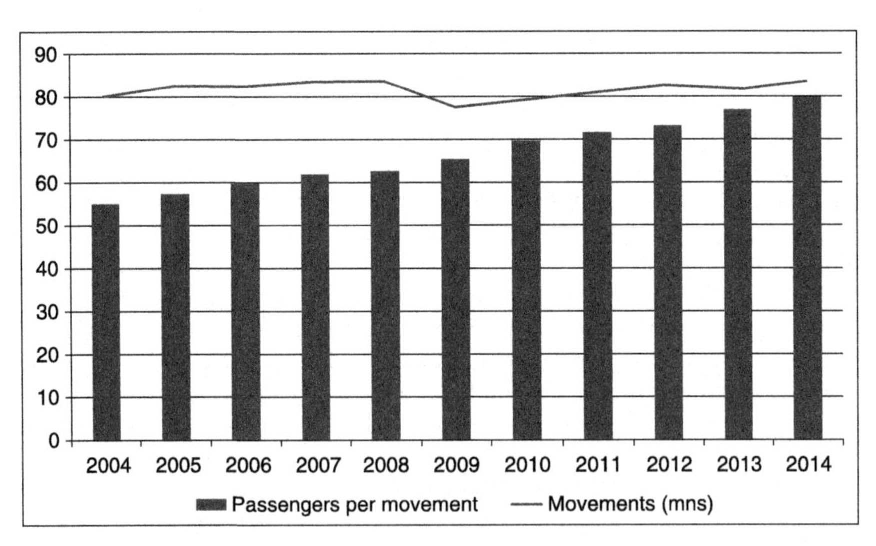

Figure 1.2 Global aircraft movements and average aircraft size 2004–2014

Source: ACI (2015a).

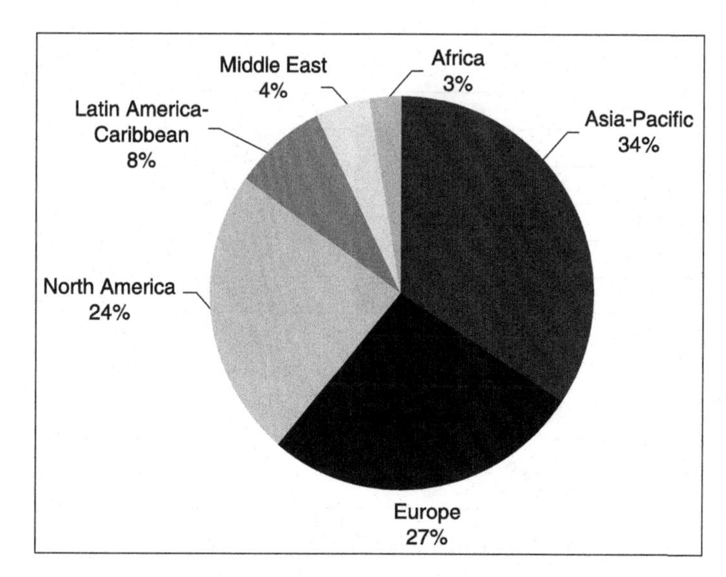

Figure 1.3 Passenger numbers at world airports 2014

Source: ACI (2015a).

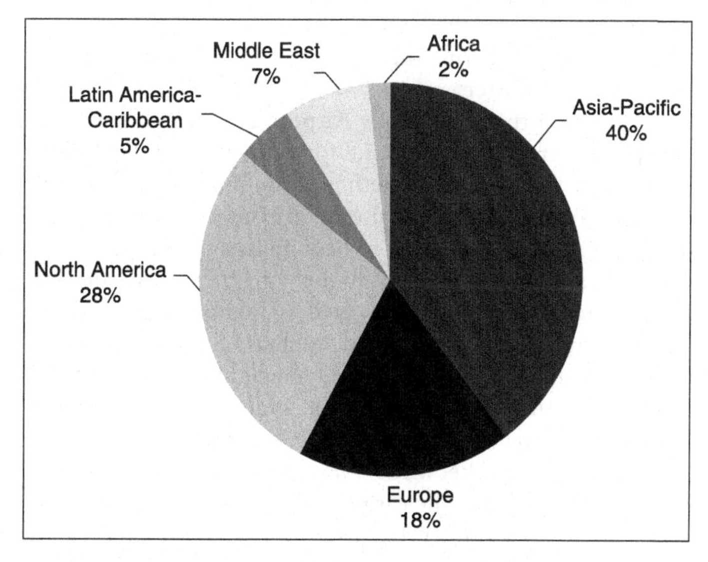

Figure 1.4 Cargo tonnes at world airports 2014

Source: ACI (2015a).

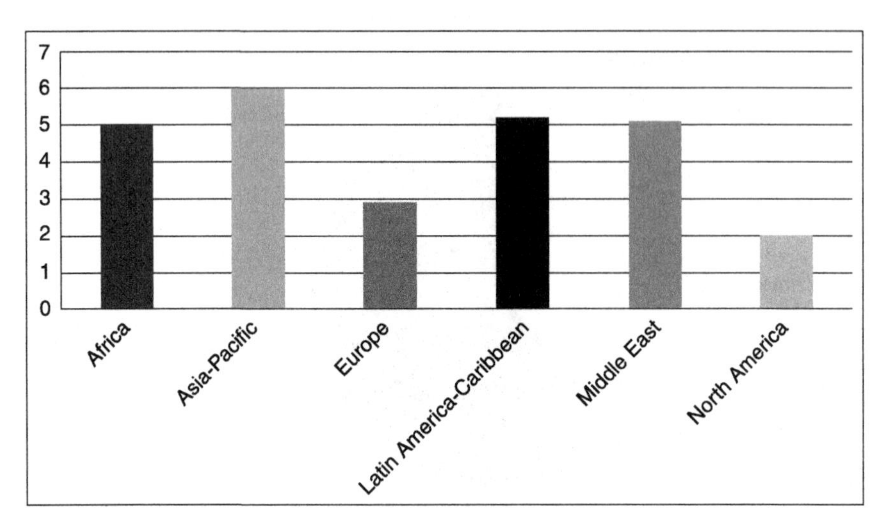

Figure 1.5 Forecast passenger growth per annum to 2031 (%)

Source: Airport World (2012).

at airports within emerging/developing economies rather than advanced markets and the Asia-Pacific region will account for over 40 per cent of the traffic. Figure 1.5 demonstrates that the largest annual growth rates expected are for Asia, the Middle East and Latin America – again a similar situation is predicted by Boeing and other forecasts.

In relation to individual airports, Atlanta Airport remains the world's largest airport in passenger terms, as it has done for many years, followed by Beijing Airport which only ranked in twentieth position in 2004 (Table 1.1). Dubai Airport, now positioned sixth, has also been rising up the rankings and in 2014 it overtook London Heathrow in becoming the world's busiest airport in international passenger terms. A number of other Asian airports such as Guangzhou, Shanghai and Jakarta, as well as Istanbul, have moved into the top 20, whilst a number of US airports, such as Houston, Phoenix, Detroit and Minneapolis, have dropped out. Overall the world's top 30 airport cities handle more than one third of the global passenger traffic with London and its six airports having the highest market share with 147 million passengers, followed by the three New York airports handling 116 million passengers (ACI, 2015a). The cargo market is even more concentrated with the top 30 air cargo hubs processing 53 per cent of the cargo tonnes. Three out of the top four airports are located in Asia – the large cargo volume at Memphis airport reflects its position as FedEx's headquarters and major US hub. By contrast eight of the ten largest airports by aircraft movements are in the US which is indicative of the fact that the average size of aircraft is smaller due to competitive pressures, shorter sectors and the dependence on domestic traffic.

Table 1.1 The world's top ten airports by traffic 2014

	Passengers (millions)		*Cargo (000s tonnes)*		*Aircraft movements (000s)*
Atlanta	96,178	Hong Kong	4,416	Chicago O'Hare	882
Beijing	86,128	Memphis	4,259	Atlanta	868
London Heathrow	73,408	Shanghai	3,182	Los Angeles	709
Tokyo Haneda	72,826	Incheon	2,558	Dallas FW	680
Los Angeles	70,663	Anchorage	2,493	Beijing	582
Dubai	70,475	Dubai	2,368	Denver	566
Chicago	69,999	Louisville	2,293	Charlotte	545
Paris CDG	63,813	Tokyo Narita	2,134	Las Vegas	522
Dallas/FW	63,554	Frankfurt	2,132	Houston	500
Hong Kong	63,121	Taipei	2,089	London Heathrow	473

Source: ACI (2015a).

1.4 Airport investment

As a result of these growing and forecast traffic levels, there has been considerable pressure on the airport industry to increase its capacity and invest in new infrastructure. As of January 2015 there were over 2,300 airport construction projects (expansion or new projects) identified worldwide, representing over US$500 billion investment (CAPA, 2015a). Some of these are for very long periods of time with lengthy master plans, for example Mexico (to 2069), Rome (to 2044) and Stockholm (to 2043), but some are also very short-term. Table 1.2 shows this investment split by region. Europe has the greatest number of construction projects whilst Asia-Pacific ranks first for investment. This is primarily because of the considerably greater value of projects in Asia-Pacific (and the Middle East), especially related to new airports. Indeed in July 2015 it was estimated that 340 of the airport

Table 1.2 Airport construction projects by region 2015

Region	*Number of projects*	*Investment (US$billion)*
Asia Pac	543	190.8
Europe	751	103.6
N America	485	91.4
M East	64	84.5
Africa	173	39.7
Lat Am	305	33
Total	2321	543

Source: CAPA (2015a).

construction projects were new airports with 178 in the Asia-Pacific region. Fifty-four of these were in China, 39 in India and 30 in Indonesia. There were just under 50 in Europe, situated mostly in central and eastern regions, and only 10 were in North America (CAPA, 2015b).

Clearly the choice between building new airports and/or expanding existing ones is dependent on many factors, especially government policy and its long-term objectives in relation to the development of air transport. The economic appraisal for airport investment needs to take account of all these factors (Jorge-Calderon, 2014). In many emerging economies where greater than average traffic levels are being forecast, many current airports are unable to cope with the traffic volumes and this, combined with both a general desire to use air transport to support economic development and generally less resistance to expansion from an environmental angle, has encouraged the building of new airports. By contrast in more developed or advanced economies the difficulties in finding suitable new sites, as well as greater opposition because of environmental concerns, often mean that expanding current airports is the more favoured option. In fact an analysis of large projects planned for 2014–2020 shows that for advanced economies 438 are for existing airports and 23 for new airports, whereas for emerging and developing economies the corresponding numbers are 570 and 261, respectively (ACI, 2015b). However, many argue that this will not be sufficient to meet the forecast demand. For example within Europe, Eurocontrol (2013) undertook a survey of 108 European airports responsible for 83 per cent of total European flights and found that only 17 per cent were planning a capacity increase by 2035, which was viewed as inadequate to cope with the forecast demand.

1.5 Airport financial characteristics

Whilst all of this book is focused on airport finance, it is useful at the start to identify some basic financial characteristics of airports. Firstly, airports have fixed infrastructure which involves long-term investment, which is both physically and financially 'lumpy' and does not usually have alternative uses. They are less substitutable than airlines, although the degree of competition that exists between airports has increased significantly in recent years. They have high fixed costs, being capital-intensive businesses, and many of their operating costs, particularly associated with safety and security, are fixed and unavoidable in the short-term, or vary little with the scale of operations. Meanwhile many of the airport revenues increase with traffic volume. So financially it may be advantageous for airports to handle more traffic if they have the capacity as the revenue benefits may well exceed the increased costs, but on the other hand if traffic falls and there are revenue losses, these may well translate disproportionately into reduced profits (Copenhagen Economics, 2012).

Secondly, airports generate revenues from two major sources, namely aeronautical and non-aeronautical, with the commercial airport paradigm which has replaced the traditional public sector airport model changing the balance between these two different revenue sources and giving non-aeronautical revenues much greater prominence. Overall airports can be considered as two-sided businesses, such as with credit cards or newspapers, where the businesses provide platforms for two distinct sets of customers who both gain from being networked through the platform. Airports serve both passengers and airlines and the positive interdependence between these two markets means that airport operators will be incentivised to compete for airline traffic and passengers as these will influence both their aeronautical and non-aeronautical revenue. If passengers stay away this will affect the airlines who might have to leave the airport. If airlines reduce or withdraw their services, this will reduce passenger numbers and consequently the non-aeronautical sales (Gillen, 2011).

Thirdly, the airport industry overall has relatively healthy profit margins. Table 1.3 shows the operating margin (operating profit including depreciation

Table 1.3 Financial performance of top 20 airport groups by revenue 2014

Airport operator	*Country*	*Total revenues (US$m)*	*Operating margin (%)*
Heathrow Airport Holdings	UK	4,425	3.7
AENA Aeropuertos	Spain	4,172	33.2
Aeroports de Paris	France	3,679	26.2
Fraport	Germany	3,156	20.2
Port Authority of New York & New Jersey	USA	2,479	34.5
Hong Kong International Airport	Hong Kong	2,111	54.3
Schiphol Group	The Netherlands	1,943	27.3
Narita International Airport Corporation	Japan	1,834	19.0
Avinor	Norway	1,674	21.6
Incheon International Airport Company	South Korea	1,664	49.7
Changi Airport Group	Singapore	1,661	43.7 (2013)
Munich Airport	Germany	1,582	22.1
Japan Airport Terminal	Japan	1,566	5.7
Airports Authority of India	India	1,514	30.1
New Kansai International Airport Company	Japan	1,388	28.8
State Airports Authority (Turkey)	Turkey	1,381	43.5
TAV Airports	Turkey	1,296	32.6
Infraero	Brazil	1,267	–25.6
Beijing Capital International Airport Group	China	1,241	31.2
Airports of Thailand	Thailand	1,230	38.4

Source: Airline Business (2015).

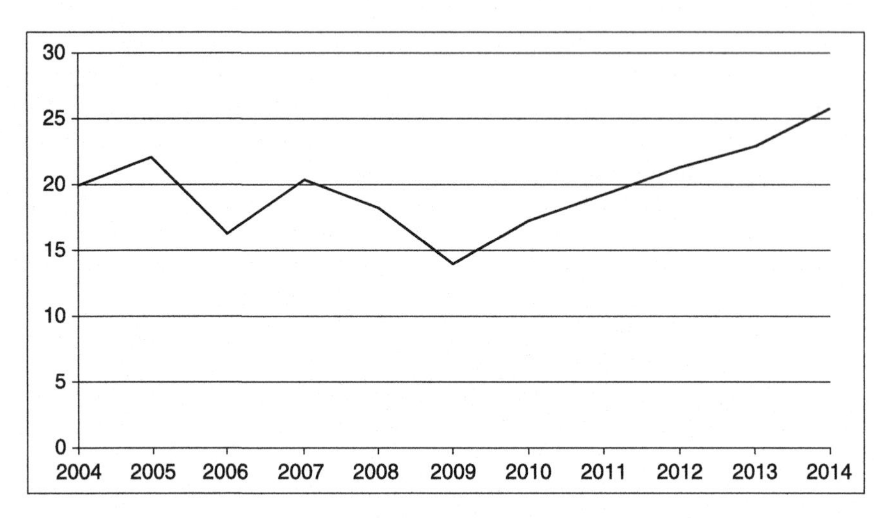

Figure 1.6 Operating margin at top 100 airport groups 2004–2014 (%)

Source: Airline Business (2008, 2015).

as a percentage of total revenues) for the 20 top airport groups by revenue in 2014 and for the vast majority of them an operating margin in excess of 20 per cent was achieved. Moreover Figure 1.6 shows the operating margin for the largest 100 airport companies for the last ten years. Whilst the margins have fluctuated and fallen in years when the external environment has been difficult, notably in 2008 and 2009, generally the margins have remained sound. They are much higher than the airline industry which achieved a global operating margin of 5.5 per cent in 2015 (IATA, 2015b), and even this airline figure is higher than in many years. This reflects many factors including the less intensive competitive circumstances for airports, different cost and revenue structures, and so generally the lower inherent financial and business risks of airports, which also reduces the cost of capital (Tretheway and Markhvida, 2013).

However, a different situation exists with smaller airports. For example within Europe, the European Commission (EC)'s view (which is further discussed in Chapter 9) is that airports under 1 million passengers find it hard to cover all of their operating costs, let alone their capital costs. At a size of 3–5 million they should be able to cover all their costs to a large extent, whereas beyond 5 million they should be profitable (EC, 2014a). The latest financial results of the European airports for 2013 published by ACI-Europe support the EC's view of this challenging financial situation. For airports handling 3–5 million annual passengers, 14 per cent were loss-making both in operating and net profit terms. The corresponding shares for airports handling 1–3 million passengers were 16 and 35 per cent, respectively. These proportions increased dramatically for airports handling less than 1 million passengers, with 79 per cent of these recording an operating loss and with 77 per cent experiencing a net loss (ACI-Europe, 2015b).

There is evidence to show that the same situation exists for airports in other regions. As a result, because there are many more smaller airports than larger airports in the world (ACI estimates that over 80 per cent of airports have traffic of less than 1 million passengers per annum) there is an overall situation in the industry where the net profits of a minority of large airports exceed the net losses of the majority of smaller airports. In fact over 98 per cent of the recorded net losses in 2013 were for airports of traffic with less than 5 million, with 93 per cent being for airports with less than 1 million (ACI, 2015b). The reasons for this situation are discussed in further detail in Chapter 2 but this is primarily because small airports have insufficient traffic to drive down costs and achieve economies of scale, or to exploit non-aeronautical revenue generation opportunities. The fixed costs associated with providing large infrastructure such as runways and terminals are very difficult to cover until a certain critical mass (generally argued to be at least 1 million) is achieved. However, for some markets, such as the UK, there is contradictory evidence that even small airports can make reasonable profits in certain market conditions (Starkie, 2008a).

The challenging financial conditions for smaller airports are one of the reasons why it is quite common to find groups of airports, or all airports, in a certain region or country operated as a system, with the profitable larger airports cross-subsidising the losses of smaller airports. Examples of such systems can be found in numerous places such as Scandinavia (Avinor – Norway, Swedavia – Sweden, Finnavia – Finland), and other countries such as Argentina, Thailand and Malaysia. In Brazil 73 per cent of airports operated by the Brazilian airport organisation Infraero reported net losses and the corresponding figure for the Airports Authority of India was 74 per cent (ACI, 2015b). Figures 1.7 and 1.8 illustrate the situation for AENA, the Spanish operator that operates over 45 airports. It may be seen that only 16 of these had positive operating margins.

1.6 Airport business models

One of the key results of the deregulation and privatisation developments for airlines has been changes to the structure of the airline industry and the emergence of completely new and significantly modified airline business models, which in turn has had a considerable impact on the structure of the airport industry. Instability associated with airline structures has produced more uncertainty for airports, as they cope with the modern-day airline business models, more airline consolidation and new route networks which have emerged. For airports this has had an impact on aeronautical charging, non-aeronautical revenues and costs, as well as on the airport–airline relationship. It has meant that the days when airports offered a fairly common

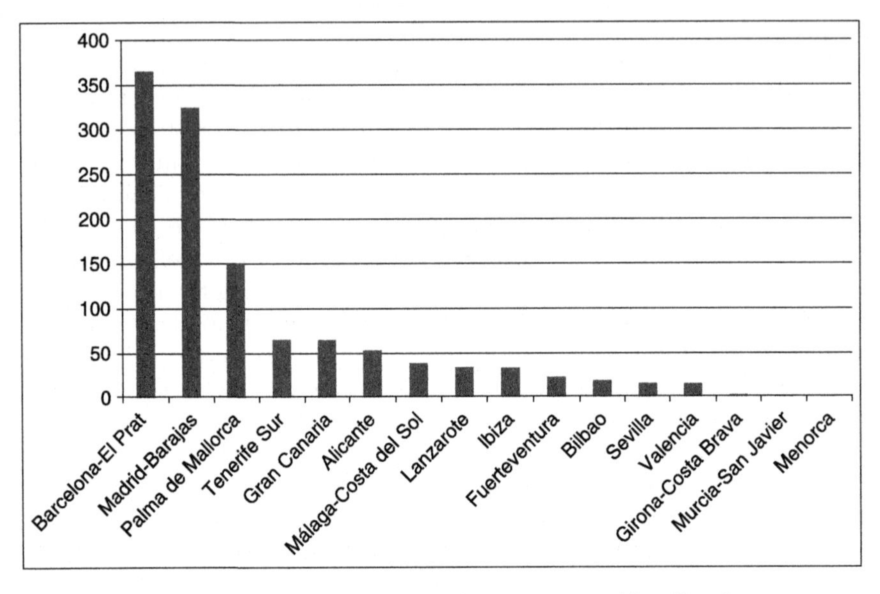

Figure 1.7 Operating profits at AENA Spanish airports 2014 (€ millions)

Source: AENA (2015).

set of services and facilities with a 'one-size-fits-all' approach seem definitely behind them.

There has been the emergence of the large network (or legacy) carriers such as British Airways, Air France, Lufthansa, Cathay Pacific and Singapore Airlines that concentrate on long-haul operations and large hub operations. These may have consolidated their operations by being a member of one of the three global alliances (Star, oneworld and Skyteam) and/or by participating in airline joint ventures, either within an alliance which is common on the transatlantic and transpacific routes, or outside alliances, with a notable example being the ten-year joint venture agreement between Emirates and Qantas. Consolidation has also occurred with mergers and acquisitions, either domestically (e.g. American/US Airways, Air India/Indian Airlines, Olympic/Aegean) or internationally (e.g. British Airways and Iberia, LAN and TAM).

This consolidation has brought both opportunities and challenges to airports. It can bring access to larger markets and a chance to serve more widespread destinations. However, in order to operate as an effective hub for such large-scale operations, such major airports need to ensure that they fully serve the needs of such airlines, for example by being capable of handling all aircraft types and effectively managing transfer traffic with reliable and appropriate infrastructure and competitive minimum connect times (MCTs). Many large hubs also have to be able to satisfy the needs of global alliances

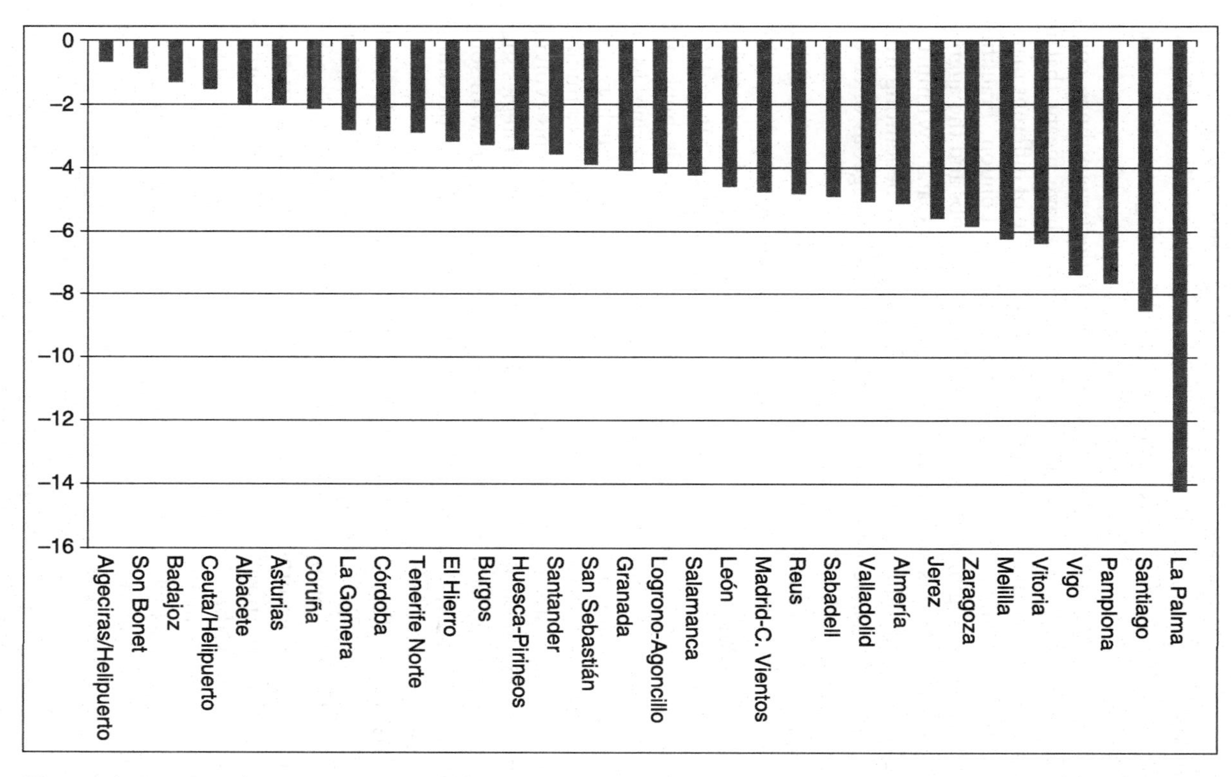

Figure 1.8 Operating losses at AENA Spanish airports 2014 (€ millions)

Source: AENA (2015).

so that the members can achieve cost economies and brand and operation benefits from operating joint facilities, such as check-in and lounges, and, where possible, have adjacent stand parking. If such airports were designed and built before the current structure of alliances was firmly established, this may be challenging to achieve and may well have significant financial consequences.

The business strategies and competitive strength of the large airlines, combined with airport capacity restrictions when relevant, have meant that in some areas there has been a shift in the relative importance of different major hub airports. For example, the main European hubs of London, Frankfurt and Paris are competing more with the Middle Eastern hubs and the aggressive expansion of carriers such as Emirates, Etihad and Qatar. Within the same region Istanbul's airports and Turkish Airlines are also benefitting from an increased market share which will become more advantageous once the new airport in Istanbul is opened.

However, other smaller airports may have lost out with the airline consolidation process bringing the realignment of schedules and capacity, and even the dropping of a hub entirely to avoid duplication and to streamline services. There have also been airports such as Birmingham, Barcelona, Milan Malpensa, Athens and Budapest in Europe which have de-hubbed as the result of airlines becoming bankrupt, downsizing or restructuring. Many smaller secondary hubs dependent on smaller network carriers (such as SAS, TAP Air Portugal, Gulf Air, Qantas) have had a challenging time as a number of these airlines have struggled to find a role for their services in this evolving airline industry. Such smaller carriers have adopted a variety of strategies such as reducing their long-haul networks, focusing on niche markets with some competitive advantage, merging with large network carriers or becoming feeders for large network carriers.

As a result many of these smaller hub airports have also changed their role (Redondi et al., 2012). Some have managed to attract more point-to-point traffic with the development of aircraft such as the B787 which is more suited for this. Some airports have been able to take advantage of their strategic geographic position, a notable example being Helsinki airport with Asian traffic. Others have tried to encourage connections with different airlines by introducing self-connecting help, for instance the 'Gatwick Connects' concept which is a paid-for additional service that allows passengers to book combinations of flights and provides self-connect help and protection against delays and cancellations. Another situation is where some of these smaller airports have become dependent on LCC traffic instead, for example Budapest airport, which lost traffic when the airline Malev collapsed in 2012 but which now has many services operated by Ryanair and Wizz.

The least successful of the smaller network airlines have lost significant market share to the LCCs which have expanded rapidly in many markets. From an airport viewpoint LCCs were traditionally useful in boosting the development of secondary airports, particularly in Europe, where there were a number of obsolete military airports such as Hahn in Frankfurt, Bergamo in Milan and Weeze in Dusseldorf. A number of secondary airports were also developed in North America such as Ontario (Los Angeles), Sanford (Orlando) and Hamilton (Toronto), although elsewhere the practice of using secondary airports was more limited with some notable exceptions such as Sharjah (UAE) and Avalon (Melbourne). Such airports were able to serve the specific needs of LCCs who generally require quick turnarounds, do not like using airbridges or airport buses, and do not need airline lounges and transfer passenger or baggage facilities (Graham, 2013).

Some airport operators have gone as far as opening new or refurbished low-cost terminals with simpler designs and lower service standards to satisfy LCC demand (Njoya and Niemeier, 2011). Certain costs, for example, those associated with the runway, navigational equipment, fire/rescue and security, will be no different for airlines using these low-cost terminals and so landing charges tend to be the same, but within the terminal the simpler design and lack of sophisticated equipment and facilities will typically have lower passenger charges associated with them. Examples include the Billi terminal at Bordeaux Airport, the mp² terminal at Marseille Airport and the KLIA2 terminal at Kuala Lumpur which is the largest low-cost terminal in the world, having opened in 2015 to replace the previous facility. Other facilities can be found in Japan (Kansai and Tokyo Narita airports) and there has been considerable interest also in China and India. However, in Europe the trend appears to be moving away from building dedicated low-cost facilities and in the US there was never much interest in this concept (Airline Leader, 2015). Whilst these facilities may arguably be able to more closely match the needs of LCCs, they can raise issues concerning cross-subsidisation of other airline charges, poor commercial revenue generation and unsatisfactory service quality levels. Moreover differentiation by terminal may cause unnecessary duplication or waste of resources and prove inflexible, all of which may have serious financial consequences. The physical separation of low-cost terminals may also create inconvenience for passengers who need to transfer flights.

Another reason for declining popularity of dedicated LCC facilities is that the LCC model has evolved considerably in recent years, with some of the basic features such as non-allocated seats being abandoned by many airlines and with others introducing new add-on features, such as priority boarding and flexible ticketing, especially for business travellers. This is causing a growing hybridisation of LCCs and network carriers. At the same time, there has been a trend towards LCCs moving into primary airports in cities such as Brussels, Glasgow and Milan. The reasons for this are numerous but include the fact that the primary airports are more convenient, are more attractive to business travellers and can thus enable a pricing premium to be gained. They may also allow LCCs to compete head-on with network carriers or feed or code-share with long-haul services of network carriers.

A number of other airport models exist, or are evolving, all of which will have an impact on an airport's financial situation. For instance, in addition to primary hubs, secondary hubs and low-cost airports, Kalakou and Macario (2013) identified business and cargo airports. Business airports, such as London City in the UK or Le Bourget in France, aim to provide good city access, quick processing times and higher quality facilities for business travellers. This may push up the costs of such airports, but the less price-sensitive customers can bear this. Cargo airports, such as Leipzig/Halle Airport, East Midlands Airport, Paris Vatry and Liege Airport, focus on providing reliable and secure connecting processes plus other appealing features such as good connections to motorways and no night curfews. Feldman (2009) argues that other airport business models are 'multimodal ports' such as Amsterdam or Hong Kong, or 'airports as a destination' such as Singapore Changi, Las Vegas or Athens. The term destination airport refers to airports at major tourist destinations or connecting to the bases of cruise ships.

There is an option to develop the airport as an airport city serving the needs of passengers but also local businesses and residents. These exist when an airport expands beyond the boundaries of the traditional business in the terminal and diversifies by developing facilities such as office complexes, business parks and free trade zones; distribution and logistics centres; sport, cultural and entertainment amenities, such as shopping centres; and medical services. In some cases airport cities have continued to develop outwards with the boundaries between the airport and its surrounding urban area becoming increasingly blurred and as a consequence a new urban form, known as an aerotropolis, has appeared. It is estimated that there are 38 such developments in North America, 20 in Europe, 17 in Asia-Pacific, 7 in Africa and the Middle East and 1 each in Central and South America (Kasarda, 2013) including examples such as Hong Kong, Beijing, Kuala Lumpur, Seoul Incheon, Dubai, Amsterdam, Paris CDG, Washington Dulles, Dallas Fort Worth and Chicago O'Hare. However, whilst such airport strategies can increase the commercial revenue of the airport and increase its attractiveness to airlines and passengers, they cannot really be considered as a standalone airport business model as they cannot be pursued on their own without consideration of the strategies of the airlines that serve the airports.

Generally as airline and airport models have evolved, so too has the balance of financial risks taken by both partners. In some instances (as discussed in Chapter 2), airport operators have placed more emphasis on the passenger-related aeronautical charges which link the passenger revenues that drive the airlines' own revenues and profitability, and less on aircraft weight-related charges which can be viewed as much more of a fixed cost for the airlines. Moreover (as discussed in Chapter 9) a number of airports and airlines, particularly LCCs, are entering into long-term agreements concerning pricing and service quality. For the airport this can lock in airlines to a certain airport for a fixed period of time with the aim of coping with the volatility of the airline industry and its increasingly footloose nature. For the airline this can guarantee the level of charges to be paid for a certain period of time, and it can 'control' one of its major uncontrollable costs.

Overall the evolution of the structure of the airline industry and different airline business models has meant that in turn airports have had to look to their business models to ensure that they satisfy the needs of their airline customers. However, an important point to make is that this does not necessarily mean that airports have to focus purely on one airline model exclusively and indeed many co-exist quite successfully at one airport. In some cases this has encouraged the payment of extra charges for additional services and facilities which is in fact somewhat similar to the trend observed in the airline industry where the product has been unbundled, with passengers having the option to pay for additional services that they may want.

1.7 Summary

This chapter has provided the background context for the rest of this book. It has discussed how the airline industry has become increasingly deregulated, and at the same time the airport sector has become very much more commercialised. This, combined with major environmental, security and technological developments, has created more challenging operating conditions for the airport industry, especially at a time when the airport passenger is seeking a better quality experience. This chapter has also shown how global airport traffic is currently concentrated in North America, Europe and Asia but in the future higher growth is expected in Asia and other emerging economies. As a result, much of the new airport investment is taking place in these areas.

As an introduction to airport finance aeronautical and non-aeronautical revenues have been defined and there has been some discussion of the relevance of the concept of two-sided businesses. In addition, it has shown how major airports are in a relatively healthy financial situation, but this is often not the case with much smaller airports. Finally to conclude the chapter, it has been argued that airports are increasingly moving away from 'one-size-fits-all' approaches and developing a range of different business models, which have major consequences for the financial characteristics and performance of the airports. Having introduced all these key issues affecting the airport operating environment, it is now possible to explore different aspects of airport finance in detail, starting with a full consideration of airport revenues and costs in the next chapter.

2 Airport revenues and costs

2.1 Introduction

This chapter provides a detailed assessment of airport revenues and costs. It starts by considering revenue structures and the mix between aeronautical and non-aeronautical revenues. It then looks, in turn, at each of these revenue streams. This is followed by a discussion of the airport cost structures. The remaining part of the chapter explores the factors that influence airport revenues and costs, ranging from outsourcing practice to the volume and nature of traffic and other locational and institutional features.

This chapter draws heavily upon the data collected by ACI in its latest annual economics survey (ACI, 2015b). This is the most comprehensive source of airport financial data that exists. It is also important to note that the International Civil Aviation Organisation (ICAO), the United Nations governmental agency responsible for worldwide regulation and governance of civil aviation, also publishes some important documents related to airport finance. The most significant reports cover airport economics (ICAO, 2013) and charging policies (ICAO, 2012a).

2.2 Revenues

2.2.1 The aeronautical and non-aeronautical mix

As identified in Chapter 1, airport revenues are usually classified into two main categories: aeronautical (or aviation) and non-aeronautical (or commercial). The aeronautical revenues are generated directly from the operation of aircraft, whereas the non-aeronautical revenues are gathered from commercial activities within and outside the terminal. There are then the non-operating items such as interest income, subsidies, grants and asset divestments. Some activities, especially ground handling, can be considered as either aeronautical or non-aeronautical revenues, depending on whether the airport operator provides this service (when it is treated as an aeronautical revenue) or whether it is undertaken by handling agents or airlines (when it is treated as non-aeronautical revenue). Another discrepancy can exist with fuel and oil throughput charges received from aircraft fuel companies or airlines, which again can be treated as either an aeronautical or a non-aeronautical item.

As the airport sector evolved from a public utility into a commercial business, the share of revenue generated from non-aeronautical sources increased. This development was most evident in the 1980s and 1990s (Freathy and O'Connell, 1998). For example, at European airports data from the annual reports shows that the share of non-aeronautical revenues rose from 41 per cent in 1984, to 44 per cent in 1989, 46 per cent in 1994 and 50 per cent in 1999 (Graham, 2014). However, since 2000 there does not generally seem to have been a significant increase in the proportion of non-aeronautical revenues since growing these revenues has become much more challenging. The latest revenue data for 2013 (although this time using the ACI dataset, which is not totally comparable) shows a global industry average 60:40 split for aeronautical: non-aeronautical revenues.

In considering the relative share of these two revenue sources, it is important to note that in some countries aeronautical charges are set at a common rate for all major airports, regardless of whether this relates to the individual costs of each airport. Another key issue is that the generation of aeronautical revenues is often subject to economic regulation at both international and national levels (see Chapter 10). By contrast airport operators typically have much more freedom when it comes to generating non-aeronautical revenues. However, both types of revenues are interrelated due to the two-sided nature of airports as discussed in Chapter 1.

2.2.2 Aeronautical revenues

Aeronautical revenues are classified according to the different charges which the airport operator levies. Most of the revenues come from a weight-based landing or runway charge (to cover areas such as the runway, taxiways, lighting, fire and rescue) and a charge dependent on passenger numbers (to cover terminal activities). The landing charge may be a fixed amount per tonne (or lb) regardless of the size of the aircraft, or there may be a more complex situation where the unit weight charge declines or rises as the overall weight of the aircraft increases. However, whilst higher aircraft weight causes more runway damage and greater maintenance costs, not all airfield costs are related to the size and weight of the aircraft, but clearly airlines with larger aircraft (and hence more passengers) will usually be in a better position to pay higher landing charges.

There has been considerable debate over time as to whether landing charges should be designed more to cope with runway congested airports (for example see Levine (1969) and Morrison and Winston (2007)). At congested airports, one option is to have a landing charge based purely on movements, irrespective of the size of the aircraft, as this may be more appropriate since the cost of occupying the congested runway will be the same for each movement. However, such charging is unpopular with the smaller airlines and there are very few examples of this practice, the most notable being London Heathrow Airport. A less radical step is to have a minimum landing charge to encourage general aviation traffic, and airlines with small aircraft, to move away from congested major airports. Sometimes landing charges will cover the approach and departure air traffic control (ATC) (or terminal navigation) although alternatively this may be covered by a specific charge, which is levied by either the airport operator or some other agency which provides the navigation services.

The passenger charge or passenger service charge (PSC) is usually billed to the airlines but shown as a separate cost (with taxes) on the passenger's ticket. It is levied per passenger and typically varies by passenger type (e.g. domestic vs international, EU vs non-EU) to reflect the different costs involved with handling these types of passengers. For example, the costs related to international passengers will tend to be greater than domestic ones, as these passengers tend to spend longer in the terminal and have more bags, as well as there being a need for more space for services such as customs and immigration. Many airports also charge less or nothing at all for transfer passengers, which arguably is cost-related as these passengers do not incur costs in the landside area, although they may require more complex passenger and baggage handling. However, this is primarily a marketing initiative to encourage transfer traffic. The passenger charge may also cover security, or there may be a separate charge. The extent to which the total costs of security are covered by the passenger and/or security charge will be very much dependent on who is responsible for providing the security – usually the choice being between the airport operator, the airline or the state.

In addition to these major sources of aeronautical revenue, there is a parking charge which is typically based on the weight of the aircraft or less commonly the aircraft wingspan. Most airports have a free parking charge, usually ranging from one to four hours, to allow the airline to turnaround without being charged (although this may not exist at very congested airports). After this free period, parking revenues will tend to be based on hourly or daily occupation. Another additional source of aeronautical revenue may come from ground handling, if the airport operator chooses to offer such services directly. There may also be other charges such as a movement based infrastructure charge, which will cover the use of infrastructure facilities such as check-in areas, baggage sorting and aerobridges, or a separate cargo or lighting charge. For more details about the variety of other charges see ICAO (2012a).

In recent years airport charging has tended to become more transparent with the separating out of individual services such as navigation and security. Such transparency may enable airlines with different business models (e.g. low-cost carriers) to have the option to only pay for services which they really want. Moreover airport charges have also become more complex through time, with an increasing number of airport operators levying peak charges during certain hours of the day to reflect the congestion caused

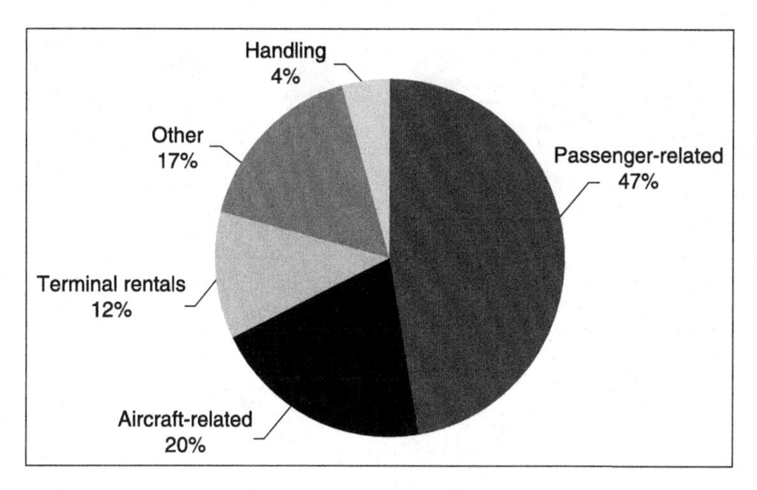

Figure 2.1 Aeronautical revenues at world airports 2013

Source: ACI (2015b).

during these periods. However, there is little evidence to suggest that the existence of peak/off-peak differentials is sufficient to have a significant effect on the airlines' behaviour, as is debated in some of the theoretical research.

Figure 2.1 shows the average breakdown of aeronautical revenues globally for 2013. The dominance of aircraft-related (mostly landing and parking) revenues and passenger-related (mostly passenger and security) revenues can clearly be seen. Passenger-related charges make up nearly half the revenue. Terminal rentals are the revenues generated from space used by airlines, which is mostly associated with North American airports where these are categorised as an aeronautical or aviation revenue item. They are usually determined with a cost-recovery approach and calculated using a weighted rate based on the type of space that is rented. Figure 2.2 shows the breakdown by world region and the importance of this source for North American airports is clearly evident. The higher direct involvement in handling at European airports can also be seen.

There are three notable trends related to airport charges. Firstly, an increasing share of airports is taking account of noise disturbance by charging considerably more for noisier aircraft, for night flights, or both. Generally there are three ways in which airports levy their noise charge: directly related to the noise category of the aircraft, a noise charge related to the landing charge, or a noise charge related to a noise threshold. In addition a small but growing number of airports (for example in the UK, Germany, Denmark, Sweden and Switzerland) have emission charges usually based on the amount of NOx emitted.

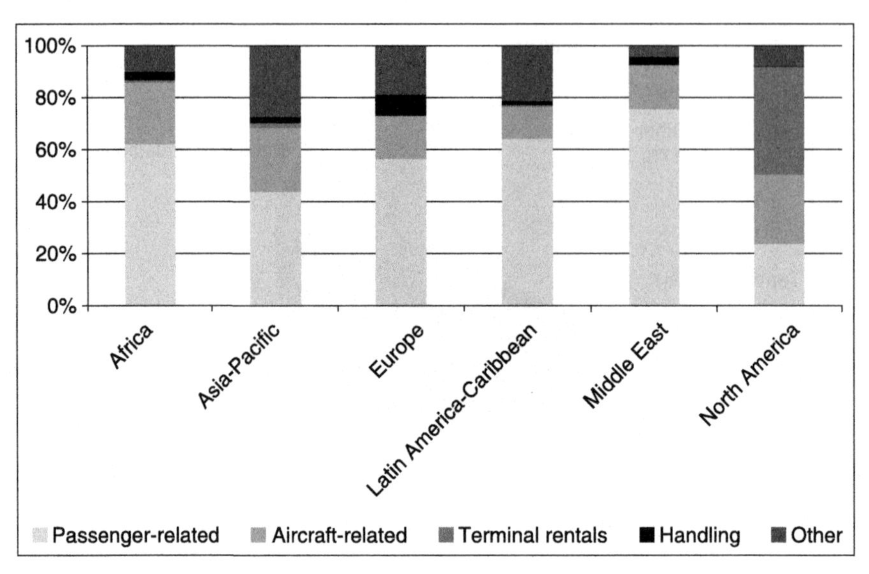

Figure 2.2 Aeronautical revenues at world airports by region 2013

Source: ACI (2015b).

Secondly, the passenger-related element of the charges has been becoming relatively more important. To a certain extent, the aircraft-related charges can be viewed as a fixed cost for the airline (assuming that the aircraft does not change), which is payable irrespective of the traffic volume, whereas the passenger charge can be considered as the variable cost. By shifting more relative weight onto the passenger charge, it can be argued that the airport operator is sharing more of the risk with the airline. This has been important in recent years with airport competition increasing, and with traffic volumes becoming more vulnerable and subject to greater fluctuations. Some airports have gone one step further, for example the major Australian airports, by removing the weight-based charges totally for international services. Other airports, for instance Brussels South Charleroi Airport which focuses on low-cost carrier (LCC) operations, have also abandoned having an aircraft-related charge. Overall ACI has observed that the ratio of aircraft-related: passenger-related charges changed from 45:55 in 2008 to 38:62 in 2013.

Thirdly, there has been an increase in airports and airlines working together to negotiate prices, particularly in Europe, which again is a reflection of the more challenging operational and competitive environment. This means that the published standard charges are becoming less relevant. This practice may include incentive schemes, available to all, where charges are reduced for new services or frequencies (see Malina et al., 2012; Jones et al., 2013). Additionally, or alternatively, the airport operator may enter into a long-term bilateral commercial contract with an individual airline to suit their individual needs. As discussed in Chapter 9, these can be used as a substitute for some formal economic regulatory process. Whilst information about negotiated charges tends to be scarce because of commercial sensitivities, an ACI-Europe study of airport charges in 2014 did find that 84 per cent of airports offered some form of charges discount, via either formal incentive schemes or commercial contracts. Forty-two per cent of the airports said that they had some commercial contracts but these airports accounted for only 24 per cent of total European traffic, indicating that this practice is more common at smaller airports, which arguably face some of the toughest competition (ACI-Europe, 2015a).

Whilst definitions can vary, it is usual to differentiate between airport charges (which are levied by airport operators to cover facilities and services which they offer) and taxes which are levied by governments (either to cover a certain service or an environmental cost, or to raise airport investment funds, or more generally just to support public sector spending). The taxes may be applied across the entire country or just at an individual airport. An example of a countrywide tax is the Air Passenger Duty in the UK which is used as general taxation income by the government. Whilst both charges and taxes are airport costs from an airline and passenger viewpoint, and indeed passenger charges and passenger taxes tend to be shown as just one item on the passenger's ticket, from an airport finance viewpoint, taxes should not be considered as aeronautical revenues. However, in some airport profit and loss accounts they are shown as pass-through revenues which are handed over to the government.

Arguably the most complex situation has been in the United States (Ashford and Moore, 1999). There is a landing fee but no general passenger fee as these are illegal, primarily because of fears that revenues from these might be diverted away from the airport for non-aviation purposes. However, there is a passenger-related charge called the Passenger Facility Charge (PFC), which airports are allowed to levy for identified airport-related investment projects. These have to obtain Federal Aviation Administration (FAA) approval and the maximum charge allowed is $4.50 per passenger per sector (FAA, 2015a). In addition, there are a number of government taxes which go into the Federal Airport and Airway Trust Fund which provide the finance for airport investment grants under the Airport Improvement Program (AIP). The most significant of the taxes is the domestic passenger ticket tax which accounts for around half of all the trust fund (FAA, 2015b). The PFC revenues and AIP grants are often treated as non-operating revenues although the PFCs are included as aeronautical revenue in the ACI data. Some other countries, such as Canada, also have an airport improvement or development passenger fee for specific investment, which is also usually defined as aeronautical revenues.

Figure 2.3 shows airport charges for a representative aircraft type (B737–800) for a selection of world airports. It may be seen that for most of the airports, the passenger-related fee is much greater than the aircraft-related one.

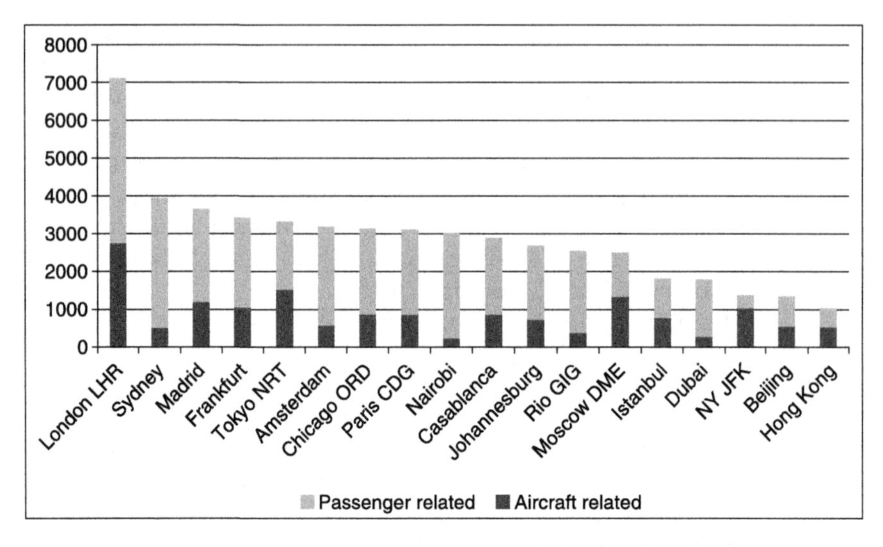

Figure 2.3 Airport charges for a 737-800 at selected world airports 2013 (£s)
Source: Mott MacDonald (2015).

There is a large variation in charges, with London Heathrow having the highest value, which is primarily related to the movement rather than weight-based landing charge which is less favourable for small aircraft types such as the B737. For illustrative purposes a summary of actual charges for five of these airports is also provided in Table 2.1. Whilst each airport

Table 2.1 Examples of airport charges at selected airports 2015

New York JFK Airport
Landing charge: US$6.33 per 1000 lbs weight (additional US$100 between 3pm and 10pm)
Passenger facility charge (PFC): US$4.50
Passenger ramp/apron area: First 15 minutes US$50 and then US$100 every additional 15 minutes
Aircraft parking (for each 8 hours): <100,000 lbs weight = US$45; 101,001–200,000 lbs = US$70; each additional 25,000 lbs = US$25
Dubai Airport
Landing charge: <4.5 tonnes = AED 13.0 per tonne; 4.5–45 tonnes = 15.1 per tonne; >45 tonnes = 16.4 per tonne
Passenger service charge: AED 75
Passenger security and safety fee: AED 5
Aircraft parking: Narrow bodies (1 hour 30 minutes free) = AED 235 first hour, AED 383 additional hours; wide bodies (3 hours free) = AED 353 for first 3 hours, AED 648 additional hours

Nairobi Airport

Aircraft weight (kg)	*Landing charge (US$)*	*Parking charge (US$)*
<1,500	10	6
1,501–2,500	20	6
2,501–5,000	25	6
5,001–10,000	40	6
10,001–20,000	65	10
20,001–40,000	102	10
40,001–80,000	223	15
80,001–120,000	585	25
120,001–180,000	820	40
180,001–300,000	1,345	50
>300,000	1,750	130
Night take off = one fifth of day		First six hours are free
Night landing = five fourths of day		
Passenger service charge: International = US$20, domestic Ksh 300		

Amsterdam Airport

Landing (per 1,000 kg for the base aircraft, three other noise categories exist):
With airbridge = Day (landing/take-off) €4.57, night (landing) €5.80, night (take-off) €6.86
Without airbridge = Day (landing/take-off) €3.66, night (landing) €4.64, night (take-off) €5.48
Cargo = Day (landing/take-off) €2.38, night (landing) €3.02, night (take-off) €3.56
Passenger service charge: terminal €13.92, transfer €5.84
Security service charge: terminal €12.17, transfer €6.81
Parking (per 1,000 kg per 24 hours): €1.60

London Heathrow Airport

Landing:
<16 tonnes = £2,934
>16 tonnes (day) = £1,430 (Chapter 4 Base), £2,934 (Chapter 3 Base)
>16 tonnes (night) = £3,576 (Chapter 4 Base), £7,335 (Chapter 3 Base)
(six noise categories exist in total)
Emission charge per kg of NOx = £8.57
Terminal navigation: £80.53 per landing and £1.08 per tonne
Passenger charge (terminal): European £29.59, other £41.54
Passenger charge (transfer): European £22.19, other £31.16
Parking (narrow bodies – 90 minutes free): £51 per 15 minutes
Parking (wide bodies – 30 minutes free): £21 per 15 minutes
(Charges are rounded to the nearest £)

Sources: Individual airport websites.

broadly has the same types of charges, it may be seen that the specific details and charging criteria vary quite significantly.

2.2.3 Non-aeronautical revenues

Turning now to non-aeronautical items, there are again a number of different revenue sources. Usually the most important item is associated with the commercial facilities offered within the terminal. Typically the airport operator will outsource these facilities to industry specialists (such as retailers, food and beverage (F&B) providers and car hire firms). This revenue is often called concession revenue because these third-party concessionaires will pay a concession fee. If the airport operators choose to contract out the car parking facilities, the revenue from this may also be included in concession revenues. Otherwise it will be a separate revenue item which can be quite substantial, especially in countries where the car is the dominant mode of transport, such as the US and Australia. However, in many countries such revenues are becoming more difficult to grow due to the combined effects of more off-airport competition, together with more passengers being encouraged to use public transport for environmental reasons. Advertising is often another small but important source, since airports are viewed as being attractive sites because of the high volumes of passengers, and the cosmopolitan and higher socio-economic status of many travellers. However, with the widening of passenger demographics as more and more people fly, arguably airport passengers are not quite as valuable now.

This concession revenue may be generated in a number of different ways. Typically the concessionaire will pay a percentage of its sales to the airport, often in addition to agreeing a minimum annual guaranteed amount or rent. This percentage commonly varies according to the individual product categories. Rather like aircraft-related and passenger-related charges, the guaranteed minimum is a relatively fixed revenue source whereas the sales percentage is variable, and so this is where the airport operator shares the risk with the concessionaire. If the minimum guarantee is too high it will be a burden to the concessionaire and this may affect its performance. Typically the sales fee for F&B providers is 10–20 per cent, with the Airport Commercial Revenues study of 2014 for 120 airports around the world showing an average of 13 per cent in North America and 19–23 per cent in Europe/Asia (Moodie International and the SAP Group, 2014). Speciality retail can be similar but duty- and tax-free shops pay a much higher percentage which can be well over 30 per cent.

Rental revenue for airport operators can also be very significant. This can include revenues from renting or leasing of terminal areas such as offices, business lounges, ticket desks and check-in desks, as well as off-airport space, both airside (e.g. fuel farms, maintenance hangars, cargo terminals) and landside (e.g. hotels/conference centres, training centres, light industrial buildings, offices). The revenue may vary according to the type of facility

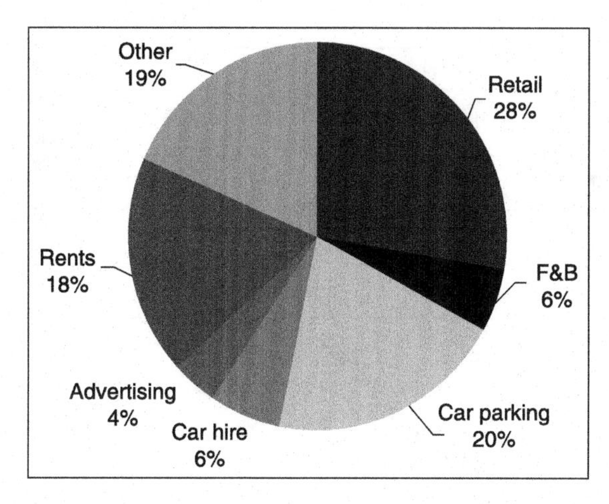

Figure 2.4 Non-aeronautical revenues at world airports 2013

Source: ACI (2015b).

or property, its age, its quality, its location and competing off-airport rents. There may also be rents and/or concession fees from other activities such as fuelling, handling and in-flight catering. In addition there may be pass-through revenues for utility and energy consumption (e.g. water, heating, air-conditioning and electricity).

Figure 2.4 shows the average breakdown of non-aeronautical revenue globally for 2013. Retail is the most important item followed by car parking. However, the split of revenues varies considerably by region as can be seen from Figure 2.5. Of note are the Middle Eastern airports that generate half their revenue from just the retail source. By contrast retail revenue at North American airports is relatively less important, whilst the revenues from car parking and car hire are very significant – reflecting the much greater reliance on car use in this continent. F&B is also of equal importance as retail here whereas elsewhere it makes up a much smaller share of the revenue.

As previously noted, the increase in the relative share of non-aeronautical revenues has generally halted in the last ten years or so. There are a number of reasons for this (Graham, 2009; Sevcik, 2014). Firstly, within the EU, intra-EU duty and tax-free products have not legally been available since 1999 which lowered overall sales, and continues to have an impact every time new countries join the EU. The last decade has also seen new and more rigorous security requirements being introduced, which have had an impact on not only the passengers' confidence to buy restricted items such as liquids, aerosols and gels (LAGs), but also on the dwell time available for using commercial facilities. In addition, PC and mobile check-in may have reduced the time that passengers feel they have to spend at airports. Moreover many

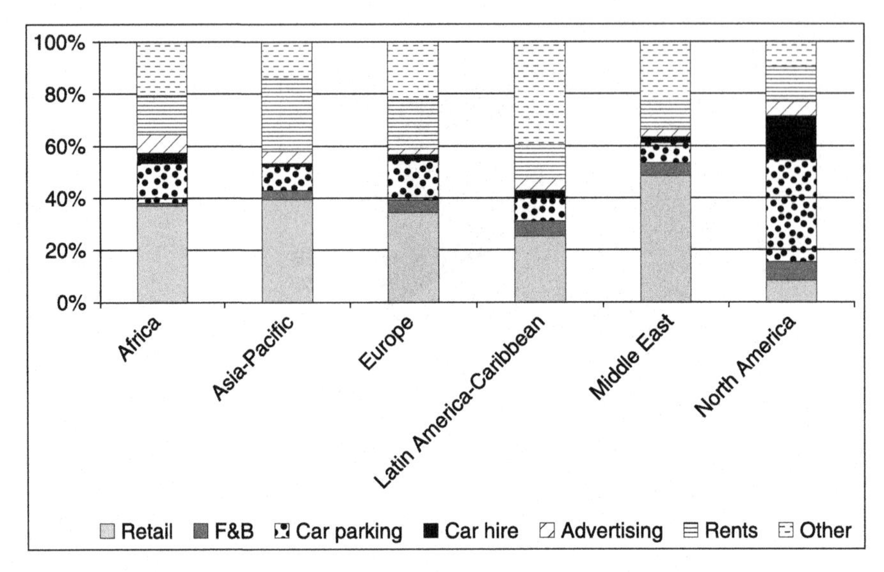

Figure 2.5 Non-aeronautical revenues at world airports by region 2013

Source: ACI (2015b).

airports seem to have reached a 'mature' stage in exploiting many of the commercial opportunities that exist, and as a result growing revenues has become that much more difficult, particularly with the increase in off-airport competition, especially from the Internet.

2.3 Costs

Whereas many of the revenue items are unique to the airport industry, this is not the case for costs and so airports have a variety of ways in which their costs are reported. Typically these are classified as staff, depreciation/amortisation (or capital charges) and 'other', with costs such as interest and tax payments being considered as non-operating items. Figure 2.6 shows the ACI world breakdown of costs with interest payments (which ACI includes in its definition of capital costs) excluded. It may be seen that staff and depreciation costs represent about half of the total costs. The most important other costs are contracted services outsourced to third parties; communications, utilities and energy; and general and administration. It is worth highlighting that depreciation and other accounting policies at airports can vary quite significantly. For example it is shown in Chapter 3 how the depreciation periods for a sample of airports vary considerably.

As discussed in Chapter 1, airports have a relatively high share of fixed costs which are associated with the provision of infrastructure (such as the runway and terminal) and certain services (such as safety and security), which

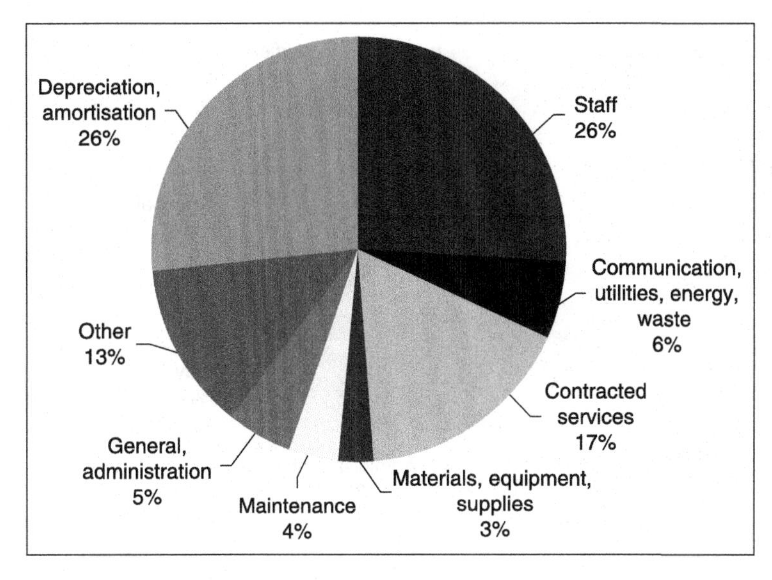

Figure 2.6 Cost breakdown at world airports 2013

Source: ACI (2015b).

will be incurred relatively independently of the traffic levels. As a result total operating costs do not change in full proportion to traffic increases or decreases. For the UK situation it has been calculated that there is a cost to passenger demand elasticity in the region of 0.3 to 0.5. In other words this indicates that if passenger demand increases by 10 per cent the costs will only rise between 3 and 5 per cent, although there is some additional evidence of greater cost elasticity responsiveness if the traffic is declining (Steer Davies Gleave, 2012). The implications of having relatively high fixed costs will mean that the costs of accommodating extra traffic will be low, as long as there is spare capacity, but additional revenue may be gained from this from airport charges and from the passenger spending on commercial facilities.

There are many other ways of categorising costs. One can be by function which is illustrated in Figure 2.7 for European airports. Unsurprisingly the two most important costs are aircraft movement areas/lighting and passengers/cargo terminal facilities, but security costs come in a close third position, representing 16 per cent of costs. One of the other most salient trends in costs has been the decrease in the relative significance of staff costs. For example at European airports staff costs went from representing 43 per cent of total costs in 1989, to 35 per cent in 1999 and then 31 per cent in 2009 (Graham, 2014). This is due to a number of factors such as more outsourcing, improvements in labour productivity, and the adoption of various new technologies which has reduced the need for as many staff.

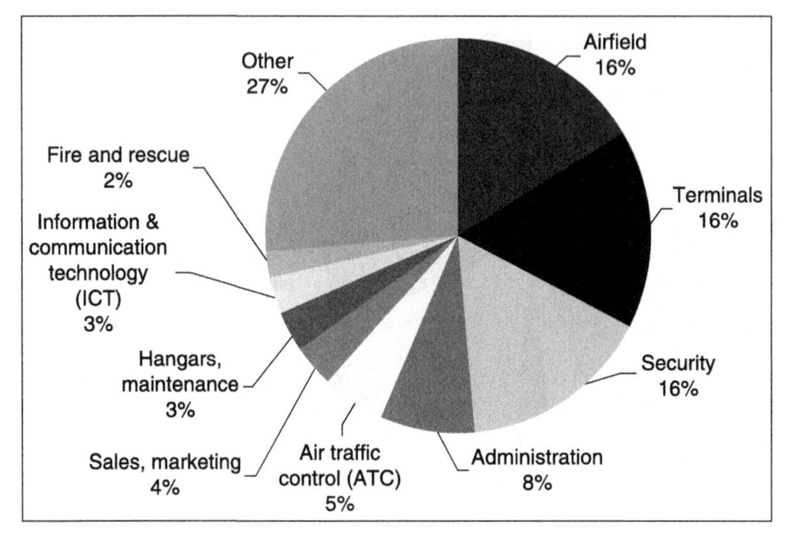

Figure 2.7 Costs at European airports by function 2013

Source: Adapted from ACI Europe (2015b).

2.4 Activities undertaken by airport operators

An important issue that needs to be considered in relation to airport finances is the extent to which airport operators provide all services and facilities themselves as opposed to outsourcing them. Practice around the world varies considerably although (as discussed previously) it is very common to outsource commercial facilities. In general in the US there tends to be a high degree of outsourcing in all areas, particularly with airlines getting involved with many activities. Elsewhere differences occur typically with activities such as handling, ATC and security. Moreover the situation is more complex than in many other industries as it is not just the fact that the airport outsources certain activities that remain a cost to the airport operator (e.g. cleaning), but also that other activities (such as handling) may be passed over totally to another organisation (typically an airline or handling agency) – leaving the airport with very little financial involvement (except perhaps for generating a rent or concession fee). In the former case the level of costs would be expected to be broadly similar (although differently split between labour and other operating costs), whilst in the latter case the lack of direct involvement in certain activities would significantly reduce the costs (and revenues) involved. Here the third party will charge for the service it is contracted to offer and the cost to the airport operator is the revenue foregone less any rents or fees. The extreme cases are when whole facilities are operated by different bodies, for example at certain US airports such as New York JFK where major airlines run their own terminals, or in Japan where at most airports separate companies are responsible for operating the

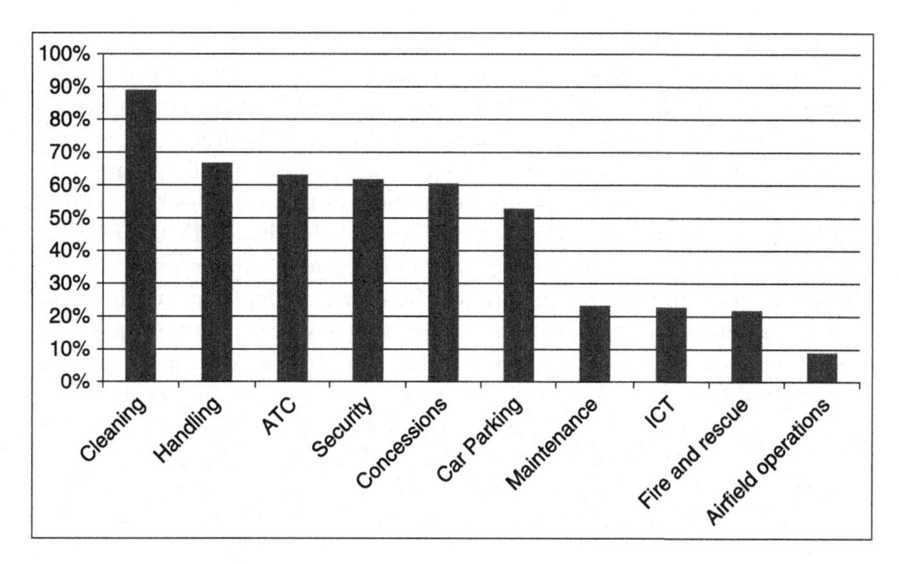

Figure 2.8 Proportion of world airports that outsource specific airport activities 2013

Source: ACI (2015b).

Note: Excludes North American airports.

terminals and commercial facilities. Figure 2.8 shows the typical situation globally. The most common activities which are undertaken by third parties are cleaning, with two thirds of airports also outsourcing handling, ATC and security. By contrast core activities such as fire and rescue and airfield operations are rarely provided by others.

There are many reasons for this varied situation. Firstly there are the generic arguments in favour of outsourcing, such as lower costs and greater flexibility, and gaining access to expertise from specialist companies who may also be able to take advantage of scale benefits and higher productivity. These can be applied to the more general activities such as cleaning. However, many of the functions of an airport need more specific consideration. Security is a particular case in point, where there is considerable debate as to whether it should be the airport operator or state's responsibility to protect the travelling public. As a result practice varies considerably with the involvement of different bodies, such as the airport operator, the airlines, third-party security operators, the police and other state agencies. In Europe there is an inconsistent approach to providing security but generally the airport operator and its customers bear more of the costs related to security compared with other areas, for example the United States. In some countries, security and other essential services such as ATC may be provided by government agencies but below the normal commercial rate.

In other cases there may be competition reasons for the provision of services. For example, within the EU by law major airports are required to have more than one organisation responsible for providing ground handling to ensure that there is adequate competition (see Chapter 9). This has encouraged the increased use of large third-party independent handlers such as Swissport and Menzies. These can benefit from significant economies of scale through serving many airports and can sign multi-airport contracts with airlines. On the other hand, if airport operators provide handling themselves they may be able to exploit synergies between ground handling and other operational functions, offer the airlines a contract that includes both airport and handling charges, and develop a closer relationship with their airline customers. It is also worth noting that independent handlers may not be interested in small airports because of their size, which may result in the airport operators having to provide these services instead, often at a loss. Figure 2.9 shows the revenue and cost structures for two European airports (Vienna and Geneva) which are of a relatively similar size and located close to each other. Vienna Airport provides some handling services itself whereas Geneva does not. The impact on the mix of revenues can clearly be seen but also at Vienna Airport, staff cost is representative of a larger share of costs, which may well also be due to the handling activity which tends to be rather labour intensive.

Overall, empirical evidence related to industry outsourcing is rare although there is some limited research which shows that outsourcing has improved airport economic efficiency in both Italy (Abrate and Erbetta, 2010) and

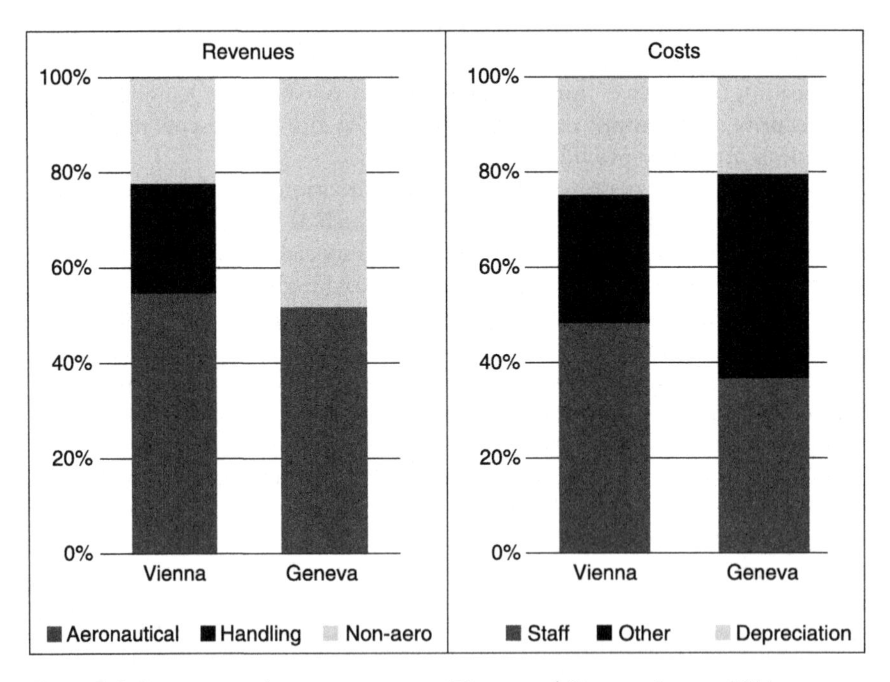

Figure 2.9 Revenues and costs structures at Vienna and Geneva airports 2014

Source: Annual reports.

Spain (Tovar and Martin, 2009). In general, it is likely that smaller airports will tend to do less outsourcing, and indeed the ACI data shows that airports with less than 1 million passengers have staff costs which account for 43 per cent of total operating costs (excluding depreciation) compared to 12 per cent dedicated to contracted services, whereas with airports of 25–40 million passengers, both cost items represent around 25–30 per cent of costs.

Arguably the most complex situation is with commercial facilities, with the most popular option being to contract these out to specialist retail, F&B and other commercial companies. This is usually a lower risk and more profitable strategy as the airport operator will not normally have a detailed understanding of the market environment, the specialist skills required, the bulk buying power and the well-established supply infrastructure which the specialist companies will possess. However, with such an approach the airport operator may lose considerable control over the management of these facilities.

There are different ways that concession agreements can be arranged (for details see Kim and Shin, 2001; LeighFisher, 2011). Airport operators can enter into agreements with individual concessionaires or they can employ a master concessionaire who will then sublease some of the facilities to other operators. Two other approaches are using prime operators, which is when an airport operator will package together the facilities and then offer them to two or more 'prime' concessionaires, or using a developer/manager who will have an agreement to develop/lease and manage the concessions without operating any directly. Westfield Concession Management is an example of a developer which manages concessions at a number of US airports at cities including Boston, Chicago, Houston, New York, Los Angeles, Miami and Washington. In selecting the most appropriate option, the airport operator needs to consider the relative trade-off in terms of competition, capital investment, airport administration costs and financial returns (LeighFisher, 2011). In 2014 in North America, 57 per cent of airports used individual concessionaires, 7 per cent used a master concessionaire, 20 per cent a prime operator and the remaining 16 per cent a developer/manager (ACI-North America (ACI-NA), 2014).

An alternative to using some kind of concession model is a management contract, which is popular with car parks, where the airport operator handles all the revenues and costs and pays a company a fee, which may be performance-related, to manage the facility. There is also the option to enter into a joint venture which will share the risks and rewards associated with certain activities and give the airport operator more influence over areas such as service quality. Delhi Duty Free Services is an interesting example which is 49.9 per cent owned by the airport operator, 17.03 per cent owned by GMR Airport Limited (which is one of the major shareholders in the airport) and 33.07 per cent owned by Yalorvin which is a subsidiary of AerRianta International, which is wholly owned by the Dublin Airport Authority

(DAA). Another example is ATU, Turkey's leading duty-free operator chain, which is run as a joint venture between the airport operator TAV and the retailer UNIFREE.

There are a few airport operators, for instance Dubai Airport, DAA, Malaysia Airports and Hyderabad Airport, who have chosen to provide some commercial facilities themselves, such as duty- and tax-free outlets, either directly or through a wholly owned subsidiary. They will often do this if they have developed a considerable expertise in this area. Moreover a significant share of very small airports provide their own facilities since they cannot attract the external specialists, and because of their size this may be the simplest approach. Overall the choice of approach depends on many factors, with the financial return, together with the amount of risk and control for the airport operator, being key considerations.

2.5 The influence of the volume and type of traffic

The volume and nature of traffic has a very significant influence on airport costs and revenues. Most evidence shows that for small airports, as they increase their traffic, their costs per unit of traffic, or unit costs, tend to decline. In other words these airports experience economies of scale. For small airports the fixed costs associated with the provision of infrastructure and certain services, incurred irrespective of the traffic levels, will push up the unit costs. As traffic increases these costs will not change and so the unit costs will reduce as the costs are spread over more traffic. Indeed the ACI data shows that total operating costs (excluding depreciation) per passenger in 2013 for airports of less than 1 million were US$14.04 compared with the overall average of US$10.55.

However, views are mixed and numerous as to whether scale economies are exhausted, or whether returns to scale change, at a certain level of traffic. For example an early study of UK airports (Doganis and Thompson, 1973) found decreasing unit costs up to around 3 million passengers or WLUs (WLUs, work load units, are defined in Chapter 5). By contrast, in their study of Spanish airports Martín and Voltes-Dorta (2011) found that the scale economies were not exhausted at any level of traffic. In Europe Pels et al. (2003) found that there were decreasing returns to scale with their aircraft movement efficiency model for some airports above a 12.5 million annual passenger number threshold, but increasing returns to scale for their passenger efficiency model for airports that had passengers above the same threshold. Meanwhile Salazar de la Cruz (1999) observed that airports were subject to constant returns to scale from between 3.5 and 12.5 million passengers and then there were decreasing returns to scale. Therefore some of the research suggests that in financial terms there might be an optimal size of airport. This may be due to a number of disadvantageous factors for larger airports, such as the need to efficiently co-ordinate or duplicate services and facilities, particularly when multiple terminals are involved, the scarcity of cheap land and labour (due to higher unionisation and local shortages), greater costs associated with mitigating the environmental impacts and difficulties associated with ensuring that there is adequate surface access to/from the airport (Kamp et al., 2007).

As regards revenues, it is likely that these will increase as the traffic rises, especially on the non-aeronautical side. This is because larger airports will normally be able to provide a greater range of commercial facilities and services. In addition typically larger airports will have a higher proportion of international passengers, who will tend to have a longer dwell time at the airport and so will spend more on commercial facilities, especially on duty- and tax-free goods and F&B, whilst waiting for their flights. It is also quite common to find smaller airports dominated by a few airlines and if this is the case such airlines may be in a powerful position to negotiate preferable deals on airport charges, thus reducing aeronautical revenue. Overall the ACI data shows that total operating revenues per passenger in 2013 for airports of less than 1 million were US$14.32 compared with the average of US$20.02.

As a result of these inherent cost and revenue disadvantages, small airports tend to face greater challenges to be profitable as discussed in Chapter 1. In addition in many countries there may be an oversupply of small airports which have been built by local governments for broader prestige or political reasons rather than just commercial motives, and this, combined with increased airport competition, may lead to underutilisation. Some small airports may also be more likely to have highly peaked operations (due perhaps to seasonal holiday traffic or morning and evening domestic business services), which will make it more difficult to achieve the best use of resources. In addition, as discussed these airports may be less attractive for third-party outsourcing which arguably could improve their financial performance, and their airline customers may be more price sensitive due to their smaller operations which may drive down airport charges.

Costs and revenues will also vary depending on the type of traffic at the airport. International passengers not only have a longer dwell time and access to duty- and tax-free but (as discussed previously) there will also normally be a higher passenger fee for international passengers because of the higher costs involved. A number of airport economic efficiency studies, including those undertaken by the Air Transport Research Society (ATRS), confirm that the proportion of international traffic does have a significant impact on airport economic performance (e.g. see Oum et al., 2003).

Typically LCCs and their passengers will have a preference for more basic facilities without the need for additional services, such as airline lounges and transfer facilities. Therefore airports aiming to attract LCC business may have lower costs. In a few cases this has encouraged airports, such as in Copenhagen or Kuala Lumpur, to develop partial or whole terminals specifically for LCC needs. However, a more basic terminal may encourage less spending because of a more limited range of commercial facilities and/or the lack of a shopping mall with a relaxed atmosphere or experience to encourage passenger spending. On the other hand, LCC passengers may spend more on F&B because of the limited offer on board. Empirical evidence related to this is mixed. Moodie International and the SAP Group (2014) found that over 70 per cent of the airports reported that LCC passengers spent less than other passengers on retail and over 45 per cent observed less spending on F&B. Likewise Lei and Papatheodorou (2010) found that the non-aeronautical spend of LCC passengers was on average £2.87 compared with £5.59 for full service passengers and Castillo-Manzano (2010) observed that LCC passengers spent 7 per cent less. By contrast Francis et al. (2003) noted that the revenue per passenger in shops for a case study airport under consideration was €8 for LCCs compared with an average of all passengers of €5.5, whilst Gillen and Lall (2004) observed that non-airline revenue per passenger increased from $9.70 to $10.55 at Albany Airport when the LCC Southwest started services. Generally it seems that it is difficult to generalise about the commercial spend of LCC passengers because it depends very much on their specific demographics but it is certainly true to say that not all of these types of passengers are budget spenders.

Hub airports and their transfer passengers also require different consideration. A 'wave' pattern of flights, with well-defined peaks and troughs of traffic, will probably be more costly to handle than a more even spread of traffic. As discussed above, the costs associated with transfer passengers will also be different and the same will be true of their spending habits. They will not need car hire or car parking facilities but may have more time to linger in duty- and tax-free shops. Overall the evidence as to whether a hub role has improved or reduced economic performance is again mixed, one example being Oum and Yu (2004) who observed a lowering of performance with hubs.

Clearly other passenger characteristics such as travel frequency and seasonality, travel purpose, length of haul, inbound/outbound mix and general passenger demographics can have a significant impact on revenues, especially from non-aeronautical sources, and in some cases on the costs of the provision of infrastructure and certain services. The amount of cargo handled is also likely to have an effect as may the average size of aircraft. Passenger nationalities can be another variable; for example the major international gateway airports located on the US west coast have much higher duty-free sales than elsewhere in the US due to their proximity and convenience for Asian travellers (LeighFisher, 2011). Likewise Thomas et al. (2013) reported that the spending power of Chinese travellers at Frankfurt Airport was 4.9 times the average whilst at the Paris airports Chinese travellers spent on average €80 on retail compared to an overall average of €17.

Finally the presence of other customer groups such as employees, family, friends, local businesses and residents within the terminal, or using other facilities that have been developed surrounding the airport, may contribute to non-aeronautical revenues as well as potentially having an impact on costs. For instance, a survey of a US west coast international airport found that 45 per cent of employees used the F&B facilities daily and 26 per cent used them weekly, with equivalent shares of 4 and 18 per cent for retail (LeighFisher, 2011).

2.6 Other important factors

There are many other factors that will have an impact on airport finances. These include ownership patterns, privatisation, competition and economic regulation which are considered in detail in other chapters. Among other effects these can influence the airport operator's funding arrangements and the cost of capital. Another relevant issue is the position of an airport in the investment life cycle since airport investment tends to be long-term, large and 'lumpy' rather than continuous and gradual. Capital costs will be high when a major development has been completed, and poor utilisation, as a result of overcapacity until the traffic builds up, is likely to increase the operating costs. Both types of costs are likely to decrease through the cycle. Thus, as with other industries, there may be economic benefits of operating close to, or even in excess of, the design capacity of an airport, although the resultant lowering of service standards may not be acceptable to the customers. Indeed Oum et al. (2004) found that capacity constraints or congestion had a positive impact on economic performance in their global study of airports.

Moreover, the use of cutting edge technology, and the level of physical and service standards, can have a major impact. There will be resource implications for higher standards, but also greater revenue trade-offs if an airport decides to focus on a more upmarket product to appeal to high-yielding airlines or passengers, for example as at London City Airport. Providing more space or high-quality facilities may be costly but it may encourage more spending on commercial facilities. At the other extreme, as already discussed, an airport may offer lower standards than normal to accommodate LCC traffic. In short, the type(s) of business model adopted by the airport (which were introduced in Chapter 1) will be fundamental in defining the economic characteristics of individual airports.

The actual location of an airport and its geographic situation will play a major role. Inevitably this will have a very significant impact on the volume and nature of traffic. However, the location may also determine any physical constraints at the airport site which may affect its layout, or environmental restrictions which may, for instance, result in the banning of night flights. These factors may limit the airport operator's ability to make the best use of its resources. Certain weather conditions, such as a strong prevailing wind or regular snow storms, may also push up costs. Finally, more general national economic conditions, such as the cost of labour, land and other resources, currency fluctuations, or government policies and taxation regimes, can also have an influence. For example, airports in the United States are exempt from most business taxes unlike many other airports, whereas in Europe the cost of labour and materials is expensive, and with high levels of unionisation this can push costs even higher. Moreover non-aeronautical revenues will reflect the spending power of the resident population. This latter factor, together with less advanced commercial strategies at some airports in the less developed regions of Africa and Latin America/Caribbean, may help explain why the 2013 ACI data showed that these two regions had the smallest shares of non-aeronautical revenues (27 per cent and 34 per cent, respectively).

Overall, it is very apparent that there are numerous factors that influence an airport's economic characteristics and performance. Reinhold et al. (2010) classify these as external exogeneities (caused by the environment, e.g. geographical constraints), endogenous heterogeneities (due to differences in economic regulation, security and safety regulation) and internal heterogeneities (due to managerial decisions). Figure 2.10 summarises some of the key factors.

Figure 2.10 Factors affecting airport economic performance

2.7 Summary

This chapter has identified the main revenue and cost items at an airport. Typically most aeronautical revenues will come from aircraft weight or passenger-related charges, with the latter becoming more important. Aeronautical charging is also becoming more complex and transparent, and incentive schemes are now very common. Meanwhile non-aeronautical revenues have been becoming more significant in the aeronautical: non-aeronautical mix until the most recent years when this has become more challenging to achieve. In comparison to revenues, the cost structures of airports are not unique. A major feature is the high proportion of fixed costs.

It has been shown that there are many factors that affect revenues and costs at airports. These include the amount of outsourcing that exists, the volume and nature of traffic, ownership and regulation, specific locational factors and many others. Having gained an understanding of airport revenues and costs, and how these are influenced, the next chapter now moves on to show how financial statements can be constructed and used to measure the financial performance of an airport.

3 Financial statements of airports

3.1 Introduction

A detailed financial accounting and bookkeeping system is a necessary part of the management of any separate legal entity; airports that are separate entities are no exception, although some airports may still form part of a government department and thus follow non-commercial methods of financial control. This chapter provides an understanding of the three major financial statements that are built up from the more detailed records. These are generally provided on an annual basis, and often on a quarterly and more frequent basis as well. They are often published, with a legal requirement to do so for those with stock market listings.

The second part of this chapter introduces the main financial ratios that are used to analyse airports, and which are based on figures that can be found in one of the three main financial statements: the Profit and Loss (P&L) statement, the balance sheet and the cash-flow statement. Some of those take figures from one statement while others draw from two.

3.2 Fundamentals of financial accounting, reporting and management

3.2.1 Tasks and objectives of financial management and control

Financial management and control requires access to financial data that is up-to-date and of sufficient detail for the various tasks that have to be performed. This will vary according to the level needed, but this chapter will focus on the higher-level financial statements and ratios that can be evaluated both internally and externally to the company or airport concerned. Before financial ratios or benchmarks can be calculated, the analyst needs a good understanding of the published accounts and financial statements. This chapter will do this by using worked examples from London Heathrow Airport, together with some comparisons with other airports. This choice was based on the need to work with published accounts that:

- are in the English language
- provide a reasonable amount of detail and clear supporting notes
- reflect the most recent recommendations and standards from accounting bodies.

The accounts describe the financial position of the airport or airport group at a particular moment or between two points in time. They are thus central to evaluating the performance of the management of the airport's finances. They enable the management and owners of an airport to answer two main questions:

- Is the airport operating at a profit?
- Will the airport be able to meet its financial commitments as they fall due, and so not have to close down because of lack of funds?

The second question above is perhaps unlikely, with regard to closing down through lack of funds, but good financial management should translate into lower borrowing costs and improved performance. If an airport does close down its shareholders might also benefit from the valuable land holdings that many airports have, being close to larger cities.[1] The system of accounts is not, however, ideally suited for management tasks such as pricing or product costing and planning, or for deriving economists' measures such as value added.

The record-making part of accounting is usually called *bookkeeping*, performed by means of a *double-entry* system. The purpose of this chapter is not to explain how this is done, but rather how to make use of the *published* results of this system at a more general level. This analysis and interpretation of the published accounts of airports could be the aim of the following interested parties:

- shareholders
- banks, other debt holders and creditors
- financial analysts
- industry regulators
- employees.

Many companies are secretive about their financial data, usually for competitive reasons, and only release the minimum required by company law or stock exchange rules. Larger government-owned airports are usually run as legally constituted corporations, and generally do publish annual accounts in some form, even though they may only be available a considerable time after the end of the financial year. Airports with stock market quotations are usually required to release financial information that is timely, in sufficient detail and available to all at the same time. Fraport, for example, announces their results for the year ending 31 December in March of each year and publishes its annual report and accounts soon after. Heathrow Airport publishes its year end December results in February, while Airports of Thailand presents its annual results for the year ending 30 September in February.

Publicly quoted airports generally control the release of information through an investor relations department, posting reports, webcasts and press releases on their websites (e.g. www.fraport.com) and giving periodic presentations to the investment community and analysts. Regulated airports will need to provide detailed financial information to their regulators which will include the timely provision of financial statements. The directors of an airport will contract with a firm of auditors to examine the books and annual financial statements of the company on behalf of the shareholders. They will then issue a report which will conclude with their opinion as to whether the accounts give a true and fair view of the state of affairs of the company or group on a certain date, and whether they comply with company legislation. The way the auditors are hired (by management rather than directly by shareholders) has led to criticism of the objectivity of their opinions in certain cases. One answer to this has been for boards to appoint an audit committee composed largely of non-executive directors. However, it could be argued that these directors owe their position to the executives in the company in the same way as the auditors.

3.2.2 International harmonisation of standards

Much progress has been made in aligning standards and financial reporting by countries around the world. The International Federation of Reporting Standards (IFRS) Foundation and its standard-setting body the International Accounting Standards Board (IASB) have no power to force a country to adopt its standards, but approaching 150 countries require IFRS for almost all publicly accountable entities. The European Union adopted IFRS from 2005 but the USA still uses its own GAAP standards, Japan a combination of its own, US GAAP and IASB standards and China its own standards. However, Chinese companies that have a Hong Kong stock market quotation generally use IFRS (e.g. Beijing Capital Airport).

All publicly quoted European Union country airports are required to use IFRS, including Zurich Airport, and so do many in other parts of the world such as Auckland Airport and Malaysia Airports (both using national standards that are harmonised with IFRS). IFRS describes itself as a globally recognised set of standards for the preparation of financial statements by business entities. Those standards prescribe:

- the items that should be recognised as assets, liabilities, income and expense;
- how to measure those items;
- how to present them in a set of financial statements; and
- related disclosures about those items.

International standards often leave more detailed decisions such as depreciation periods or valuation of non-quoted companies to judgement by the board of directors. However, almost all of the airports discussed in the following sections have adopted IFRS and use comparable approaches to depreciation.

3.2.3 Problems of comparison and interpretation

The next section will introduce the main financial statements: income/P&L, balance sheet and cash flow, as well as the statement of changes in equity. Comparisons between airports at this stage are impossible, given differences in reporting currencies, subsidiaries included and periods reported. Financial ratios allow much better comparisons to be made, especially across different currencies, and these are described in the subsequent section. However, there are a number of problems that remain to cloud the benchmarking process (for a more detailed discussion of commercially oriented benchmarking, see Chapter 5).

The first problem is the 12-month period that is chosen for the annual statement. Many airports now use the calendar year, but many UK airports use year to end of March, and Airports of Thailand uses end of September. Thus the overlap between airports included in a comparison might be up to six months out; combined with a major event such as the closure of European airspace this would render comparisons relatively worthless.

The second problem is the nature of the businesses consolidated in the statements that are to be analysed. Ideally these should be largely airport operating companies, with limited benefit derived from comparing an airport operator or real estate company with one that specialises in ground handling.

Ratio analysis used to assist judgement

It is impossible to generalise as to whether one particular ratio by itself is good or bad. For example, a high quick ratio shows a strong liquidity position, but the firm may not be earning a high enough return on its total assets. The airport analyst should therefore use a number of ratios together. In a study of the performance of US firms over a 20-year period, Peters and Waterman used 6 indicators to identify 43 excellent companies. They were asset growth, equity growth, market to book value, return on capital, return on equity and return on sales (Peters and Waterman, 1982).

Window dressing

Balance sheets are only a snapshot on a particular date and firms can employ techniques to make their position look better on that day. An example of this is delaying payments due over the last few days of the company's reporting year to improve the cash balance on the balance sheet. This would improve current assets (cash) but also inflate accounts payable under current liabilities. Sometimes P&L accounts can be made to look worse: if the year's results are poor, make them worse by provisions for redundancy and restructuring and the next year's profits will look good by comparison.

3.3 The set of financial statements

Financial statement preparation is guided by a number of key accounting principles. These are:

The Going Concern Principle: The assumption that the business will continue in operation for the foreseeable future, i.e. that there is no intention to curtail or significantly reduce the scale of operations. If the company's financial situation is such that the auditor believes the company will *not* be able to continue trading, the auditor is required to disclose this opinion. The going concern principle allows the company to defer some of its prepaid expenses until future accounting periods.

Matching Principle: This accounting principle requires companies to use the accrual basis of accounting. The matching principle requires that expenses be matched with revenues. For example, sales commissions expense should be reported in the period when the sales were made (and not reported in the period when the commissions were paid). Wages to employees are reported as an expense in the week when the employees worked and not in the week when the employees are paid. If a company agrees to give its employees 1 per cent of its 2014 revenues as a bonus on 15 January 2015, the company should report the bonus as an expense in 2014 and the amount unpaid at 31 December 2014 as a liability. Because we cannot measure the future economic benefit of things such as advertisements (and thereby we cannot match the ad expense with related future revenues), the accountant charges the ad amount to expense in the period when the advert is run.

Materiality: A subjective judgement of the extent to which any amount is significant in the context of the financial position of a business as described in the balance sheet or its reported profit or loss. For example, the purchase of a $100 item may be expensed rather than depreciated over a number of years.

Revenue Recognition Principle: Under the accrual rather than cash basis of accounting, revenues are recognised as soon as a product has been sold or a service has been provided, regardless of when the money is actually received. For example, if an airline used the runway and other facilities of an airport on 31 December 2015 (before the end of its financial year that ended on that date), the cost of this landing will be 'recognised' or included in the P&L for FY2015, even if it was only charged for these services by way of an invoice dated 31 January 2016.

Consistency: Accountants are expected to be consistent when applying accounting principles, procedures and practices. For example, if a company has always used a certain method for recording and valuing stocks or fixed assets on the balance sheet it should continue to use these methods in the future. Any changes such as different depreciation periods would only be made after careful consideration of the new circumstances.

3.3.1 The Profit & Loss account

The Profit and Loss Account, Income Statement or Statement of Earnings summarises the revenues and expenses of the airport for the accounting period.

Revenue: Conversion of real assets into cash. Under the accrual basis of accounting, cash receipts are allocated to the period in which the related service took place. In other words the revenue from an aircraft landing fee is allocated when the landing took place and not when the invoice is presented or paid.

Expenditure: Conversion of cash into real assets (some short-lived). Expenses are charged to the Profit and Loss Account in the same accounting period as the one in which the related revenue is recognised. Certain large expenses will need to be charged over a number of years, since these assets will provide the potential to generate revenue over a period of time that extends well beyond the current accounting period, for example:

- airport facilities such as runways, taxiways and aprons, passenger terminals, car parks and other buildings and equipment
- software development costs
- goodwill through the acquisition of other companies.

This process of allocation is called *depreciation* for tangible assets such as runways and other physical structures, and *amortisation* for intangible assets such as goodwill and software.

The P&L and other financial statements will usually be published for the airport operating company; however, this legal entity (limited company) may also own other operating companies as a majority or minority shareholder, and these companies may specialise in other areas such as ground handling or car parks. Where the airport holding company has a majority share and controls another company it is called a 'subsidiary' and its accounts will be consolidated or combined with those of its parent holding company. This means all the revenues and expenses of both parent and subsidiary will appear in the parent company P&L. Minority-held companies, where the holding is above 10 per cent but below 50 per cent, are called 'associates' and not consolidated, but their shares of profits or losses are included in proportion to the shares held, regardless of whether these are distributed in dividends. Profits of holdings of less than 10 per cent are usually only included if they are distributed as dividends, these being shown in the parent P&L as income from trade investments.

A good example of this is group financial statements of Fraport AG: Table 3.1 shows the significant contributions to its group revenues from ground handling services, something that many airports leave to the airlines and third-party suppliers. It also has a number of investments and management contracts in other airports around the world that generate revenues. Examples that are majority-owned and thus consolidated are: Jorge Chavez Airport (Peru), 70.01 per cent; Varna Airport (Bulgaria), 60 per cent;

Table 3.1 Fraport AG group portfolio FY2014

	Revenue €m	*Revenue share*	*EBIT €m*	*EBIT margin*
Aviation	884	36.9%	116	13.1%
Airside and terminal management				
Corporate, safety and security				
Airport security management				
Retail and real estate	456	19.0%	275	60.3%
Retail activities				
Parking facility management				
Real estate leasing and marketing				
Ground services	656	27.4%	8	1.2%
Ramp handling				
Passenger and baggage handling				
Cargo services				
External activities	399	16.7%	85	21.3%
Global investments and management				
Facility management				
Information and telecoms				
Corporate infrastructure				
Total group	**2,395**	**100.0%**	**484**	**20.2%**

Source: Fraport (2015).

Dakar Airport (Senegal), 100 per cent; and Ljubjana Airport (Slovenia), 97.99 per cent. Fraport's airport associates are Antalya Airport (Turkey), Hanover Airport (Germany), Pulkova Airport (Russia), Delhi Airport (India) and Xian Airport (China). It also generates income from a number of US terminal services companies or concessions.

It can be concluded from the above that Fraport AG group accounts will not necessarily just show how its principal airport operation at Frankfurt is performing, although, as Table 3.1 showed, some segment data is published and some ratios can be calculated. Detailed financial statements, however, are only given for the group as a whole.

A detailed breakdown of sources of revenues can be found in ICAO's Airport Economics manual (ICAO, 2013) (see also Chapter 2). The same document identifies the key constituents of airport expenses. Another source is the ACI annual airport economics survey. This moves depreciation from 'operating expenses' to join finance or interest expenses and revenues (in contrast to the usual P&L format). Its EBITDA (earnings/profit before interest, tax, depreciation and amortisation) is thus total revenues less reported operating costs, which are synonymous with 'operating expenses'. EBIT is thus EBITDA after subtracting depreciation and amortisation, and is identical to operating profits (discussed in an industry context in Chapter 1). Its 'bottom line' is 'net profit/(loss)', calculated by taking EBITDA less 'capital costs' and 'taxes and other fees', which is often called 'after-tax profit' in financial statements. ACI also provides definitions for the main items in a glossary, as well as financial ratios which will be discussed in section 3.3.

Airport example: Heathrow Airport Ltd

A less complicated airport to take as an example is London Heathrow, which has few subsidiary or associate companies of any size, leaving the published financial statements to focus on the performance of Heathrow Airport itself (see breakdown of revenues in Table 3.2). In fact its only subsidiary of

Table 3.2 Heathrow Airport Holdings Ltd, consolidated statement of comprehensive income FY2014

	FY2014 (£m)	*Share*
Aeronautical	1,706	63.4%
Retail	503	18.7%
Property & facilities	285	10.6%
Heathrow Express	129	4.8%
Other	68	2.5%
Total revenues	2,691	100.0%
Fair value gain on properties	46	
Employment costs	460	26.5%
Depreciation and amortisation	586	33.8%
Maintenance costs	196	11.3%
Utility costs	100	5.8%
Rents and rates	137	7.9%
General expenditure	293	16.9%
Retail expenditure	23	1.3%
Police	29	1.7%
Own work capitalised	(88)	–5.1%
Total operating costs	1,736	100.0%
Finance income	237	
Finance costs	(980)	
Loss on financial instruments	(153)	
Pre-tax profit	105	
Profit from discontinued operations	237	
Taxation	(34)	
Consolidated profit for year	308	
EBITDA	1,567	
EBIT	955	

Source: Heathrow Airport Holdings (2015).

significance was its 100 per cent ownership of Heathrow Express which provided frequent rail services to central London. The largest minority shareholders in Heathrow Airport were as at end FY2014: Ferrovial (25 per cent), Qatar (20 per cent), Caisse de dépôt et placement du Québec (13.29 per cent), the Government of Singapore Investment Corporation (11.88 per cent), Alinda Capital Partners (11.18 per cent), China Investment Corporation (10 per cent) and Universities Superannuation Scheme (8.65 per cent).

Table 3.2 shows the income statement for Heathrow Airport with two additional measures of profit calculated at the bottom: EBITDA and EBIT. Both of these are used in ratio analysis (addressed in the next section). EBITDA approximates to cash operating profit, arrived at by adding back depreciation (£586m) to total operating costs and adding back a further £26m of exceptional items that had been included under various expenditure headings.[2] EBIT is usually taken to be operating profit (revenues less operating costs), but it could also be pre-tax profit before subtracting finance or interest costs. Discontinued operations refer to the disposal of Glasgow, Aberdeen and Southampton airports which generated a profit of £200m (the remainder of the income statement entry of £23m being from the sale of another subsidiary).

Operating a large airport at near capacity involves large capital expenditure and the capital intensive nature of airports is reflected in the share depreciation takes in total costs (almost 40 per cent). The table also shows that high operating profits are necessary to cover large finance costs, in this case the result of the completion of two major expansion projects: first Terminal 5 and then the overhaul of Terminals 2 and 4.

The remainder of the P&L or income statement includes finance costs (e.g. interest payable on debt and finance leases), finance income (e.g. interest received on bank deposits and short-term securities, as well as cash deposits lodged as security for finance leases) and any profits or losses from the sale of fixed assets. It should be noted that, like most other large European airports, Heathrow does not itself offer ground handling services, and most of its retail outlets are operating as concessions. The latter will appear in the accounts under retail income, which may be broken down into a fixed rental and a percentage of turnover (discussed in Chapter 2).

3.3.2 The balance sheet

The balance sheet (also called Statement of Financial Position) provides a classified summary at a particular date (end of the financial year or quarter) of where an airport has acquired its funds (liabilities) and how it has deployed those funds (assets). It also shows whether the funds have been borrowed on a long-term basis (for periods of greater than one year) or short-term basis (less than one year). The balance sheet shows the position at a particular date, while the P&L account shows the results of transactions occurring between two dates.

The balance sheet can be presented in *Account* format or *Net Asset* format. The account format generally shows assets and liabilities on separate pages each with their own total, while the net asset format shows them on the same page with a total of assets less current liabilities being identical to the total of shareholders' equity or funds. The balance sheet shows what the airport *owes* as liabilities, and what the airport *owns* as assets. These must balance, or in other words total assets must always equal total liabilities (e.g. line G equals line H below):

Net asset format balance sheet

A. Fixed (property & equipment) and other non-current assets
B. Current assets
C. Current liabilities
D. Net current liabilities (B – C)
E. Total assets less current liabilities (A + D)
F. Long-term (fixed) debt and other long-term liabilities
G. Total assets less fixed & current liabilities (E – F)
H. Capital & reserves or shareholders' funds (= G)

Account format balance sheet

Assets	*Liabilities and shareholders' equity*
Current assets	Current liabilities
Fixed assets	Long-term debt
(Property & equipment)	Other liabilities
Other non-current assets	Shareholders' equity (funds)
Total assets	Total liabilities

Most airports that follow international standards adopt the net asset format approach, albeit with some differences in the order of the main items, while the account format is used by all US companies and one or two Asian airports. The first does not have a total assets line, whereas the second does.

Fixed assets or non-current assets: These are the physical and financial items that are intended to be used for the longer-term operations and business of an airport. They should not therefore vary much from day to day. They can be converted into cash, but not always easily (or individually) or at short notice. They can be divided into:

- tangible assets: physical property, plant and equipment (e.g. runways, aprons, buildings and equipment)
- intangible assets: long-term financial investments, goodwill, patents, computer software, etc.

Current assets: These are those assets that are expected to be consumed or converted into cash in the near future over the 12 months following the end of the financial year. They consist of stocks or inventory, accounts receivable or debtors, and cash. Stocks are short-life items such as office supplies, maintenance spares and materials that are only kept for a short time. Accounts receivable covers amounts that will be paid within one year's time and normally within around 30 days from issue of invoice. This money will be due mainly from airlines and concessionaires. Finally cash will consist of petty cash and cash not yet deposited to the bank and demand deposits held in banks and similar accounts that can be used in payment of short-term obligations.

Long-term or non-current liabilities: These consist of bank borrowings and other long-term debt such as bonds and securities issued. Finance lease obligations would also be included here. Provisions for future payments of uncertain timing or amount are estimated and with growing unfunded pension liabilities, these could be a significant amount, as could be another of this category of liabilities, namely provision for derivative contracts and tax payments.

Current liabilities: These are short-term obligations such as creditors or accounts payable (e.g. to outside contractors and utility companies), wages payable, or accrued liabilities that are expected to be settled over the 12 months following the end of the financial year. This would include the short-term part of long-term debt liabilities and the short-term elements of the provisions found in non-current liabilities.

Airport example: Heathrow Airport Ltd

Table 3.3 gives what used to be described as the balance sheet for Heathrow Airport: this is the position on the last day of the reporting period, namely 31 December 2014. This is in contrast to the income statement (Table 3.2) which includes the 12-month period up to 31 December 2014. The first thing to note is the long-term nature of the assets, with 'Property, plant & equipment' (also called fixed assets) accounting for two-thirds of total assets. The amount recorded here will be the original cost less accumulated depreciation; this is its book rather than market value, the latter impossible to establish even with the sale of the airport. Investment properties are acquired specifically to earn a rental and not integral to the airport operation (e.g. car parks); they are periodically re-valued to give a close to market value on the balance sheet in contrast to fixed assets. 'Intangible assets' such as goodwill and software costs, like fixed assets, are booked at cost less amortisation (essentially similar to depreciation).

Fixed assets and investments are closely matched by long- and short-term financing. Long-term borrowing is very high relative to shareholders' equity for two main reasons: borrowing has been necessary to finance the very high capital expenditure programme over the past few years; and any cash from operations and sale of other airports in the group (e.g. Stansted, Glasgow,

Table 3.3 Heathrow Airport Holdings Ltd, consolidated statement of financial position (as at 31 December 2014)

Assets	*£m*
Non-current assets	
Property, plant & equipment	11,571
Investment properties	2,054
Intangible assets	2,894
Available for sale investments	26
Derivative financial instruments	172
Trade and other receivables	116
	16,833
Current assets	
Inventories	10
Trade and other receivables	426
Derivative financial instruments	2
Restricted cash	10
Cash and cash equivalents	323
	771
Total assets	17,604
Liabilities	
Non-current liabilities	
Borrowings	–12,195
Derivative financial instruments	–1,334
Deferred income tax liabilities	–935
Retirement benefit obligations	–228
Provisions	–11
Trade and other payables	–6
	–14,709
Current liabilities	
Borrowings	–929
Derivative financial instruments	–1
Provisions	–27
Current income tax liabilities	–17
Trade and other payables	–441
	–1,415
Total liabilities	–16,124
Net assets	1,480
Equity capital and reserves	
Share capital	2,666
Other reserves	–317
Retained earnings	–869
Total shareholders' equity	1,480

Source: Heathrow Airport Holdings (2015).

Aberdeen and Southampton airports) has been distributed to shareholders as dividends. This is also reflected in the negative retained earnings which have been eroded by a large loss in 2010 and a smaller one in 2011, as well as high dividend payments.

Trade and other payables were £441m compared to trade and other receivables of £116m. The payables figure included £176m of capital payments due. It should also be noted that 'cash and cash equivalents' provided a cushion of £323m to meet short-term liabilities. But a further amount is available in credit and liquidity facilities that were undrawn as at the end of December 2014. Cash flows, cash and cash equivalents comprise cash at bank, cash in hand and short-term deposits with an original maturity of three months or less. Short-term deposits with an original maturity of over three months are shown within current trade and other receivables. Note that the cash position of the balance sheet is updated as a result of the cash movements over the year, as shown in the cash-flow statement in the next section.

Depreciation is provided on operational assets, other than land and assets in the course of construction, to write off the cost of the assets less estimated residual value (not given), by equal instalments over their expected useful lives (i.e. 'straight-line' depreciation) as set out in Table 3.4. The original

Table 3.4 Heathrow Airport fixed asset lives FY2014

Terminal complexes: fixed asset lives	
Terminal building, pier and satellite structures	20–60 years
Terminal fixtures and fittings	5–20 years
Airport plant and equipment	
Baggage systems	15 years
Screening equipment	7 years
Lifts, escalators and travelators	20 years
Tunnels, bridges and subways	50–100 years
Airport transit systems	
Rolling stock	20 years
Track	50 years
Airfields	
Runway surfaces	10–15 years
Runway bases	100 years
Taxiways and aprons	50 years
Rail	
Rolling stock	8–40 years
Tunnels	100 years
Plant and equipment	
Motor vehicles	4–8 years
Office equipment	5–10 years
Computer equipment	4–5 years

Source: Heathrow Airport Holdings (2015).

asset cost is sometimes adjusted for 'impairment' which essentially accelerates the writing off process. Land and buildings might also be re-valued (up or down) following an estimate of their market value. Assets in the course of construction are transferred to completed assets when substantially all the activities necessary to get the asset ready for use are complete and the asset is available for use. Work in progress is normally included in current assets and when completed moves to fixed assets and is then subject to normal depreciation.

An asset that comes under the definition of a 'non-monetary asset that lacks physical substance' will be classified as an intangible asset and amortised rather than depreciated (essentially the same straight-line process). Concessions for retail outlets are now included as intangibles but the method of valuing such contracts relies very much on judgement. The number of years remaining on the contract will be important, with the amortised value close to what the current concessionaire could get by selling the remaining concession to another party (if allowed). It is similar to an operating lease with a variable commercial rather than financial return. Software costs are capitalised and amortised over periods ranging between three and five years. Other intangibles were goodwill and retail contracts. An example of software intangibles is Aéroports de Paris: the airport has filed patent applications for the creation of an automatic self-service baggage drop-off system for airport passengers, and another one for measuring the slipperiness of surfaced areas such as runways and roads.

The comparison of depreciation periods in Table 3.5 shows the greater detail that Heathrow published, but none of the airports provide information on residual values.

Table 3.5 Comparison of fixed asset depreciation periods FY2014

Type of asset	*Heathrow*	*AdP*	*AENA*	*Fraport*	*Beijing*	*AOT*
Land	n/a	None	None	None	None	None
Runways, taxiways and aprons			25–44			
Runway base	100			7–99	40	
Taxiways and aprons	50			20–99		
Terminal complexes						
Terminal building, pier and satellite structures	20–60	40–50	32–40	5–40	8–45	10–50
Terminal fixtures and fittings	5–20	20–25				
Airport plant and equipment			4–22	3–33	5–15	5–10
Baggage systems	15	20				
Screening equipment	7					

(Continued)

Table 3.5 (Continued)

Type of asset	*Heathrow*	*AdP*	*AENA*	*Fraport*	*Beijing*	*AOT*
Lifts, escalators and travelators	20					
Other plant and equipment, including runway lighting	5–20					
Tunnels, bridges and subways	50–100	45				

Source: Company financial statements.

3.3.3 The statement of cash flows

The cash-flow statement compares cash used in operating the airport with the capital investment and financing activities. It provides additional useful information that the two other statements cannot provide: for example the amount of new financing raised versus existing loans repaid. The cash-flow statement is usually split into three different sources or applications: cash from operations, cash from investing activities and financing activities. The first is generally positive, and if not the airport may be running into financial difficulty. The second will normally be negative, since further assets will be acquired in the normal course of business through expansion and improvement projects. However, assets such as investments in subsidiary or associate companies may be sold and result in this cash-flow category being positive. Finally, financing activities will be negative if existing loans or bonds are repaid, or if dividends are paid; it could be positive if new loans are taken out or new bonds issued.

Airport example: Heathrow Airport Ltd

Cash used in investing activities includes £1,045m from the sale proceeds of the three airports it owned, and £746m for completed investment at Heathrow Airport (see Table 3.6).

Cash for financing includes £1,098m that was distributed as dividends, and interest paid amounted to £569m. New bonds were issued for £1,525m and £516m was used to repay maturing bonds. A further £320m was used to repay loans to the airport that had become due.

3.3.4 The statement of changes in owners' equity

The consolidated statement of changes in equity shows how the main elements that make up shareholders' equity changed from the beginning to the end of the financial year (and the preceding year).

Table 3.6 Heathrow Airport Holdings Ltd, consolidated statement of cash flows FY2014

	FY2014 (£m)
Net cash from operating activities	1,584
Net cash (used in)/from investing activities	–417
Net cash used in financing activities	–995
Net increase/(decrease) in cash and cash equivalents	172
Cash and cash equivalents at beginning of year	159
Cash and cash equivalents at end of year	331

Source: Heathrow Airport Holdings (2015).

Airport example: Heathrow Airport Ltd

For Heathrow Airport, the position at the beginning of FY2014 was, for 1 January 2014:

Share capital	£2,666m
Other reserves	(£311m)
Retained earnings	£72m
Total shareholders' equity	£2,427m

To get to the position at 31 December 2014, retained earnings were increased by the net profit for the year of £308m. This is also to be found at the 'bottom line' of the P&L statement (Table 3.2); retained earnings were further reduced by the large dividend that was paid in FY2014 of £1,098m. A loss of £152m was also deducted for pension losses. Various smaller adjustments were made to 'other reserves' due to currency, hedging and tax differences. No new shares were issued or existing shares bought back, so that 'share capital' remained unchanged over FY2014.

3.4 Airport financial ratios

3.4.1 Financial ratios as a system

The previous section explained in some detail the individual items in an airport's P&L account, balance sheet and cash-flow statement. Some idea can be gained of the airport's size, capital structure, profitability and the financing of its investments from an examination of these figures and the notes attached to them. However, performance ratios will need to be calculated in order to be able to assess past trends of a particular airport or to compare different airports. These could be helpful in evaluating a shareholder's investment in an airport, or in an assessment by banks or lessors before entering into a loan or lease agreement. The ratios can be categorised under the following headings:

- Performance/earnings;
- Risk or solvency;
- Liquidity;
- Market valuation or investment.

The first group of ratios are designed to evaluate how the airport is trading, whether in relation to turnover, assets or equity, while the second deal with the risk of the firm being unable to meet its financial commitments overall, and continue trading. The third provide a measure of the airport's ability to meet its short-term financial commitments. The last group are concerned with value, and are based on the market price of the airport's shares or bonds and can thus only be calculated for companies that are traded on a stock market. Ratios are also discussed in Chapter 5 but the focus there is on commercial and efficiency ratios or benchmarks.

Some ratios use only P&L statement account data, some use only balance sheet data and some combine data from both of these statements. The latter needs to take into account the fact that balance sheet items are measured on a particular date, whereas P&L account items are summed over a particular period (usually one year). The balance sheet items need therefore to be averaged over the same period. The cash-flow statement is also used for ratio analysis, for example determining the percentage of cash generated from an airport's own operations.

The next part of this chapter explains how the more important and widely used ratios are calculated with reference to London Heathrow Airport's last two financial years. These are compared with European and Asia-Pacific airports reporting to ACI's latest survey of airport financial performance.

3.4.2 Profitability and performance ratios

Performance ratios are focused on profits or earnings, seeking to evaluate how successful airport management is in increasing revenues while also controlling costs. Some of these ratios can be calculated using only P&L items (see Table 3.8), while others relate profits to invested capital and thus use the P&L for the ratio numerator and the balance sheet for the denominator (Table 3.9).

Success in terms of P&L performance is measured by three ratios: the first level relates EBITDA to revenues or turnover – this is more of a measure of cash profits, since it is arrived at before deducting capital charges; the second level is based on EBIT or operating ratio, which deducts part of capital charges (depreciation and amortisation) but not finance or interest charges; the last measure takes 'the bottom line' profitability after deducting finance charges and tax.[3] All these measures use revenues as the denominator of the ratio.

The last three rows of Table 3.7 show how the three ratios are calculated using Heathrow Airport's consolidated accounts for FY2014. The EBITDA and EBIT ratios were high, especially compared with many of its airport customers, but high finance charges reduced the net margin to a more 'normal' 11.4 per cent. Heathrow's net margin for FY2013 was 28.7 per cent compared with 11.4 per cent for just above 200 European airports that reported to ACI for that year, and 27.5 per cent for 100 or so Asia-Pacific airports.

Financial performance can also be evaluated using ratios that use a combination of earnings or profits from the P&L and capital or assets from the balance sheet. These are various forms of return on capital, shown for Heathrow Airport in Table 3.8.

Returns on assets and invested capital normally use EBIT as the numerator since this reflects the profits that are available to cover the interest on the

Table 3.7 Heathrow Airport – operating margins FY2014

	2014
Operating revenues (£m) – A	2,691
Operating expenses (£m) – B	1,736
Operating profit or EBIT/(loss) (£m) – C	955
EBITDA or Earnings/profit before interest, tax, depreciation and amortisation – D	1,567
Consolidated profit for the year (£m) – E	308
EBITDA margin (%) = (D*100)/A	58.2
EBIT margin (%) = (C*100)/A	35.5
Net margin (%) = (E*100)/A	11.4

Source: Heathrow Airport Holdings (2015).

Table 3.8 Heathrow Airport – return on capital FY2014

	2013	*2014*
EBIT (£m) – A_1 (year)	–	955
After-tax profits (£m) – A_2	–	308
Total assets (£m) – B (year)	15,725	16,124
Long-term debt (£m) – C (year end)	11,795	12,195
Shareholders equity (£m) – D (year end)	2,427	1,480
Return on assets (%) = $(A_1*100)*2/(B_{2014}+B_{2013})$	–	6.0
Return on invested capital (ROIC) (%) = $(A_1*100)*4/(C_{2014}+C_{2013}+D_{2014}+D_{2013})$	–	6.8
Return on equity (%) = $(A_2*100)*2/(B_{2014}+B_{2013})$	–	15.8%

Source: Heathrow Airport Holdings (2015).

debt part of capital and the dividend or increase in share value for the shareholders. Return on equity, however, takes the profit that is left for the shareholders after payment of interest and tax. Returns on assets or long-term capital are normally much lower than return on equity, reflecting the broader capital base in the denominator of the ratio. This was the case for Heathrow Airport's 2014 returns. In comparison the European airports surveyed by ACI in 2014 (FY2013) achieved an ROIC (return on invested capital) of 6.8 per cent, close to the Heathrow 2013 ROIC of 6.4 per cent (ACI did not calculate return on equity despite its common usage).

3.4.3 Ratios of risk or solvency

Solvency is concerned with the ability of a company to meet its long-term obligations. Liquidity, which is discussed in the next section, looks at the short-term position, generally up to one year ahead. The higher the amount of long-term debt, including that part of long-term debt that will mature in the year ahead (£929m in Table 3.9), relative to shareholders' equity, the greater the risk is of insolvency. This is captured by the debt/equity ratio that can be calculated either by having a simple denominator of long-term debt or by including the short-term maturities and deducting cash and cash equivalents. All the elements come from the balance sheet and can thus be expressed as at the end day of the financial year (for Heathrow on 31 December 2014). The two ratios can be expressed in multiplier form (times 8.2 and times 8.6 in Table 3.9) or expressed as a percentage of debt and equity (the numerator).

Net debt/equity or gearing ratios are often used in covenants to financing agreements: for example, Heathrow finance agreements included a covenanted maximum of 90 per cent in some agreements (the alternative formulation in the last row of Table 3.9). This is unusually high and reflects the excellent credit rating of Heathrow's owners rather than the airport

Table 3.9 Heathrow Airport – gearing ratios 2014

	31/12/2014
Short-term debt (£m) – A_1	929
Long-term debt (£m) – A_2	12,195
Cash and cash equivalents (£m) – B	323
Shareholders equity (£m) – C	1,480
Debt/equity ratio = A_2/C	8.2
Net debt/equity ratio = $(A_2 + A_1 - B)/C$	8.6
Gearing ratio = $A_2 \star 100/(C + A_2)$ or $(A_2 + A_1 - B)/(C + A_2 + A_1 - B)$	89.2% (or 89.6%)

Source: Heathrow Airport Holdings (2015).

Table 3.10 Heathrow Airport – interest cover ratios FY2014

	31/12/2014
Cash operating profit/EBITDA (£m) – A	1,567
Finance income (£m) – B	237
Finance costs (£m) – C	(980)
EBITDA/Net interest = A/(B + C) (Interest cover)	2.1
Net debt (£m) – D = ($A_2 + A_1$ – B) in Table 3.10	12,801
Net debt/EBITDA = D/A	8.2

Source: Heathrow Airport Holdings (2015).

itself.[4] Its covenant level was x 1 in terms of interest cover,[5] having a comfortable margin above that of x 2.1 in 2014 (Table 3.10). More normal levels of gearing are evident in the ACI FY2013 ratios: x 1.86 on average for European airports (still somewhat high) and a conservative x 0.71 for Asia-Pacific airports.

One indication that debt is too high would be the level of interest payments on that debt relative to earnings. Failing to pay interest is likely to trigger a loan default (although some reprieve might be negotiated for a limited period of time). One indicator is the interest paid over the past financial year relative to the cash profit or EBITDA that was available to pay these charges. This ratio uses only figures from the P&L. Normally the interest that was received is offset against the much larger interest paid (Table 3.10). Heathrow had a comfortable margin of EBITDA over net interest paid in FY2014 that was well above its covenant levels discussed above, but market rates of interest were historically low. A further look at the footnotes to the accounts would reveal what part of debt was at variable interest rates and thus susceptible to a future rise in market rates.

Net debt to EBITDA is used by some firms as an indication of leverage (not strictly correct) and its ability to service debt from current cash profits. Moody's rating agency associates a level of around x 1 in this ratio to A grade debt securities, B grade with x 5 and C at over x 6 (Moody's, 2007).

Unfortunately the ACI report calculated debt to EBITDA rather than net debt; it also showed net profit to interest rather than the more commonly used 'net debt to EBITDA' and 'EBITDA to net interest' in Table 3.10.

3.4.4 Liquidity ratios

Liquidity is concerned with the ability to meet short-term obligations when they come due. It is thus to do with working capital management, and its analysis focuses on current assets and liabilities. This means taking the latest information from the balance sheet, specifically current liabilities and the

Table 3.11 Heathrow Airport – liquidity ratios FY2014

	FY2014
Current assets (£m) – A	771
Current liabilities (£m) – B	1,415
Cash and cash equivalents (£m) – C	323
Total revenues (£m) – D	2,691
Current ratio = A/B	0.54
Quick ratio = C/B	0.23
Cash as % of operating revenues = C*100/D	12.0%

Source: Heathrow Airport Holdings (2015).

degree to which current assets can produce the necessary cash to settle the invoices that are or become due. This is captured by the two traditional ratios, the current and quick ratios.

Table 3.11 shows that even if all Heathrow Airport's current assets were converted to cash they would fall well short of balance sheet liabilities. This was because of the large part of long-term debt that will become due over the course of FY2015. The ability to meet these commitments will depend more on cash flow from operations and the absence of large dividend payments than from the historical current asset position. Balance sheet cash can be expressed as a percentage of revenues, and Heathrow's cash was relatively low on this score. Liquidity ratios are thus not ideal given the above situation. Other problems are the fact that the latest balance sheet available may be many months out-of-date and cash for example is very different from previously reported. It should be added that many firms have stand-by lines of credit from banks; these have been negotiated and can be activated at very short notice.

Heathrow's current ratio for FY2013 was 0.39 compared with the more normal 1.02 for just above 200 European airports that reported to ACI for that year, and 0.89 for 100 or so Asia-Pacific airports.

3.4.5 Stock market ratios

The final category of ratios is those that use market rather than book values of assets. The latter are based on original cost less depreciation, and usually differ significantly from market value. However, these are only possible if the airport has a stock market quotation: this can apply both to its equity shares or stocks and (less common) for its debt securities. The market price for the shares will value the whole company, rather than any particular assets it owns. This is called 'market capitalisation' and is calculated simply by multiplying the market share price per share by the number of shares outstanding.

Table 3.12 Free float as percentage of total shares issued 2015

	%
AdP	33
AENA	41
Fraport	40
Vienna Airport	50
Zurich Airport	41

Source: Lobbenberg (2015a).

Table 3.12 shows that, at least for the major European airports, there are sufficient shares that can be traded which should lead to a good market price.

Price/earnings ratio and EV/EBITDA

The price/earnings (P/E) ratio is the traditional one that relates the stock market price at any point in time to the latest annual earnings or profits per share. According to HSBC, 'For the airports, the market generally looks at EV/EBITDA and P/E multiples. In addition, dividend yield also matters and can create momentum in the stock' (Lobbenberg, 2014a). Dividends will depend on the airport's capital expenditure programme, but are generally expected to be paid from sizeable cash earnings.

EV/EBITDA differs from the P/E ratio in including debt in the valuation of the company (although the valuation is normally the balance sheet one based on original cost rather than market value). The denominator is cash profit before deductions for depreciation, finance costs, etc., whereas the P/E takes the 'bottom line' net profit. Both ratios compare an airport's value with the latest year's profits (or projected profits in the current or next year); another way of expressing this is the number of years of profits needed to equal the shares' value, assuming profitability is maintained at its recent level. Airports with higher growth prospects would thus be able to command a high ratio, but a high ratio might also be caused by a sudden drop in profits. EV/EBITDA is widely used in valuing airports which do not have a stock market listing (see Chapter 6 on valuation techniques in general, and Chapter 8 in the context of airport privatisations).

Table 3.13 compares EV/EBITDA and the more traditional P/E ratios for the major European airports that have stock market quotations. Aéroports de Paris and AENA (the Spanish airports group) have a slightly higher rating than the others, perhaps reflecting their greater growth prospects and investment programmes. Vienna Airport has a lower ratio stemming from the poor performance of its major hub airline, Austrian Airlines. It also pays a lower dividend and generated a lower dividend yield in relation to its share price on 5 November 2015.

Table 3.13 Ratios based on market share price for selected EU airports FY2014

	Fraport	*AdP*	*Vienna*	*AENA*	*Zurich**
Revenues (€m)	2,466	2,791	630	3,165	889
EBITDA (€m)	790	1,109	250	1,867	483
EBIT (€m)	483	730	120	1,052	272
Balance sheet net debt (€m) – B	3,791	2,929	528	10,734	783
Shares outstanding (m)	92	99	21	150	6
Market capitalisation (€m) – A	5,287	11,232	1,777	14,835	4,222
Share price 4 Nov 2015 (€) – C	57.34	113.5	84.6	98.9	688
Enterprise Value (EV) (€m) (A + B – minority interests)	9,013	14,161	2,305	25,507	5,003
Earnings per share € – D	2.54	4.07	3.93	4.04	31
Price/earnings ratio (C/D)	22.6	27.9	21.5	24.5	22.2
EV/EBITDA	11.4	12.8	9.2	13.7	10.4
EV/Revenues or sales	3.7	5.1	3.7	8.1	5.6
EV/EBIT	18.7	19.4	19.2	24.2	18.4
Dividend yield 4 Nov 2015	2.4%	4.1%	1.9%	1.8%	1.8%

* converted to € at €0.923 to the CHF Swiss franc (www.oanada.com).

Source: Airport annual reports and authors' ratios.

The investment community rate airports as good long-term investments. They benefit from the good growth prospects of the aviation industry, and avoid the riskier short-term fluctuations that the airlines experience. They produce relatively high cash returns, but these depend on the severity of price caps that the regulatory authorities impose (at least on the aeronautical part of their business). This is addressed in Chapter 10, but it is worth noting here that, apart from Zurich that uses a consensus type of regulation, the others are governed by dual- and hybrid-till approaches, with AENA moving from the current single-till regime to dual-till by 2018 (Lobbenberg, 2015a).

Of the five airports discussed above, AENA only recently got its share quotations with its privatisation in February 2015. It can be seen from Table 3.13 that its EV/EBITDA in November 2015 was higher than its peers' (Frankfurt and Paris);[6] on a P/E basis, however, it was lower than Aéroports de Paris. This was partly because the French airports had quite a large amount of cash that was deducted from debt, which reduced its EV and thus its EV/EBITDA; this did not affect its P/E ratio.

Dividend yield

Dividends can be paid at the discretion of the board of directors. These are paid from the latest year's profits although they can exceed the amount available in that year. Institutional investors such as pension funds and insurance companies like companies that pay dividends since they have a considerable annual requirement to pay pensions and insurance claims.

All the airports shown in Table 3.13 except AENA paid dividends in FY2014, and these provided a yield or return of around 2 per cent. Dividend yield was expressed as a percentage of the share price as at 5 November 2015. AENA intends to start paying a dividend in 2015, when it will give a yield of 2.4 per cent. Another way of looking at dividends is to compare them with profits or earnings: the dividend cover is defined as the net profit for the year (after tax) divided by the proposed dividend. This was between x 2 and x 3 for the airports in Table 3.13, all showing more than adequate cover. However, smaller or no dividends might be an option in a year ahead that foresees large cash requirements for capital investment projects.

3.5 Summary

An understanding of financial statements is necessary to assess an airport's financial strengths and weaknesses, supported as it needs to be by financial ratios. Thus the P&L, balance sheet and cash-flow statements were examined for Heathrow Airport Ltd, a relatively simplified example that did not include either other airports as part of a group, or majority holdings in other airports. These statements provided the inputs to the financial ratios which together cast some light on the financial position of the airport as at the end of its financial year. It was stressed that no single ratio could alone provide a complete enough picture of financial performance, solvency and liquidity. However, the calculation and use of a combination of ratios were discussed as well as some of the pitfalls and shortcomings arising from comparing one airport with another.

It will be seen in Chapters 6 and 9 that financial ratios are crucial in the valuation of airports, and in particular their privatisation through public offering. Debt finance in Chapter 7 also refers to ratios in the context of loan covenants. The next chapter, however, explains how the financial statements are projected into the future as part of the financial planning process.

Notes

1 One example was Plymouth Airport in the UK, which closed down but is not allowed to be developed for housing or other uses for the time being.
2 Most of this was to do with the opening of the new Terminal 2.
3 This used to be described as after-tax or net profits but is now shown as consolidated profit for year.

4 As discussed previously, large amounts had recently been paid to shareholders to pay down their debt rather than use these amounts (from asset sales) to improve the Heathrow balance sheet.
5 The definition of both gearing and interest cover were slightly different to the ones adopted for the worked example.
6 And a slightly higher EV/EBITDA than Fraport and AdP was used by the Spanish government's privatisation advisors in estimating the price at which to offer the shares to the public (see also Chapter 8).

4 Airport financial management and control

4.1 Introduction

Financial planning is the process whereby an airport's corporate goals, and the strategies designed to meet those goals, are translated into numbers. These numbers cover forecasts of market growth and airline market share, and estimates of resources required to achieve this share. Financial planning ranges from the short-term preparation of budgets to long-term planning, the latter often in conjunction with a new runway or passenger terminal project. Its main longer term financial aims are:

- the evaluation of the expected future financial condition of the company
- the estimation of likely future requirements for finance.

The first requires the estimation of items in an airport's future profit and loss (P&L) statement. The second focuses on cash flow, which might also include assumptions on long-term finance, as well as working capital or short-term financial needs. Both of these will also need to be tested for the impact of alternative strategic options.

Short- to medium-term financial planning is generally described as budget planning and control. It is concerned with the achievement of the firm's objectives, but it is also the principal way in which a company controls costs and improves the utilisation of assets. The control process involves four aspects:

- The development of plans
- The communication of the information contained in the plans
- The motivation of employees in order to achieve the plan goals
- The evaluation and monitoring of performance.

These could be applied to a particular project or to the airport company as a whole. The difference between longer-term financial planning and shorter-term budgets lies in the latter's greater detail and ability to provide a basis for the improvement in resource utilisation. It also determines immediate financial needs or surpluses. Airport assets are by their nature long-term, and involve long-term projects and thus long-term (30–40 year) plans. The remainder of this chapter will be divided into an examination of airports' approach first to shorter-term budgets, and second to longer-term financial planning, finishing with managing working capital.

4.2 Budgeting and cash-flow forecasts

The budget is a formal quantification of management's *short-term* plans. It forces managers to think ahead, and to anticipate and prepare for changing conditions. It is generally prepared for the financial year ahead, by month and often also by quarter. The greater the likely problems of control, the shorter the reporting period should be. More frequent reporting and analysis takes time and resources. Airports that have outsourced many of the on-airport services have a simpler task and thus might report less often. For airports, costs are likely to be reported on a monthly basis, while the less controllable traffic and revenue side is perhaps examined on a more frequent basis.

Continuous budgets are sometimes produced, with an additional month added at the end of the period as soon as one month passes, so as always to give a complete 12 months' projection. *Cash budgets* are also useful so as to avoid situations of idle cash surpluses or worrying cash shortages. A *flexible budget* can be prepared for a range of outputs based, for example, on alternative traffic forecasts and varying levels of aircraft utilisation.

The format of the budget may be broadly similar to that of the longer-term corporate or resource plan. Indeed, the first year of the longer-term plan may be the starting point in the preparation of the budget. The integration of the two is clearly important, and longer-term goals should not be abandoned for inconsistent short-term measures. Budgets are generally co-ordinated by the finance department, but their preparation involves a high degree of co-operation between departments:

- Passenger and aircraft movement forecasts (Marketing).
- Cargo forecasts (Cargo).
- Revenue projections (Marketing/Finance).
- Operations planning (Marketing, Operations, Engineering).
- Resource and manpower planning (all departments).
- Cost estimates (all departments).
- Budget finalisation (Finance).

Budgets therefore help the co-ordination between the various parts of the airport. For example, ground operations need to liaise closely with engineering on maintenance planning and scheduling of ground vehicles, and with passenger terminal staff on flight arrivals and departures.

For an existing firm, budgets are often prepared with reference to the previous year's experience. Zero-based budgets, on the other hand, take nothing as given, and consider the most effective way of achieving output targets. Budgets can be built up in various ways and with various levels of detail. They can be for the airport as a whole, by department or by activity or service.

Costs are allocated as far as possible down to the division or unit level to allow a comparison of each one's contribution to overheads. Table 4.1 is one way that this can be done, but airports might group costs in different ways. This serves as a starting point for an evaluation of the impact of removing, combining or outsourcing departments.

Budgetary control consists of comparing the estimates of revenues and costs contained in the monthly budgets with the actual revenues earned and costs incurred. Control will also be exercised through the cash and working capital budgets. The variation between forecasts/estimates and actuals will be

Table 4.1 Typical airport* management accounts – budget for April 2015

	January 2014	*January 2015*		
	Actual	*Actual*	*Budget*	*Variance*
Passengers carried (000s)	5,380	5,452	5,649	–197
Air transport movements	37,280	36,988	37,700	–712
Air cargo (tonnes)	108,200	113,100	106,036	–7,064
Total aircraft movements	37,680	37,362	38,400	–1,038
Aeronautical revenue ($m)	128	132	140	–8
Commercial/other revenue ($m)	65	68	72	–4
Operating margin (%)	18.7	20.5	24.7	–4.2ts
Expenditure by department ($m):				
Marketing	11	12	12	0
Airport Operations	94	95	98	–3
Planning and Engineering	40	40	40	0
Safety and Security	17	18	19	–1
Regulatory Affairs	1	1	1	0
Total	163	166	170	–4
Expenditure by type ($m):				
Staff costs	42	44	42	+2
Depreciation	58	60	64	–4
Materials and Services	20	20	22	–2
Utilities	12	12	10	+2
Other	31	30	32	–2
Total	163	166	170	–4

* for aviation division.

Note: costs or expenditure by department and function may vary in terms of headings and what is included, depending on the airport. Thus these accounts differ somewhat from the ACI breakdown shown in Figures 2.6 and 2.7 in Chapter 2.

calculated, and any significant differences highlighted. The likely causes of such differences should be identified and any necessary action taken.

The variance in total expenditure can be broken down into the principal explanatory factors. These might distinguish between capacity (costs would rise if traffic growth was higher and more peaked than planned) and price (staff costs were higher than budgeted and incurred more overtime pay). They might also include any exchange rate changes that had not been allowed for. Items such as rentals of space are generally easier to predict than landing fees, which depend on traffic forecasts being met. Commercial concession revenues are also tied in some way to retail revenues which also depend on passenger numbers. A further analysis might reveal:

Staff costs: + $3.2 million, or 16 per cent over budget;
Number of employees up by 5 per cent
Average wage/salary levels up by 10.5 per cent
Energy costs: – $0.7 million, or down by 17 per cent compared to budget;
Less air conditioning and average price reduction

Performance indicators should also be shown to give an idea of underlying changes in productivity or service quality. For Copenhagen Airport (2015) these included:

- Investments in improving the passenger experience, including passenger terminal expansion or reconfiguration to create more space for check-in and improved passenger flow
- Target to introduce at least one new unique brand at the shopping centre each year
- Target of 85 per cent passenger check-ins taking less than five minutes
- 86.8 per cent of traffic at the airport arriving on time (target 85 per cent)
- 87.6 per cent of all baggage delivered within 35 minutes (last bag)
- 91 per cent of all passengers security screened in less than five minutes (target 85 per cent)
- Passenger satisfaction with check-in, cleaning, shopping centre, terminals and baggage delivery 86.3 per cent (target 87 per cent).

The above focuses on the more operational part of the airport, and a fuller discussion of a fuller range of performance measures is given in Chapter 5. Some of the differences between actual and budget figures will be due to factors beyond the control of management: for example, bad weather or a security alert. The inclusion of a very high demand period such as Easter in the budget period which fell in a later period the year before will also cause distortions. A distinction should therefore be drawn between controllable and non-controllable costs.

Budgets are the basis for expenditure limits within a particular department or division for a particular period, usually the financial year. Most budgets

Table 4.2 Example of airport cash budget

US$ (000s)	*January*	*February*	*March*	*April*
Total revenues	1,000	1,300	2,100	2,800
Direct costs	1,500	1,450	1,600	1,800
Payroll costs	50	50	50	50
Other costs	20	30	30	40
Net cash from operations	–570	–230	420	910
Net capital movements	–200	–150	–	–
Net cash surplus/(shortfall)	–770	–380	420	910
Opening balance	1,500	730	350	770
Monthly movement	–770	–380	420	910
Closing balance	730	350	770	1,680

lapse at the end of the period, so that funds that were allowed, but not spent, cannot be carried forward to the next period. This has obvious advantages in cost control, but can result in the budget-holder finding ways to spend the remaining funds before they are withdrawn.

The budget can be in account or accrual format, or in terms of cash. The latter is vital in determining future working capital needs, which are described in the next section of this chapter. For the cash budget, assumptions will be made on the delay between the date on which the passenger is carried (the accounts) and the date of receipt of the funds. For airports, this would be around a one-month delay on settlement of invoices, and around the same period for expenditure on credit. Cash sales and revenues would be received and incurred in the same month as shown in the accounts.

Table 4.2 highlights the seasonal variation of an airport in Europe with a high share of leisure traffic. The table includes the net inflow or outflow of capital which is obtained from the capital budget, with capital investment above a certain amount requiring an investment appraisal (see later in this chapter) and board approval. If the closing balance is too low, short-term funding may be required, but in this example the cash balance builds up after March. This budget would also show capital movements, such as debt and equity financing.

4.3 Financial planning

Financial planning deals with the longer-term financial condition of the airport, and in particular the generation of investment proposals, and the process of the analysis and selection of projects from these proposals (capital budgeting). The term *capital* refers to fixed assets, which for the airport is likely to be runways, aprons and passenger terminals,[1] but could also be a major computer or maintenance hangar project. These have a useful life of anything between 5 and 50 years, and to evaluate whether such investments should be made it is necessary to prepare cash-flow forecasts over a longish period.

Table 4.3 Examples of drivers of airport aeronautical revenues

Revenue category	*Driver*
Passenger fees	Passenger numbers (terminating, transfer and transit) Domestic/international split
Landing fees	Aircraft landings Aircraft MTOW
Aircraft parking	Aircraft arrivals/departures
Environmental charges (if separate)	Landings by aircraft type
Fuel throughput charges (often classified as non-aeronautical revenues)	Aircraft departures Flight sector length Tankering

The starting point for the cash-flow forecasts are projections of traffic and revenues. Similarly, operating costs will be estimated from capacity planned to meet the traffic forecasts, as well as input price projections. The revenue streams will be linked to their main drivers which for aeronautical revenues are shown in Table 4.3.

These drivers give some idea of the level of detail that the traffic forecasts need to address. For example, landing fees are usually linked to the aircraft Maximum Take-off Weight (MTOW), so the forecasts of number of take-offs or landings would need to be split into MTOW categories or bands. Stand occupancy time might be determined from the type of flight, with low-cost airline short/medium-haul flights assigned a relatively fast (30-minute or even less) time slot. Long-haul aircraft will typically occupy the stand for a number of hours, and are sometimes towed to remote stands for longer periods of time.[2] The aeronautical charging structure for the particular airport will also dictate the level of detail required.

Forecasts are required of operating costs, some of which are passed on to airlines, lessees or concessionaires (e.g. heating and lighting), and thus also in revenues. The split between labour and other costs will be initially determined by the degree to which different services are outsourced. For example, many airports outsource car parks and passenger terminal retail outlets. These will provide revenue in concession fees and rentals but costs will be limited to managing the contracts (see Table 4.4 and also section 2.4).

An airport's own staff costs will depend on productivity growth, wage inflation and payroll (Table 4.5). Productivity growth might be based on past trends, while wage (and other) inflation could be linked to government inflation projections. Non-employee costs will be driven by the size of facilities to be maintained, heated or cooled, and in the case of security whether it is centralised or distributed. Security can be provided by the airport in which case the cost is passed on to airlines, or by government with charges passed through (see Chapter 2). Whichever way obtains, the relevant

Table 4.4 Examples of drivers of airport commercial revenues

Revenue category	*Driver*
Own outlet spending	Passengers
Concession spending	Passengers
Car parking	Modal split
	Type of trip
Other	Passengers
Rents	Space (square metres)
	Location

Table 4.5 Main drivers of airport operating costs

Staff costs	*Cost drivers*
Management staff costs	
Security staff costs	Productivity growth
Fire staff costs	Wage inflation
Maintenance staff costs	Staff numbers
Other staff costs	
Maintenance	Number of terminals
Rents, rates & utilities	Terminal areas and volumes
Security	Terminals; gate versus centralised
Insurance	Terminals, size or value

costs and revenues need to be based on sound assumptions in order to ensure that reasonably accurate cash-flow forecasts are made.

Capital investment projections will be based on providing sufficient capacity to meet forecast demand. Because additional capacity can often only be provided in discrete and relatively large blocks, timing and phasing are crucial to avoid paying for large amounts of unused capacity. Capital will be a key part of the essential cash-flow forecasts as well as depreciated in the P&L statement.

Net cash receipts (receipts less disbursements) are then subtracted from the initial cash balance to give the subsequent cash surplus or cash requirements in each period. If there is a cash shortfall, then the methods of financing and its phasing should be considered, and the schedule of capital and interest payments incorporated in the cash-flow forecasts.

The pro forma (projected) P&L and balance sheet can be derived from the cash-flow forecast. For the P&L, the capital expenditures will need to be removed and replaced by a depreciation charge. Book or balance sheet profits or losses from asset sales will be substituted for the cash proceeds from such sales.

The pro forma balance sheet will be estimated for the end of each forecasting period. The initial balances of fixed assets, current liabilities, etc.

will be updated using information from the P&L and cash-flow statements for each period. Thus the future financial position of the airport will be estimated, and its ability to raise further long-term capital.[3]

In summary, the following financial statements are likely to be prepared in conjunction with any major terminal expansion or runway extension study or other corporate planning exercise:

For investment appraisal

- Investment schedule.
- Cash-flow statement.

For financial evaluation

- Loan disbursement schedule.
- Summary of finance charges.
- Debt service schedule.
- Debt repayment schedule.
- Cash-flow statement.
- Net income or P&L statement.
- Balance sheet.

For the investment appraisal, it is not necessary to know likely future sources of finance for the investment being evaluated. For a fuller financial evaluation, however, sources of finance can be evaluated, and their impact on the cash flow, net income or P&L statement and balance sheet determined.

4.4 Investment appraisal

The next part of this chapter will deal with the investment appraisal. For this it has been assumed that the airport investment options have been narrowed down to two or three future scenarios. The investment or project could be an airport as a whole that was being valued either by a potential purchaser or by the seller; or it could be a major expansion plan for one airport, and it could be undertaken by a company that controlled a number of airports (e.g. Macquarie or Hochtief and more recently Vinci or AENA).

The projections in the theoretical (but realistic) example in Table 4.6 are not shown over the entire 30-year period, making it easier to understand the calculations in the absence of a PC spreadsheet. Capital expenditure (CAPEX) has been assumed to be heavier in earlier years to reflect an additional runway or terminal investment. But investment is required continuously to update existing facilities and add smaller amounts of capacity through

Table 4.6 Airport investment appraisal cash-flow forecasts (US$m)

US$ million	*2015*	*2016*	*2017*	………	*2044*	*2045*
Capital cost (CAPEX)	16.5	24.7	12.0	………	13.7	13.7
Residual/terminal value						0.0
Cash operating revenues		158.5	187.4	………	525.9	537.2
Cash operating costs		120.0	125.0		163.4	165.4
Cash operating result (EBITDA)		31.1	58.2	………	362.5	371.8
Net cash flow after CAPEX	−16.5	13.8	50.4	………	348.8	358.1
NPV @ 8%	176.6					
IRR (%)	23.4					

the construction of new piers and gates. Usually an alternative scenario will also need evaluation, such that a decision can be made on whether for example to expand an existing terminal/apron area or move to a new site on the other side of the main runway.

Cash flows in Table 4.6 should be net of expected tax payments which could have a large impact on cash flow, as well as likely dividends. At the end of the forecasting period, consideration should be given to including a residual or terminal value of the investments or company. In this example it was assumed to be zero. This value would be the present value of the future cash profits generated from 2045 onwards. If a zero value is adopted it is assumed that future profits are likely to be close to zero, and profit forecasts are often tapered to zero over the last ten years of the forecasts.

Expected profitability, or net cash flow, is an essential element in the selection of investment projects, and the following techniques reduce the net revenue streams of different projects (or fleet planning options) to a common measure. This provides a quantitative basis for comparison, although the final selection of investment may include other non-quantifiable elements. Net cash flows for financial appraisal can be stated in constant or base year prices. This avoids the problems of forecasting inflation rates for the various cost and revenue items. Above-average rates of inflation for particular items will then be reflected in higher real or constant price increases in the item (e.g. fuel costs). Alternatively, all revenues and costs could be forecast in current prices, with appropriate inflation assumptions for the various cost items.

4.4.1 Decision criteria

Various measures are used to combine the project cash flows (or profits) for comparison with the initial investment required. These are used to decide whether or not to go ahead with a particular project (comparison with the without project case), or to compare a number of different projects.

Table 4.7 Example of accounting rate of return

US$ (000s)	*Project A*	*Project B*	*Project C*
Investment	10,000	10,000	10,000
Annual profits:			
Year 1	4,000	1,000	2,500
Year 2	3,000	2,000	2,500
Year 3	2,000	3,000	2,500
Year 4	1,000	4,000	2,500
Year 5	0	0	2,500
Total profits	10,000	10,000	12,500
Average annual profit	2,500	2,500	2,500
Return on investment (%)	25	25	25

Accounting rate of return: The average rate of return technique measures the average profit per year and expresses this as a rate of return on the capital invested.

The example in Table 4.7 shows three projects of similar initial investment but varying profits and project duration. Apart from difficulties about how to measure profits (pre-tax?) and whether to take the average investment over the life of the project, this technique does not differentiate between profits earned at the end of the first year and profits earned, say, after 20 years. The particular example has been chosen to produce identical rates of return and no preference for any one project; however, even if one project had produced the highest rate of return, selection on this basis might have been misleading due to the different timing of profits.

This ratio cannot be calculated from the data in Table 4.7, since accounting items such as depreciation would have to be deducted from cash profit to get accounting net profit. The ratio is useful in that returns can be compared with the overall return on assets or investments for the firm as a whole, but it is not widely used in investment appraisal.

Payback period: This technique measures the length of time that a project takes to recoup the initial investment. Here, cash flows (profits before depreciation) are measured rather than accounting profits. The timing of profits is more important than in the first technique, but no consideration is given to cash flows received after the payback period.

Project A is selected by this method, although it is possible that the rate of return over its whole life is zero or negative. This illustrates the problem of using this technique, which should only be used as an initial screening device in certain cases. For the airport example shown in Table 4.8, the payback period for the project is complicated by the continuous nature of investment. This makes it difficult to apply in practice. However, the Accounting Rate of Return has been applied by airport regulators to the Regulatory Asset Base (RAB) to calculate the airport charges cap (CAA, 2013). This is examined in more detail in Chapter 10.

Table 4.8 Example of payback period

US$ (000s)	*Project A*	*Project B*
Investment	10,000	10,000
Net cash flows:		
Year 1	4,000	1,000
Year 2	3,000	2,000
Year 3	3,000	1,000
Year 4	0	1,000
Year 5	0	3,000
Year 6	0	3,000
Payback period	3.0 years	5.7 years

Discounted cash flow: Discounted cash flow (DCF) techniques take into account the differing timings of cash flows and the variation in project lives. The only mathematical manipulation required is the reciprocal of compound interest.

The essential objective of DCF is to value each year's cash flow on a common time basis. This is usually taken to be the present, although it could equally well be at the end of the period. Profits earned in year 1 could be reinvested in each of the three subsequent years on a compound interest basis; conversely, profits earned in future years can be discounted back to the present, the mathematics of which is given in the following general formula:

$$\textit{Net Present Value} = \sum_{t=0}^{n} \frac{CF_t}{(1+i)^t}$$

where CFt = Net cash flow in period t
i = Discount rate or cost of capital
n = Project life (years).

The Internal Rate of Return (IRR): The discount rate (i) required to equate the discounted value of future cash flows with the initial investment, or to reduce net present value to zero. This can be calculated by trial and error; for a project requiring an initial investment of $10,000, followed by cash benefits of $6,500, $5,500, $4,500 and $3,500 at the end of the first, second, third and fourth years, this amounts to solving the following equation:

$$0 = -10,000 + \frac{6,500}{(1+i)} + \frac{5,500}{(1+i)^2} + \frac{4,500}{(1+i)^3} + \frac{3,500}{(1+i)^4}$$

The IRR (sometimes referred to as the DCF rate of return of the investment) in this example is 40 per cent. Projects can be ranked according to rate of return, and a project selected if its IRR is greater than a specified cut-off value. The major drawback of this technique is the possibility of finding two solutions to the above equation, or two IRRs for the same investment (this occurs when there is a change of sign to negative for future cash flows, as in the case of the need to decommission a nuclear power station at the end of its useful life). For the example shown in Table 4.6, the IRR is 23.4 per cent.

Net Present Value (NPV): Instead of calculating the discount rate required to equate the NPV to zero, the rate of return or discount rate is specified and the NPV is calculated. Projects may be selected with a positive NPV, and the discount rate chosen as a minimum target rate of return, ideally based on the weighted average cost of capital to the firm (WACC – see next section). Projects may also be ranked according to NPVs. This is the preferred technique in investment appraisal, although it does require the prior selection of the discount rate. One answer to this is to compute NPVs with more than one discount rate to see how sensitive the outcome of project ranking is to changes in this parameter. For the example shown in Table 4.6 the NPV was US$176.6m using an 8 per cent discount rate.

Profitability Index: This is the ratio of the project's benefits to the project's costs, both discounted to present values at the appropriate discount rate. It is similar to the NPV approach, but has the possible advantage of being independent of the relative size of the projects. This ratio may be useful where there are a number of investments that might be made, but limited capital is available for investment (i.e. capital rationing). In this case, projects could be ranked by profitability index, and selected from the top of the ranking until the available capital was used up.

4.4.2 Discount rate calculation for NPV

The discount rate is selected to represent the cost of capital to the airport or airport group, although it should also be appropriate to the particular project that is being evaluated. Since investors do not usually have the opportunity to signal their needs in relation to a particular project, in practice past returns to investors in the airport are taken as a proxy for future returns to the airport and project. This is calculated for both equity and debt finance, or a weighted average based on a past or target future debt/equity ratio.

The cost of debt can be obtained by taking a weighted average rate of interest of existing balance sheet debt.[4] Another approach would be to take the current LIBOR plus the premium suggested by the airport's current credit rating, although that might be affected by shorter-term factors which may not persist over the entire project life.

The cost of equity is computed using the Capital Asset Pricing Model (CAPM). This assumes that equity markets are 'efficient' in the sense of current stock prices reflecting all relevant available information. Finance theory asserts that shareholders will be compensated for assuming higher risks by receiving higher expected returns. However, the distinction should be made between systematic risk, which is market risk attributable to factors common to all companies (e.g. impact of 9/11 on air traffic and all airports), and unsystematic risk, which is unique risk specific to the company or a small group of companies (e.g. the bankruptcy of an airport's key customer such as Malev at Budapest Airport). CAPM models the expected return related to the systematic risk. According to portfolio theory, unsystematic risk can be diversified away through portfolio selection, and thus no reward is received for assuming this risk.

The covariance between the company's return and the market's return is the company's β value, and is a measure of the systematic risk of the company. From the β value, CAPM can be used to calculate the equilibrium expected return of a company. The equilibrium expected return of a company, *Re* is the sum of the prevailing risk-free rate, *Rf*, and a 'risk premium' dependent on the β value and the market risk premium ($Rm - Rf$). This can be expressed as follows:

$$R_e = R_f + \beta (R_m - R_f) \tag{1}$$

In order to estimate β, the following regression equation is used:

$$R_e - R_f = a + b_b (R_m - R_f) \tag{2}$$

where

Re = the return on equity *e*,
Rf = the risk-free return,
a = constant,
Rm = the return on the overall stock market,
be = the equity β.

Although the calculation of β involves a covariance relationship between company return and market return, the exact methodology of estimating β is not explicitly indicated for published values, nor is it apparently unique (Morrell and Turner, 2003). The risk-free return is needed for the above formula, and the yield on government bonds is taken as a proxy for this, adjusting for the expected future rate of inflation. Index-linked government bonds can be used for this, or the inflation rate subtracted from the bond yield. Recent estimates for this have ranged from 0.25 per cent to 0.75 per cent, down from 2.5 per cent to 3.5 per cent a few years earlier.

An estimate of the equity risk premium is also required. The UK Civil Aviation Authority (CAA) have used a range of 4–5% in past regulation of airport charges, which they later revised down to 3.5–4.5%. Earlier work for the CAA and other UK regulators proposed a range of 3–4% for the equity risk premium, and 2½% for the risk-free rate (Wright et al., 2003). The latest estimates are higher at 5–6% (CAA 2014a, 6.18), slightly higher than the Competition Commission's 4–5% (CAA 2014a, 6.19).

Table 4.9 CAA WACC calculation for London Heathrow Airport from 2014

Risk-free rate:	0.5%
Equity beta	1.1
Equity risk premium	5.75%
Post-tax cost of equity	6.83%
Pre-tax cost of equity (20.2% tax rate)	8.56%
Pre-tax cost of debt	3.20%
Gearing	60%
Pre-tax real WACC	5.35%

Source: CAA (2014a).

The formula for WACC uses the β values obtained from the above CAPM methodology:

$$WACC = g.(r_f + \rho)(1-T) + (1-g)(r_f + ERP.\beta)$$

where:

g is the gearing for the airport expressed as ratio of debt to (debt + equity)

r_f is the risk-free rate

ρ is the debt premium

T is the airport's rate of corporate or profits tax

ERP is the equity risk premium

β is the beta value estimated from the CAPM regression.

Gearing (g) can be the airport's existing ratio, or more usually a target future ratio. The first (debt) part of the equation can be replaced by the airport's average existing debt interest rate.

Table 4.9 gives the WACC that the Regulator (CAA) used for the 2014 to 2019 price cap for Heathrow Airport. The risk-free rate has declined significantly since the banking crisis, while the equity risk premium has increased.

4.4.3 Which criterion to choose?

The first two criteria discussed above (payback period and accounting rate of return) do not take into account the time value of money, and can thus be rejected. Both NPV and IRR are valid methods of comparison used in industry, but a different conclusion may be drawn depending on which is used. IRR is however widely used, and it is easy to see why this is so, especially in large organisations: the spreadsheet calculations will be done at a lower level of management than those making the decision (which for larger projects will be at board level). There might also be a time lag between evaluation and decision. It is thus easier for the board to be given the preferred project IRR and then decide on their target or cut-off rate, taking into account the project's risk and timing of the decision, rather than specifying the discount rate to be used for each NPV calculation.

Table 4.10 Financial evaluation of alternatives

	Airport A	*Airport B*
Payback period (years)	n/a	n/a
Net present value:		
(NPV @ 8% in US$m)	177	205
Internal rate of return (%)	23.4	15.6

For independent projects, the NPV and IRR criteria always lead to the same accept/reject decision. This is shown for the hypothetical example in Table 4.10 where both projects could be accepted based on positive NPVs, while both IRRs are greater than the target IRR or the investor's cost of capital. On the other hand, if only one project can be selected the choice will depend on whether the investor uses IRR or NPV. Where the gap is narrow, risk analysis might result in the selection of a project with a slightly lower NPV but less influenced by more pessimistic assumptions.

The best decision criterion to use is NPV, assuming that the airport can borrow sufficient funds at the discount rate or cost of capital to finance the investment. For an airport investor the NPV would have to be positive and higher than other opportunities at the time. This would ensure the greatest contribution to the value of the company that was investing. In an airport context this could be another airport, an airport operating company or a pension fund. However, the result may be close and the following section describes the various ways of testing the outcome for shocks to the assumptions that were used in the forecasting.

4.5 Financial risk management

The forecasts that were prepared for a project or company in the previous section were underpinned by numerous assumptions. Some of those would have been economic and depended on economic growth and development. Others would have been related to the aviation industry and more specifically to the airport or airports considered. The future is clearly uncertain and cannot be precisely quantified; forecasts, however, produce expected values which are essential for planning, and the risk of the assumption being wrong can often be quantified. Where it cannot be quantified mathematically or statistically, the assumptions can be varied upwards or downwards to determine how the outcome alters.

Probability (risk) analysis: This relatively complex task involves the estimation of ranges of values and probabilities of the financial inputs to each project. Thus, for each airport expansion option, these must be estimated for forecasts of traffic, revenues and costs. A series of rate of return calculations is then produced in the form of probability distributions for the rate of return for each option. The project with the highest probability of exceeding a given rate of return is chosen.

Sensitivity analysis: Sensitivity analysis tests the effects on the financial outcome or ranking of projects of changes in some of the key assumptions used in making the projections, assuming other factors remain unchanged. These tests should be applied in areas of greatest uncertainty such as traffic forecasts, aircraft size estimates, fuel prices or rates of exchange. Judgement would be required to determine which parameters to change and the range of values to be explored. Sensitivity analysis does not involve the assignment of probabilities to changed assumptions: for example if the central plan assumed fuel prices to be constant in real terms over the forecast period, the alternative might be tested of an increase of 3 per cent per annum in real terms. Sensitivity analysis would determine the resultant change in NPV, but would not consider the likelihood of the alternative assumptions. In the example in Table 4.6 above, the outcome would change significantly if it had been assumed that some of the capital expenditure could be delayed without affecting airport capacity; it would not have changed much if a residual value had been placed on the airport 30 years into the future because the discounting process would have reduced this to a small present value.

Scenario analysis: This technique considers the sensitivity of the NPV or IRR to changes in the key variables and also the range of likely variable values. Thus a pessimistic set of variables might be chosen to determine the NPV, or an optimistic set, to give a range of outcomes. The optimistic set might include fuel prices declining or remaining constant in real terms, a high GDP forecast, and high market share or low yield dilution. The pessimistic scenario might take a high fuel price increase, low GDP growth and low market share. It is important that the assumptions for the key variables are consistent with one another for each scenario, e.g. low fuel price escalation is consistent with high GDP growth. The analysis may involve much work on generating alternative assumptions, as well as workshops where these are challenged and honed into a shortlist of scenarios to be evaluated.

In conclusion, it needs to be emphasised that investment decisions based on the framework and criteria recommended above are only as good as the assumptions used in the evaluation. As many of the relevant factors as possible should be quantified and included in the appraisal, some sort of risk analysis undertaken, and, where appropriate, other unquantifiable factors should also be addressed.

Monte Carlo simulation is a procedure whereby random numbers are generated using a normal probability distribution of the expected values of the assumptions that were used for the cash-flow forecasts. This is similar to probability analysis described earlier, but where the probabilities are not known.

A survey of CFOs found that, of those using the NPV technique, almost two-thirds raised or lowered the discount rate to allow for risk, rather than changing the cash-flow forecast assumptions using the techniques described above. This is clearly easier, but does not provide the discipline of re-visiting the major assumptions upon which the evaluation is based.

4.6 Credit control and working capital management

The management of an airport's capital can be divided into short-term working capital management (up to one year) and longer-term capital budgeting. The former is the outcome of budgeting discussed in section 4.2 above and the latter in the section on financial planning. The appropriate level of working capital is determined by the levels of current assets (cash, marketable securities, receivables and stocks) and current liabilities (overdrafts, short-term borrowings, accounts payable, and sales in advance of carriage).

The way in which an airport's assets are financed involves a trade-off between risk and profitability. In general, short-term borrowings cost less than long-term borrowings, and short-term investments earn less than long-term ones; thus on the basis of profitability, the aim should be for a low proportion of current to total assets, and a high proportion of current to total liabilities. However, this would result in a very low or negative level of working capital, and a high risk of technical insolvency (an airport unable to meet its cash obligations).

Ideally, each of the airport's assets would be matched with a liability or financing instrument of approximately the same maturity. This would ensure that cyclical and longer-term cash needs were met (i.e. zero risk) at minimum cost. In practice, a cushion would be required because of the difficulty in forecasting cash flows with a high degree of accuracy. This would imply a level of current assets somewhat higher than current liabilities. Airports also face the problem that their assets are very long-term and it is difficult to find debt finance for the same 30–40-year term (see Chapter 7).

4.6.1 Current assets – stocks

Manufacturers tend to hold high levels of stocks or inventories, which include materials, work-in-progress and finished goods. The finished goods tend to be sold on credit. Retailers, on the other hand, carry only finished goods, which are sold for cash. Airports, and other service industries such as hotels, carry low stocks (mostly materials or consumables) and no finished goods. They sell almost entirely on normal credit terms (30 days).

Work-in-progress is a major item at airports, especially at times when a large capital investment programme is under way. The interest paid on loans that are purely financing the work-in-progress can be capitalised and placed on the balance sheet. However, this is normally placed in fixed and not current assets. Once the investment is completed and the facility operational the capitalised interest and remaining cost will be placed in fixed assets and depreciated along with the existing assets.

One stock ratio (cost of sales divided by stocks) would be under ten times for a manufacturer, but is not relevant to service industries such as airlines or airports: the latter's ratio was 52x for Fraport and 154x for Heathrow (both excluding capitalised interest).

4.6.2 Current assets – debtors or receivables

Almost all an airport's customers settle on a monthly basis based on invoicing terms. This involves a cost to the airport of administration, the opportunity cost of the funds not yet received, and the possibility of bad debts (with failed airlines or lessees). The average collection period is calculated by expressing the 'trade debtors' or 'trade receivables' amount on the balance sheet date in terms of the number of days' sales:

$$\textit{Average collection period} = \frac{\textit{Trade debtors}}{(\textit{Credit sales} \div 365)}$$

Ideally, it should be calculated using the number of days' credit sales, but this information is rarely available from the financial statements, and so 'total sales' or turnover is used. For London Heathrow Airport Ltd, the average collection period using figures for total sales was 31 days in its financial year to the end of December 2014, up slightly from 29 days in the previous year. Copenhagen Airport's was also 31 days with Zurich Airport somewhat higher at 39 days in FY2014. On the other hand, the Fraport Group converted their revenue into cash slightly quicker at 27 days in FY2014.

Trade debtors (or trade receivables) generally include a deduction for bad debts that will never be collected, and sometimes draconian measures are adopted to force a settlement by physically preventing the take-off of one of the aircraft owned by the airline in question.

4.6.3 Current assets – cash and marketable securities

Cash holdings would usually cover only money that is immediately available, i.e. petty cash and current account balances. However, funds might be placed on short-term deposit with banks for a term of anything between overnight and one year. These funds will earn interest, and the very near term deposits could be considered as quasi cash.

There will be an opportunity cost of holding cash in the interest or higher interest income foregone. At times of high inflation, cash holdings will lose their purchasing power. The major reason for holding cash is the unpredictability of cash flows, and the need to have funds available to meet unexpected demands. Some airports accumulate cash during the peak season or periods of low capital investment, and retain this (or place it on short-term deposit with banks or in government securities) to meet demands in the low season.

An overdraft facility gives airports the possibility to reduce cash holdings, but this is an expensive form of borrowing, and should be used to cover events such as airport closure or sharp downturns in traffic and revenue which cannot be predicted. However, Copenhagen Airport had only DKK47.1m in cash and marketable securities on its balance sheet at the end of 2014, giving it only 6 days of expenditure. It also had lines of credit available from banks of DKK1,886m, which would provide 229 days of cover, but at a cost.

An airport might build up cash and marketable securities, either because it plans major investments in airport infrastructure in the near future, or to fund acquisitions or investments in other companies.

Removing depreciation, amortisation and currency adjustments from operating expenditure gives a rough figure for cash spend: for Heathrow Airport this was £1,540m for the 12 months to 31 December 2014, or an average of £4.2m per day. Thus Heathrow's end 2014 cash and cash equivalents of £323m would cover 77 days of cash expenditure at this rate. For the same financial year Fraport's cover would have been 64 days and Zurich Airport's a much longer 188 days. Zurich has a number of capital investment projects under way, such as the upgrading of Terminal 2, and keeps higher cash reserves in spite of paying a dividend to shareholders.

4.6.4 Current liabilities

The two key items of working capital in current liabilities are trade creditors and short-term loan repayments. Overdrafts were discussed in cash earlier, and there will also be other short-term creditors such as the government (taxes due) and shareholders (dividends payable). Trade creditors are a source of short-term finance which depends on suppliers' terms. A free period of credit will generally be extended to customers, after which interest may be charged on late payment. Delaying payments too long might put critical supplies at risk.

The average settlement period can be calculated in the same way as the average collection period. There is, however, a similar problem in obtaining data from published accounts on credit purchases.

$$\textit{Average}\ \text{settlement}\ \textit{period} = \frac{\textit{Trade creditors}}{(\textit{Credit purchases} \div 365)}$$

Assuming that credit purchases approximate to operating expenses less staff costs and depreciation, then Heathrow Airport's average settlement period was 40 days for FY2014, and Copenhagen Airport's 52 days, Fraport Group's only 21 days and Zurich Airport's 36 days for the same financial year.

4.7 Summary

Financial planning and control is an essential discipline for any company but for an airport it is perhaps harder to modify the plan if the forecasts are not met. Crucially, a combination of the long-term and fixed nature of airport assets makes it difficult to adjust capacity to significant changes in air services. An example of this was the planned expansion of London Stansted Airport in the 1990s to cater for a mix of long-haul and network carriers with shorter haul leisure flights (in those days largely charters). First, the forecasts had not foreseen the rapid expansion of low-cost airlines at Stansted due to limited and more expensive capacity at the other London airports. Second, the long-haul and wide-bodied aircraft flights at Stansted did not materialise, mainly due to lack of feeder flights.

Short-term financial planning or budgeting is undertaken to ensure that the finance department has sufficient funds to meet immediate needs and determine how much money needs to be raised to finance investments. However, as with long-term planning, projections can be upset by delays to payments or spikes in construction costs; these are dealt with more easily through the use of lines of credit or overdrafts with banks. The budget combines the cash from operations with the CAPEX forecasts to enable funds to be available at the right time, thus avoiding higher financing costs.

Short-term projections will also be required by the economic regulator, where regulation is based on price caps or rate of return allowed. This often excludes certain assets or facilities from the evaluation.

Working capital management focuses on the short-term part of the balance sheet and enables the identification of the cash that is expected from airline charges and the invoices that are due from suppliers.

Long-term financial planning is usually linked with the master planning of the airport's infrastructure; it is required by buyers and sellers of airport companies (control or minority stakes) or long-term concessions. A 30- to 40-year period may be considered, although the detail diminishes over the last decade. Forecasts of operating revenues and costs are required, as well as the CAPEX needed to ensure that sufficient capacity is available to meet the traffic forecasts over the period.

Once the net cash stream has been forecast for the project or alternative projects they need to be discounted to present values using an appropriate discount rate for the investor. Alternatively the internal rate of return (IRR) can be calculated and compared with the investor's hurdle rate. The discount or hurdle rate is usually the weighted average cost of capital (WACC). This combines the required return on equity with that for debt by means of an average that is weighted by current or target future level of gearing. The WACC is essentially backward looking and thus assumes that investors will be happy with a future return that matches past experience.

The next chapter also evaluates the past in order to improve efficiency and provide management targets. This focuses on commercial ratios which can be analysed over time and by comparison with other airports' performance and also assesses the academic research which has been undertaken in this area.

Notes

1 Cargo terminals are often built by third parties on land rented to them by the airport.
2 At the airline's home base they may be towed to the maintenance hangar or cargo apron area.
3 Balance sheets are usually prepared more frequently (quarterly or half yearly) in the first two years as part of the budgeting process.
4 If debt is on variable rate terms it will be necessary to forecast LIBOR or whatever the variable rate is linked to.

5 Airport benchmarking

5.1 Introduction

This chapter considers the increasingly important practice of benchmarking. As airports have been transferred into business enterprises, there is now worldwide acceptance that the use of benchmarking, not only for airport operators but also for other interested entities such as investors, regulators and users, is a fundamental aspect of airport management for evaluating and improving performance. Most airport activities (e.g. service quality, safety and security, the environment) can be included in benchmarking analyses (see Graham, 2005; ACI-Europe, 2015c) but the focus here is on the economic and financial areas. However, the trade-off between different performance areas (e.g. service quality vs cost levels) needs to be fully taken into account. Moreover, airports have very specific characteristics and differ in many aspects (e.g. large vs small airports, private vs public airports). This will mean that airport operators are likely to prioritise the measurement of the various aspects of economic and financial performance in different ways.

A detailed understanding and knowledge of both airport revenues and costs and the nature of financial statements, as discussed in Chapters 2 and 3, is crucial for the successful use of benchmarking tools. Some standard financial ratios have been described in Chapter 3 but this chapter goes further by identifying specific ratios unique to the airport industry that are best used when assessing its performance. The chapter begins with a discussion of why benchmarking is needed and which organisations can benefit from its use. This leads on to a consideration of key benchmarking concepts and the complex area of measurement issues. This then allows for a detailed examination of the different benchmarking approaches and their practical applications in the remaining part of the chapter.

5.2 The types and uses of benchmarking

Essentially benchmarking performance is concerned with evaluating performance against a standard or 'benchmark'. Without a benchmark, any measure will be meaningless. Therefore this means that the usefulness of any performance evaluation will depend almost entirely on the appropriateness of the benchmarks that are set.

There are two main types of benchmarking:

Internal or self-benchmarking: With this approach, benchmarks are set based on some internal past performance and an assessment of performance is undertaken through time. This can show trends over the years and give indications as to the direction in which the airport is heading. However, the inherent weakness here is that the airport is considered in total isolation with all the evaluation related entirely to its own sphere of operation. As a consequence, it will not be possible to identify areas of performance which are substandard compared with other airports or to be familiar with what is actually achievable in the industry.

External or peer-benchmarking: This key weakness associated with self-benchmarking can be overcome by making external assessments with other peer airports. Benchmarks can be associated with an industry standard (e.g. an average) or best practice (e.g. the best-performing airport). The comparisons are most commonly made at a single point in time but they can also cover a period of time using inter-airport data for a number of years (in statistical terms known as panel data). This external evaluation is more complex because of the heterogeneous nature of airports which, as discussed later, introduces both problems of comparability and challenges involved with choosing the most suitable sample of peer airports.

There is little firm evidence concerning the relative popularity of these two methods but it is generally thought that the simpler internal processes are used more often. Indeed this is confirmed by a recent survey of benchmarking methods (for all airport activities) of 50 airports in Europe which found that 80 per cent of airports used internal survey data and around 58 per cent used internal audit data, compared with corresponding shares of around 40 per cent for external surveys and audits (ACI-Europe, 2015c).

The primary users of benchmarking techniques must be the airport operators themselves. To varying degrees, all benchmarking activities will help management gauge how effectively they are using resources to produce the required outputs in terms of traffic or revenue generated. Benchmarking should be able to identify shortcomings in the airport production process which can stimulate corrective action. From the benchmarking findings, management can decide what levels of performance are desirable and build these into their financial planning and management. Benchmarking techniques can also help airport management gauge the impact of future major planning or investment decisions. However, the extent of benchmarking that the airport operator actually undertakes will depend on many factors including data availability, ownership and governance structure, competitive forces and the resources involved.

ICAO (2013, appendix 1, p. 8) identifies six key uses of performance comparisons and benchmarks, stating that they can:

a) improve transparency of a performance management process;
b) provide insight into the opportunities for the improvement of individual airports' performance (learning opportunities, setting performance targets);
c) highlight best practices for delivering improvements in performance through the identification of highly efficient or high-quality service facilities and/or processes;
d) support more effective regional coordination and planning, thereby rationalizing and avoiding duplication of efforts;
e) support constructive dialogue with users and other interested parties; and
f) provide global reach to expand the knowledge base.

Clearly airport benchmarking measures can also be of use to other bodies that will have various perspectives on, and usually somewhat different objectives for, assessing performance. Governments, regulators and other policymakers can use them to ensure that the optimal use is being made of public resources (if the airports are publicly owned) and that the airports are providing their users with the services the users need at a fair and reasonable price. Shareholders, investors and financiers of airports can evaluate airport-specific benchmarking measures to identify possible business opportunities and to inform their airport investment decisions, in addition to using more generic financial ratios that they would consider for any business purchase. Finally users of airport services and facilities, particularly airlines, are often keen to have access to airport benchmarking findings in order to evaluate whether airports are operating efficiently in terms of average or best practice and are delivering value for money to their customers. Such measures may be used to add weight to negotiations related to airport fees and the services offered.

5.3 Benchmarking concepts

Within an economic and financial context, performance benchmarking is primarily concerned with investigating relationships of inputs (e.g. labour, capital) and outputs (e.g. goods and services). These inputs and outputs can be measured in either physical or financial terms. Such input–output relationships (e.g. output per unit of input) are typically defined as productivity measures or ratios.

The notion of economic efficiency is related to the input–output relationship. From a theoretical viewpoint there are three main types of efficiency. Firstly, there are the closely related concepts of technical and productive efficiency. Technical efficiency considers the effectiveness with which a given set of inputs is used to produce an output, with technical inefficiency being more commonly known as x-inefficiency. Productive efficiency is defined as producing an output for the lowest possible costs. Secondly, there is allocative efficiency which is concerned with ensuring that society derives the most possible utility from scarce resources, with the most demanded goods and services going to those who value them the most. Both these two types of efficiency are static concepts, dealing with a specific point of time. By contrast the third aspect of economic efficiency is dynamic efficiency which is associated with enhancing technical efficiency over a period of time, by balancing a short-term focus with long-term needs to ensure that suppliers are fully able to undertake research and development and deliver innovation, new processes and technologies. Most performance measures that are used for benchmarking focus on technical/productive efficiency.

5.3.1 Inputs

In line with most other businesses, labour and capital are the major inputs of the airport system. The number of employees is the simplest physical measure of labour but this may be misleading given the common practice of shift work and seasonal employment at airports. A better measure is full-time equivalent employees or man-hours worked if this amount of detail is available. The financial measure of the labour input is represented by employee wages and salaries and associated costs. This will automatically take account of the different hours worked although there may be some discrepancy between airports as to what 'associated' costs actually include (e.g. related to expenses or pensions).

A reliable measure for the capital input is more difficult to determine. In some ways this is due to the very diverse nature of capital inputs (e.g. small pieces of equipment with short life expectancy vs long-term investments in land and buildings) and also because of the difficulties involved in assessing the loss in production due to the aging of physical assets. Measures such as the number of runways, gates and check-in counters or terminal area can be used but these are rather crude and cannot take account of detailed factors, for instance the configuration of runways. The alternative could be to define the capital input as the production capabilities or capacities of the airport (e.g. maximum capacity). However, the production capacity of an airport can be measured in relation to many different areas such as runways, terminals, gates and so on. In addition this can be assessed on an hourly, daily, monthly or annual basis.

Financial accounting practices associated with depreciation and amortisation can be used to represent the consumption of capital but clearly these are just paper exercises which may bear little relation to the deterioration of the commercial life of the assets or the economic production capability. Moreover in practical terms there are also difficulties because accounting practices associated with items such as the treatment of depreciation and asset valuation tend to vary by country and even by airport. This can be complicated by different systems of economic regulation. Adjusting the data so that it relates to a common set of accounting rules has not proved to be a feasible solution. There may also be issues related to direct and indirect state subsidies which will affect the capital input measure. As a result, many benchmarking studies tend to place less emphasis on the capital input (both physical and financial), in spite of the key role that it plays.

In addition to the labour and capital inputs, there are other inputs that are commonly called intermediate or 'soft cost' inputs. These are associated with externally purchased products such as utility costs, repair costs, building/equipment and other material costs, consultant services and outsourced activities. Due to their diverse nature they are normally only considered from a financial viewpoint and such input data is usually forthcoming as in essence it is just cost data.

5.3.2 Outputs

Airports provide a service to enable aircraft to land/take-off and passengers and freight to be loaded/unloaded, as well as offering many commercial, especially retail, facilities to appeal to passengers and other airport users. This multi-product nature of airports complicates the physical definition of outputs. Therefore typically this is measured in terms of aircraft movements, passengers or freight – although this does not capture the output of the airport as a retail facility which usually proves too difficult to include directly.

A decision has to be made as to which of the three main physical output measures should be used at an aggregate level. Unless the focus is on airfield operations, aircraft movements are not ideal as these do not differentiate between different sizes and types of aircraft. This leaves passenger and freight volume. It can be argued that the selection of passenger numbers makes sense as freight handling tends to be more of an airline activity with very little airport operator resources devoted to it, and/or many airports tend to have low volumes of freight compared with their passenger throughput. An alternative is to combine the passenger and cargo traffic into one aggregate output measure. Frequently in this situation the traffic unit or work load unit (WLU) is used which equates one passenger with 100kg of freight. This measure originated from the airline industry with the weight criterion loosely assuming that the average passenger and their baggage were equivalent to 100 kg. However, whilst easy to compute, this measure is rather arbitrary as clearly the same weight of passengers or freight does not involve the same use of resources. Other more sophisticated measures have also been used. For example LeighFisher produces an annual global benchmarking study and uses the so-called airport throughput unit (ATU), which keeps the WLU relationship of 1:10 between passengers and freight but also includes the aircraft movement component, weighting 100 passengers to be equivalent to 1 aircraft movement (LeighFisher, 2014).

The financial measurement of the outputs tends to be more straightforward. It is usually the total revenues generated, although sometimes the concept of 'value added' is used which measures the extra wealth created by the airport. This latter measure is defined as the total revenue less the costs of the intermediate inputs and so focuses on the labour and capital resources where the airport operator normally has the greatest control.

5.3.3 Comparability issues

For most organisations, the use of external or peer benchmarking will necessitate the consideration of comparability issues, particularly if the other airports are located in different countries. The specific nature of airport operations and the heterogeneity of the airport landscape have meant that these 'apples with pears' comparison problems are very significant and have undoubtedly hindered the development of effective inter-airport benchmarking in the past. As discussed in Chapter 2, one of the major difficulties is due to the varying range of activities undertaken by airport operators themselves.

As far as possible these comparability problems should be addressed by choosing peer airports that are as similar as possible, but the complex characteristics of airports mean that pure 'like-with-like' comparisons are rarely possible. In these situations two alternative approaches tend to be adopted. The first is to accept that there will be differences but to work with the raw data. The thinking behind this is that choices about whether to outsource certain activities are management decisions that should be assessed with performance studies. Any attempt to compensate for this could be viewed as unrealistic and a move away from the truth.

The other approach is to standardise or normalise the data so that each airport's performance is presented as if it undertook a uniform set of core activities. For example, if an airport operator undertakes ground handling activities itself, the assumed costs, revenues and staff numbers associated with this can be deducted in order to make the data more comparable with airports with no involvement with this activity. A hypothetical concession income from handling can then be added back to the airport's accounts. This is the method used by LeighFisher in their benchmarking work and it has also been used in a somewhat similar manner in the US when airline data has been added to airport operator finances to take into account that some airlines, rather than the airport operator, directly operate the terminal (ACI, 2006). Such adjustments, while arguably enabling a more 'like-with-like' assessment to be made, will clearly also be subject to a certain level of subjectivity related to the assumptions that have to be made.

Airports tend to be plagued with further comparability problems. For instance it often proves very difficult to compare airports which are managed individually with those that come under group operations because of possible joint costs and cross-subsidisation. Also, if the benchmarking considers just one period of time, the findings may be unduly influenced by the different positions of the airports in the investment cycle. The lumpy investment characteristics of airports mean that when there is significant investment this will not only be reflected in the valuation of fixed assets and high depreciation charges, but also in high unit operating costs which may arise due to the temporary overcapacity brought about by the new investment. A solution here is to consider more than one year if possible in order to average out these effects.

A further common problem with any inter-firm comparison involving different countries is the need to convert local currencies to a common unit. Official market exchange rates are readily available but they may not reflect the real purchasing power of each currency and they may be subject to considerable fluctuations. As a result, a number of benchmarking studies use purchasing power parity (PPP) exchange rates instead which are calculated by dividing the cost of a given basket of goods in one currency by the cost of the same basket of goods in another country. An alternative is to use special drawing rights (SDRs) which use four currencies (the euro, the US dollar, pound sterling and the yen) weighted according to the relative importance of the currency in international trade and finance.

5.4 Partial performance measures

There are two main types of performance assessment or benchmarking techniques which utilise either partial or total measures (Figure 5.1). Partial or one-dimensional measures, in use at many airports throughout the world, focus on selected areas of performance by investigating the specific inputs and outputs relationships. They are typically ratios or percentages which are relatively easy to compute and understand. They have the advantage of being able to highlight strengths and weaknesses in certain areas and to indicate where specific improvements can be made. However, since each measure will in one way or another be interrelated or dependent on each other, they

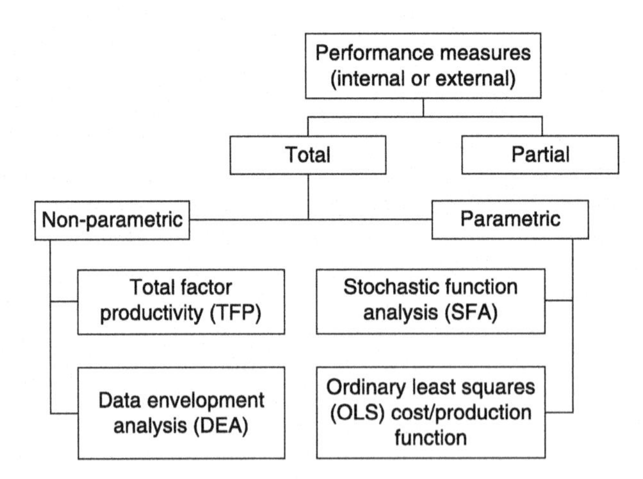

Figure 5.1 Types of performance measures

should not be considered in isolation but instead viewed collectively as a system.

Whilst most of these will investigate the input:output relationship (e.g. revenue per employee, staff costs per passenger), it is often useful to supplement these with input:input measures (e.g. staff costs per employee) and output:output measures (e.g. revenue per passenger) to provide further insight into the observed performance. In addition measures looking at the mix of inputs or outputs (e.g. staff costs as % of total costs, non-aeronautical revenue as % of total revenue) may also be informative. For illustrative purposes, Table 5.1 shows the actual indicators used in the LeighFisher study which are a mixture of input:output, input:input and output:output ratios.

Typically these measures will be divided into different aspects of performance. For instance ICAO (2013) makes suggestions for some key indicators differentiating between productivity (e.g. aircraft movements per employee,

Table 5.1 Airport benchmarking measures used by LeighFisher

Total revenue per ATM
Total revenue per 1000 ATUs
Total revenue per passenger
Total revenue per employee
Aeronautical revenue per ATM
Aeronautical revenues as a percentage of total costs
Aeronautical revenues as a percentage of total revenue
Aeronautical revenue per 1000 ATUs
Aeronautical revenue per passenger
Non-aeronautical revenue per passenger
Commercial revenue as a percentage of total revenue
Total costs per ATM
Total costs per passenger
Total costs per 1000 ATMs
Operating costs per passenger
Materials and services costs per passenger
Staff costs as a percentage of operating and staff costs
Staff costs per 1000 ATUs
Staff costs per passenger
Staff costs as a percentage of turnover
Operating profit
Operating profit per passenger
Net cash generation per passenger
EBITDA
Return on capital employed
Return on shareholders' funds
Return on invested capital
Passengers per employee
Passengers per ATM

(Continued)

Table 5.1 Continued

ATUs per employee
Total assets per passenger
Equity ratio
Liquidity ratio
Assets per employee
Capital expenditure per passenger
Capital expenditure per passenger as a percentage of turnover
Taxation effect

Source: LeighFisher (2014).

aircraft movements per gate, passengers per employee, tonnage of cargo per employee) and cost-effectiveness (e.g. total costs per aircraft movement, total costs per passenger, total costs per 1,000 air traffic units, staff costs as a percentage of turnover). Table 5.2 shows the measures suggested by ACI which are divided into the productivity/cost effectiveness and financial/commercial areas. Other evaluations may be divided into a greater number of areas – for instance Richardson et al. (2014) use cost effectiveness, revenue generation, commercial performance, profitability and capital investment. Figure 5.2 shows some of the most popular performance areas which are used. Organisations other than the airport operator will focus on areas which are of specific interest to them. For example, investors tend to concentrate on the pure financial ratios although some also consider revenues and costs per passenger.

The system of partial measure should ideally have a hierarchical structure with ratios at different levels of disaggregation, ranging from those considering broad indications of an airport's relative performance to detailed measures focused on discrete areas of an airport's operation where specific changes will usually be easier to implement. Typically the high-level indicators at the top

Table 5.2 Economic and financial performance measures suggested by ACI

Productivity/cost effectiveness	*Financial/commercial*
Passengers per employee	Aeronautical revenue per passenger
Aircraft movements per employee	Aeronautical revenue per movement
Aircraft movements per gate	% Non-aeronautical revenue/total revenue
Total cost per passenger	Non-aeronautical revenue per passenger
Total cost per movement	% Debt service/operating revenue
Total cost per WLU	Long-term debt per passenger
	Debt:EBITDA ratio
	EBITDA per passenger

Source: ACI (2012).

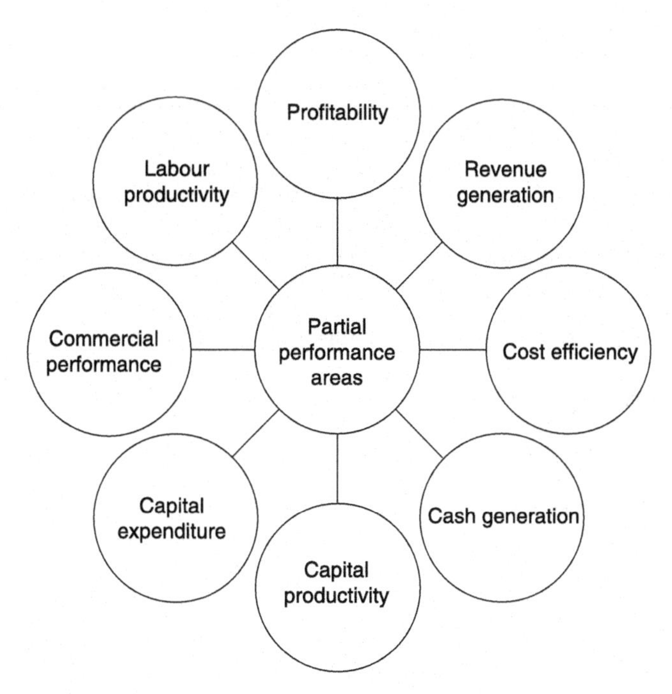

Figure 5.2 Performance measurement areas

of such hierarchical systems are called Key Performance Indicators (KPIs) or core measures, with each of these linked to the airport achieving a specified goal. Below this can be other levels of indicators, for example Hazel et al. (2011) suggest Key (Departmental) indicators which are important for the operations of key airport departments or functions (Table 5.3). Then other lower-level measures that can be useful as secondary department unit measures, at or below the manager level. When selecting the number of measures and hierarchical levels there needs to be balance between limiting the number so that the measures are relatively easy to compute and interpret, while at the same time ensuring that they are sufficient in number to cover all areas of importance. Externally high-level data is usually possible to obtain for most airports, but the more detailed data may not be published and therefore may be less readily available.

One aspect of performance which is typically analysed in considerable detail is commercial revenue generation. Figure 5.3 shows some of the measures that are commonly used. Whilst some of these are straightforward input:output measures (such as revenue per square metre), many of the others explore other relationships which can help provide greater insight into performance in this specific area.

Table 5.3 Core and key financial indicators suggested by the Transportation Research Board

Core indicators	*Key indicators*
Airline cost per enplanement	Accounts receivable aging – days
Airport cost per enplanement	Airline cost per operation
Bond rating	Airport revenue from non-passenger-dependent sources (%)
Days unrestricted cash on hand	Contract services cost as % of total operating cost
Debt per enplanement	Debt service as % of operating revenue
Debt service coverage ratio	Investment income as % of invested assets
Non-aeronautical operating revenue as % of total operating revenue	Long-term debt per enplanement
Non-aeronautical operating revenue per enplanement	Net operating income per enplanement
Operating cost per enplanement	Net working capital (operating liquidity)
	Operating cost per operation
	Personnel cost per enplanement

Source: Hazel et al. (2011).

5.5 Total performance measures

In spite of the fact that partial benchmarking measures are in widespread use within the airport industry and frequently used by financial analysts, they do have a number of shortcomings. Firstly by definition, they only give a 'partial' diagnosis of the situation and can be misleading if only a selected number or a biased collection of indicators are chosen. They can provide a valuable insight into a certain area, but to have a complete picture, many measures are needed but then the sheer number of these would be challenging to interpret. Secondly such measures may ignore the interaction between the multiple inputs used and outputs produced as they cannot take account of factor substitution (e.g. if one airport uses an employee to undertake a specific task whilst another may use a machine) or differences in input/output prices and other operating conditions. For example an airport that has high reliance on outsourcing many activities may appear to have very high labour productivity but this does not actually mean that it uses its labour inputs very efficiently. In essence, relatively good performance in one area may be at the expense of weaker performance in another area.

One way to overcome these weaknesses is by investigating the relationship between the combined inputs and outputs, using econometric techniques, to produce a single multi-dimensional performance or efficiency measure. In the last two decades there has been considerable interest within the academic environment in developing such 'total' measures although these

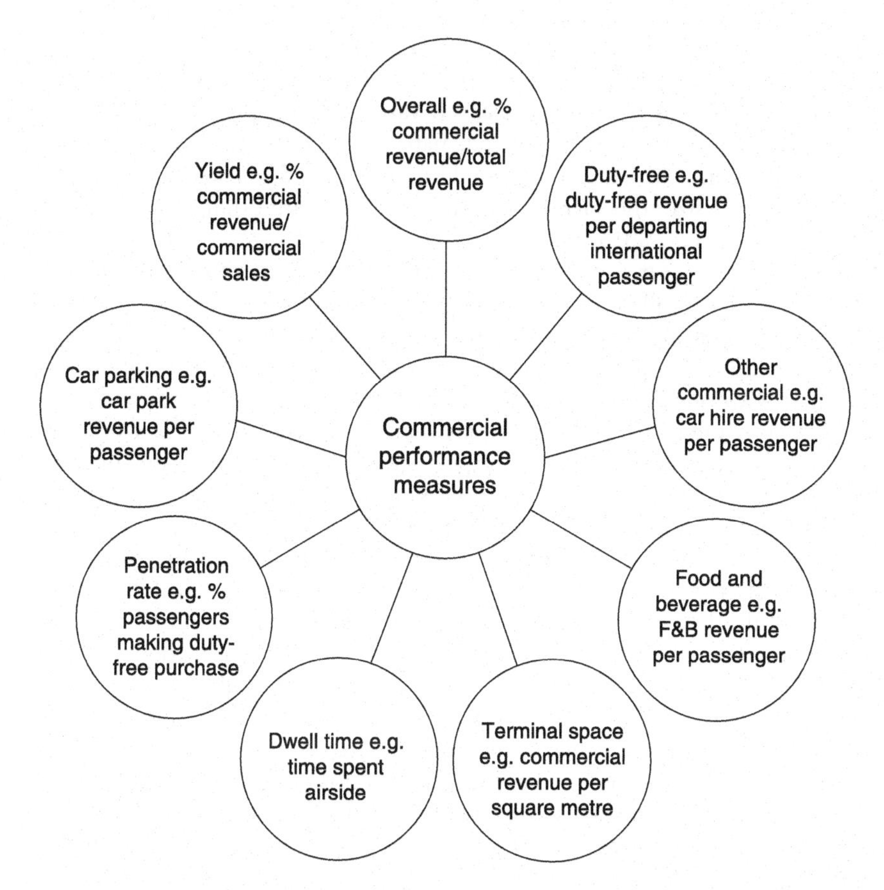

Figure 5.3 Types of commercial performance measures

have had very limited usage within the actual airport industry (usually within the context of economic regulation). These methods are based on either averaging evaluations or making comparisons with a defined efficiency frontier, and can be of a deterministic or stochastic nature (for full details of these methods see Merkert et al., 2012; Liebert and Niemeier, 2013; Lin et al., 2013).

It can be seen from Figure 5.1 that there are three key methods: two non-parametric and one parametric or statistical. The first of the two non-parametric techniques is an averaging index number approach such as the Tornqvist total factor productivity (TFP) method. With this all outputs are aggregated into a single outputs index weighted by revenue shares and all inputs are aggregated into a single inputs index weighted by input cost shares. This approach is used in the Global Airport Benchmarking Report which is produced annually by the Air Transport Research Society (ATRS). The weighted output is based on aircraft movements, passengers, cargo and non-aeronautical revenue and the weighted index is based on labour, other non-capital (soft cost) inputs, runways, terminal size and the number of gates. The capital input is excluded in most measures because of data difficulties, so most of the focus is on what is called variable factor productivity (VFP). Two measures of VFP are produced, namely the gross value and also the net/residual value which has removed factors beyond management control (such as airport size, the share of international and cargo traffic and capacity constraints) (ATRS, 2015).

The second, by far more popular, non-parametric method is the deterministic approach called data envelopment analysis (DEA). This again relates a weighted input index to a weighted output index, this time using a linear programming technique which does not require the weights to be predetermined as with the TFP non-parametric methods. These less demanding data requirements often make it a more favourable method to use. It works by assessing the relative efficiency of airports (generally called decision-making units or DMUs) in relation to the total sample. The most efficient airports are located on the so-called frontier with a relative index of 1.00.

An advantage of the DEA approach is that it can be used to measure scale effects as there are both constant and variable returns to scale models. Moreover if DEA is used with the Malmquist index, sources of productivity differences over a certain time can be identified as the index decomposes the productivity changes into efficiency changes and technical changes gained from adopting new technologies. However, DEA models are very sensitive to outliers and parameter selection and so if different inputs and outputs are selected the outcome may be very different. Furthermore, if the combined number of inputs/outputs is large relative to the number of airports, the performance may be overstated and consequently many airports may achieve the maximum efficiency value of 1.

By contrast the third method is a parametric or statistical approach which uses a production or cost function that incorporates several variables influencing performance. The cost function, for instance, typically expresses costs as a function of output, input prices and other factors affecting outputs and inputs. The function can be estimated by an averaging deterministic approach using ordinary or corrected squares regression analysis or more commonly now by estimating the efficient frontier, by using the stochastic frontier method. Compared with the other two total methods, this technique usually requires significantly more detailed data and is more complex as it requires the specific functional form to be specified.

5.6 Practical applications

When used carefully and appropriately all of these benchmarking methods can be powerful analytical tools. The total measures can provide a clear insight into the airport's overall performance. However, it can be difficult to relate this single total value to the practical airport environment and so as a consequence the findings may not be very informative for airport operators. This is not usually an issue with partial measures that are easier to interpret, although if these are too few in number they may be misleading, whereas if they are too numerous they may over-complicate the evaluation. Overall ideally total and partial measures should be used in a complementary manner to drive performance improvement by identifying strengths and weaknesses and exploring underlying factors causing these.

It may be possible to undertake some statistical analysis to examine these explanatory factors. For example with both the partial and total measures some form of regression analysis to investigate the relationship between the performance measure(s) (the dependent variable) and the explanatory factors (the independent variables) may be possible. The exact method that can be used will depend on the performance technique. For instance with the frontier approach of DEA which produces values with an upper bound of one, a Tobit model (rather than the more common ordinary squares model) tends to be used and in recent years the reliability of this has been improved by using so-called bootstrapping procedures.

As discussed in Chapter 2, there are many different factors driving performance that can be explored. Some of the common ones considered in the published literature include location, airport size, nature of traffic (e.g. connecting vs terminal, international vs domestic, LCC vs network carrier), level of congestion, ownership, governance and regulation. It may be possible to exclude some of these that are considered beyond the airport management's control as in the ATRS study. Whether or not these effects can actually be quantified, in any performance assessment it is important to differentiate between such external factors and internal factors (such as the degree of outsourcing, the quality of service and the investment cycle) which are more within the airport operator's control. Moreover, if the actual airport operator appears to have little control, an assessment of the stakeholders' influence should also be undertaken. The key point with any benchmarking exercise is that the results are not an end in themselves but a powerful tool that will raise issues that need further investigation.

Benchmarking is one element of the airport performance management process which will typically consist of a number of different generic steps. These begin with defining the business goals and the areas that are going to be benchmarked (e.g. key performance areas (KPAs)). This is followed by making decisions concerning what performance measures are to be used, what data should be used and how to set the benchmarks. Once this has been done the data can be collected and the results can be interpreted taking into account the explanatory factors. This will then lead to communicating the results to all decision makers and the introduction of strategies to improve performance. Communication is important not only internally but also with external stakeholders, obviously acknowledging commercial sensitivities. This continuous performance management process then begins again by assessing how these new strategies have influenced performance.

As regards external benchmarking, there are a number of benchmarking studies that airports can participate in, and have access to the results. Two of the most popular studies are those undertaken by LeighFisher and ATRS which have already been discussed. They have very different approaches. LeighFisher adjusts the data to account for the comparability problems associated with different activities and only uses partial measures. ATRS uses raw data in producing the VFP values, although calculates some partial measures as well. Examples of the outputs of these two studies are shown in Figures 5.4 and 5.5 for some Asia-Pacific airports for illustrative purposes. Some regional organisations of ACI (Europe, North America) are also involved with calculating partial measures, with the main results being shared only amongst the participants. For instance ACI-North America (ACI-NA) undertakes detailed benchmarking concerning commercial revenue generation amongst its members (ACI-NA, 2014). Figure 5.6 gives an example of one of the indicators used but for aggregate groupings of airport by size as only the high-level summary data is publicly available. There is also another study in the commercial area called 'The Airport Commercial Revenues Study' with the 2014 report covering 120 airports (Moodie International and the SAP Group, 2014). Figure 5.7 provides an example of an indicator used. For reasons of commercial sensitivity the report does not identify individual airports but nevertheless produces average figures by region or by airport size which can be used for broad benchmarking.

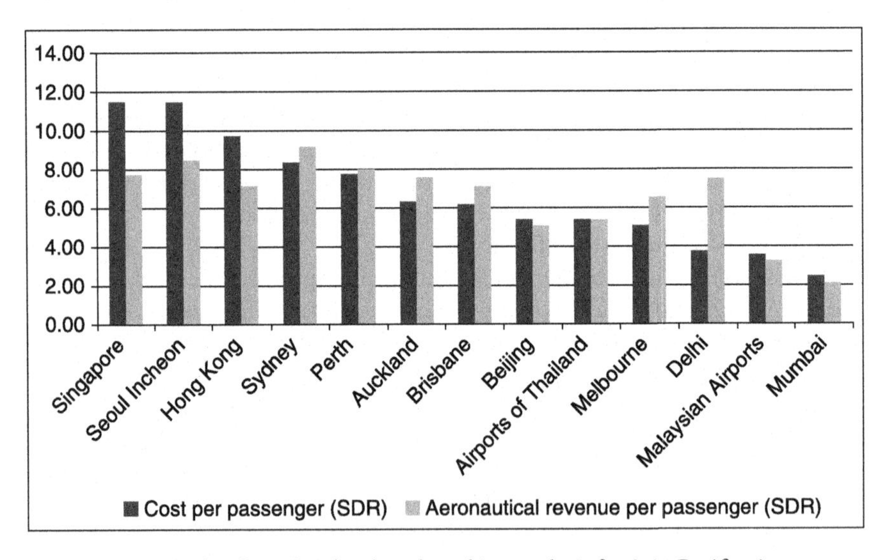

Figure 5.4 Example of LeighFisher benchmarking analysis for Asia-Pacific airports 2013

Source: LeighFisher (2014).
Note: SDR = Standard Drawing Rate (e.g. 1SDR = 1.52US$, 1.21€).

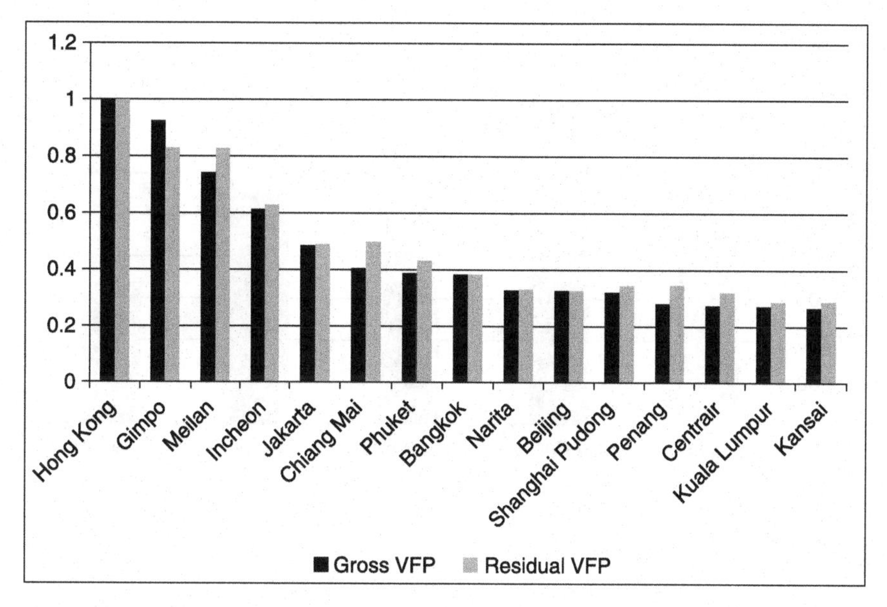

Figure 5.5 Example of ATRS benchmarking analysis for Asian airports 2013

Source: ATRS (2015).

Notes: The values are indexed with Hong Kong = 1. The higher the value the better the performance. VFP = Variable Factor Productivity and the residual values exclude the effects of the variables beyond managerial control.

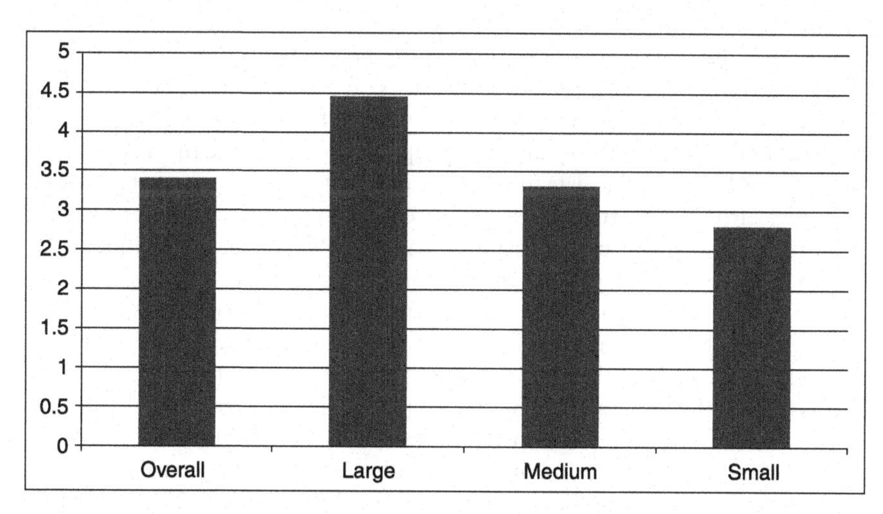

Figure 5.6 Duty-free, news, gift and speciality median gross sales per enplanement by US airport type 2013 (US$)

Source: ACI-North America (2014).

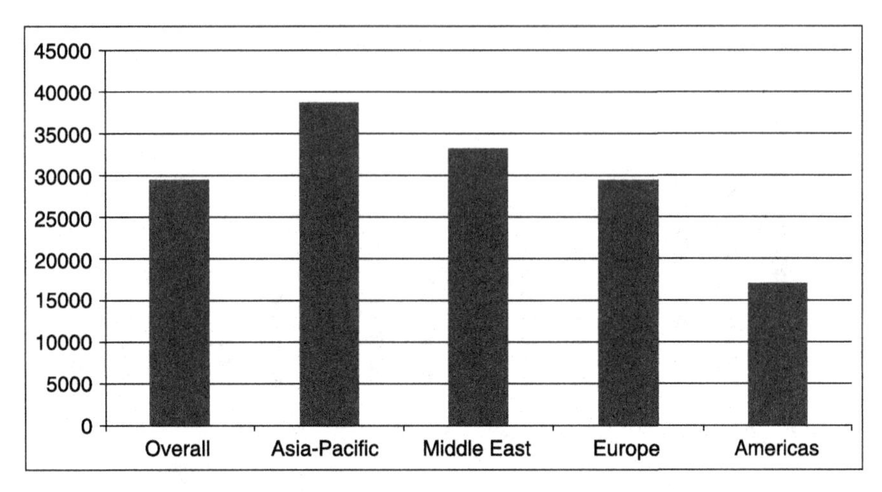

Figure 5.7 Duty-free sales per square metre by world region 2013 (US$)

Source: Moodie International and the SAP Group (2014).

However, not all airports will be able to participate in these industry studies, or will find them relevant to their own specific operations. In this case more individually designed peer benchmarking should be undertaken. To be as useful as possible, this should be carried out with as similar airports as possible to produce a homogeneous group with minimal differences in the physical environment and operational conditions. However, as discussed by Vogel and Graham (2013), it is often difficult to identify the most suitable airports and if inappropriate comparators are chosen, airports may set benchmarking targets that are unachievable. Typically one-dimensional criteria such as location, size or ownership are used to select the airports and these may be chosen for data availability or convenience reasons. However, in reality airport performance is influenced by a number of different factors with usually no single one being dominant. For example, when looking at partial measures one aspect of performance (e.g. related to costs) may be largely explained by geographical differences, such as labour costs, whereas another aspect (e.g. related to revenues) may be primarily related to traffic characteristics, such as the proportion of international traffic.

This raises the issue as to whether in practical terms peer benchmarking can be used to inform regulatory decisions (see Chapter 10). A few countries such as the UK, Ireland, Belgium, Austria and Italy have attempted to do this to a certain extent. For example in the UK in 2008–2013, the UK regulator (the CAA) used a sample of 14 UK and international airports to benchmark a number of processes that accounted for around 20–30 per cent of operating costs. They have continued to use peer benchmarking in certain areas. Also previously in Ireland benchmarking techniques were used but they came under criticism for choosing an inappropriate selection of peer airports and failing to take full account of the nature of traffic and the outsourcing that was undertaken. In theory best practice benchmarks could go much further and replace an assessment of internal accounting costs when setting regulatory controls, as is the case with some utility regulation. However, the practical problems experienced in Ireland and elsewhere due to the heterogeneous nature of the airport market have led regulators such as the UK CAA and others to not go in this direction. Nevertheless it can be argued (e.g. see Reinhold et al., 2010) that peer benchmarking can still be an insightful tool to informally aid regulatory decisions, as long as the drawbacks are fully acknowledged.

5.7 Summary

This chapter has looked specifically at airport benchmarking which has further extended some of the discussion in previous chapters concerning the basic financial characteristics of airports and the most effective ways to measure financial performance. It has described why there is a need for both internal and external benchmarking, examined the definition of inputs and outputs, and identified some of the major comparability problems that exist. It concludes by considering both partial and total benchmarking techniques. Following on from this the next chapter considers another important aspect of comparative airport financial analysis, namely the valuation of airports.

Overall in this chapter it has been argued that, in spite of the progress that has been made in the last two decades, there is still no real common consensus as to how airport benchmarking should be undertaken or used, and there are numerous impediments to effective benchmarking such as data limitations, competing methodologies and significant comparability issues. There has been considerable debate as to what is the best way forward (for example see Morrison, 2009; Adler et al., 2009). In the end it must be up to the airport operator or other interested party to make specific choices based on their goals and priorities; physical, operating, economic and political environment; and the availability of resources. The industry is likely to continue to favour partial measures and academia total measures, but there is room for both these approaches. However, for all involved, even with the limitations brought on by commercial confidentiality and competitive pressures, an open environment in which airports can co-operate with each other, share best practice and swap as much data and information as possible, can undoubtedly play a key role in benchmarking's effectiveness.

6 Valuation of airports

6.1 Introduction

Airports often evolve over many years from their original air force and defence role to commercial hubs or regional assets. This means that the value of the land and even the cost of the runway may never have been paid for by more recent owners. Valuation is generally not needed as long as the airport is fully owned by local or central government. However, once it is necessary to sell shares in an airport or group of airports a valuation is required. This may be performed by the seller or potential buyers, most likely by both. The sale may be of a minority or majority to private interests, the general public or a combination of the two. Whatever the case, the sale has been defined as privatisation (see Chapter 8).

Valuation is required for many reasons, some of them 'one off' and others with a continuing basis:

- Initial Public Offering (IPO)
- Mergers and acquisitions (how much should shareholders accept?)
- Equity analyst research (is an airport's current share price out of line?)
- Debt issues (collateral value of airport).

Airport accounts are not expected to show how much the airport is worth or even the value of its fixed assets. This is especially the case for an airport that has been operating for many years, rather than one that was constructed more recently on a greenfield site (e.g. London City Airport). Fixed assets are generally included at their original historical cost, less an allowance for depreciation. It is unlikely that this book value of tangible assets at a given date would coincide with the market or resale value of the same assets. Valuing land, which is often excluded from financial statements or included and not depreciated, is particularly problematical. Chapter 3 highlighted these differences in terms of the stock market value of an airport and its relationship to the book value of its assets.

This chapter will tackle the problem of providing an airport valuation to assist in the pricing of its shares in an IPO, placement or trade sale. It will also cover the valuation of airports which guides those bidding for longer term concession agreements such as BOT (Build-Operate-Transfer) and other similar arrangements (described in Chapter 8).

6.2 Approaches to valuation

There are three main ways of valuing airports (or for that matter any other company):

- Accounting or financial statements
- Ratios (e.g. P/E (Price/Earnings) ratio or EV/EBITDA)
- Discounted Cash Flow (DCF).

Sometimes a combination of the above is used. Where the airport already has a stock market listing the valuation can be compared with the value placed on it by the marketplace, based on the price established through recent share trades. Investment bank equity analysts that specialise in airport stocks generally use their own valuations to decide whether the market is over- or under-valuing the stock. The banks then advise institutions to buy, sell or hold shares in publicly traded airports, generating business for their share trading department. However, it can be argued that the 'correct' valuation is established by an 'efficient' market until investors have new information of relevance to airport performance.

A market price per share would be available on a day-to-day basis for an airport which is quoted on a stock market. Given the total number of shares issued, this would give a market valuation for the airport as a whole, or market capitalisation (see section 3.4.5). Such valuation would change by the minute, by the hour or day, depending on supply and demand for trading the shares. This in turn would be determined by changes in investors' desire to hold shares in general (versus cash), and their wish to hold shares in the sector and the company.

For airports with stock market quotations, the market capitalisation will show investors' valuation of the airport as a whole, but this will include intangible assets, management strength and business prospects, or what has been described as the airport 'franchise'. Few of these intangibles will be included on the balance sheet, which is the focus of the first valuation method in the next section.

The share price quotation will consist of a bid and an offer price. For a share like Aéroports de Paris which has a daily turnover of an average of some 55,000 shares per day, the spread between the two will be around ½–1 per cent. For other airports which are quoted on a stock market, but whose shares are rarely traded, the spread will be very much larger. The shares of these airports might not be traded very often, either because very few shares have been issued to the public,[1] or because private owners wish to hold on to their shares. Where turnover is low, the stock market will not be a very efficient method of valuation, only suggesting a range of values.

BAA was privatised through an IPO in 1987, the shares being offered to the public at £2.45, valuing the company at £1,225m. On its first day of trading on the London Stock Exchange the share price rose to £2.91, giving it a value of £1.455m. This meant that the investment bank advisors to the UK government had underestimated its value by 16 per cent. More recently a consortium headed by Ferrovial made a hostile bid for BAA at a price of £8.10 per share, well above its stock market price at the time of £6.40. The BAA board and shareholders rejected the initial offer and eventually accepted a bid of £9.55 per share, 49 per cent above its previous market price. So valuations can be wildly off the mark.

The next sections will address each of the above valuation methods in turn, with worked examples and the advantages and disadvantages of each one.

6.3 Accounting based airport valuation

6.3.1 Approaches to accounting based valuation

An airport can be valued by looking at the net asset value found in its financial statements. This combines balance sheet values of the assets with the external liabilities. It considers a worst case scenario where the airport ceases operations, sells its assets and settles all outstanding debts. This raises the first problem: in contrast to aircraft which can be sold off separately, many airport assets, such as runways, are not transferable. Assets such as ground handling and maintenance vehicles can be sold separately, but it would seem more sensible to sell the airport in total, as a going concern. For a large airport group such as Fraport, it would be possible to sell on some of its parts, for example its ground handling business (see Table 3.1 in Chapter 3). It could also sell its holdings in other airports or management concessions in other airports. However, its main aviation asset at Frankfurt Airport could not easily be split into parts.[2]

The choices of approach are as follows:

1 Balance sheet net asset value
2 Replacement cost
3 Lowest cost of purchasing assets that could be used to produce the same services as existing assets
4 Net realisable value
5 The market value that would be realised by the sale of an airport's assets (fair market value).

These will be described in the next sections, combining the rather similar third and fourth points above into one section.

6.3.2 Balance sheet net asset value

Most airports record the value of their fixed assets using historical cost less accumulated depreciation to date (Table 6.1). This is the starting point for valuing the airport as a whole, having the advantage that the information is readily available and no costly valuations are required. The majority of assets on an airport balance sheet will be fixed assets: for example Heathrow Airport had £10.9 billion tangible fixed assets at the end of FY2011 versus total assets of £13.0 billion, or 84 per cent. The only non-tangible fixed asset was its investment in the Heathrow Express rail operation to central London, valued at £3.8 million (valued at cost).

Tangible assets cover both the fixed or physical assets of an airport and the long-term investments in other companies or airports. The first consists largely of runways, passenger and cargo terminals and related airside and landside buildings. It will include vehicles and equipment (for example for baggage handling, ramp services or fire services). The second could be in shares of quoted companies, in which case valuation can be based on the market price. In the case of unquoted companies, the directors would provide an estimate for accounting purposes, in which case their original cost would be used (as with Heathrow Express above).

Depreciation rates were shown to vary according to the policies adopted by the airport, but generally the runways tend to have the longest depreciation period, followed by terminal buildings, the shortest being for vehicles and equipment. Heathrow Airport Ltd provided a detailed list of useful asset lives while other airports grouped assets according to more general categories (Table 3.5 in Chapter 3). Land is usually not depreciated and often not included in assets unless integral to buildings or other structures.

There are also intangible assets which include goodwill, software and payments for concessions in other airports, but these are not very significant in an airport context. They are also amortised (depreciated) over periods of up to around 25 years, software over a much shorter time. Concessions involve the right to use the asset (intangible asset method) under concession in consideration of the costs incurred to design and construct the asset, with

Table 6.1 Airport balance sheet net asset values

Listed company	*Year end*	*Airport value (US$ billion)*	*Accounting Policy*
Fraport AG	31/12/2008	4.8	Cost
Ferrovial SA	31/12/2008	25.4	Cost
Beijing Capital International Airport	31/12/2008	3.9	Cost
Airports of Thailand	30/08/2008	3.1	Cost
Airports Company of South Africa	31/03/2008	1.3	Cost
Auckland International Airport	31/06/2008	1.4	Fair value

Source: Parker (2011).

the obligation to return it at the term of the concession (discussed in greater detail in Chapter 8).

The second problem is the method of valuation of assets for the balance sheet and other financial statements. This is usually based on the original cost of the asset plus or minus any additions or depletions that have occurred since. Items such as the land value may not be included since it was originally given to the airport operator. However, the land can be valued and the historical costs can be adjusted to take inflation into account (i.e. converted to current cost accounting). Other assets can also be adjusted to present-day prices as the next three sections describe.

6.3.3 Replacement cost

Replacement cost brings historically priced assets up to present-day prices. It is thus particularly appropriate to airport terminal buildings and other equipment. However, the cost of providing these valuations needs to be assessed in the light of the importance of the asset in the total. Clearly this method would not be appropriate to land or runways.

6.3.4 Realisable value

Realisable value is commonly used for inventory or stock in order to provide an estimate of value for balance sheet purposes. It can also be used for airport assets and is defined as the value of an asset that can be realised upon its sale, less a reasonable prediction of the likely costs associated with a sale (e.g. commission or advertising).

There are practical difficulties in predicting such values, given the limited number of potential buyers and the degree to which the asset is dilapidated compared to likely offers of similar assets in the market.

6.3.5 Fair market value

Fair market value has been applied to an airport as Table 6.4 shows. One approach would be its value in the best alternative use, which for an airport close to the centre of a large city might be a shopping centre (without the security and other restrictions that it may have as an airport shopping centre). However, many cities have zoning or planning regulations that restrict alternative uses. International accounting standard IAS16 contemplates market value by appraisal from market-based evidence undertaken by a professionally qualified valuer. This was undertaken for Auckland International Airport where it was found that the fair value of the airport's land in 2008 was 1,054 per cent above its reported balance sheet cost. In the same year its buildings were 205 per cent above reported cost. The problem with this approach is that land would account for a large share of assets, in Auckland Airport's case 59 per cent of total balance sheet assets in 2009 (Oxera, 2010).

6.3.6 Valuing assets for regulatory purposes

Privatised airports will usually be regulated by a government agency to prevent them taking advantage of their monopoly or quasi-monopoly position. This is often in the form of a price cap or upper limit on airport charges based on an allowed rate of return on assets, which considers an 'economic' rather than financial rate of return on assets. The denominator of this return is called the Regulatory Asset Base (RAB), which only includes assets that are required and used by the current airline users of the airport. This is addressed in some depth in Chapter 10 where the various ways of regulation are described. Here we will focus on the asset base and its relationship to valuation.

The UK Civil Aviation Authority (CAA) is the body responsible for the economic regulation of the larger UK airports, and has applied a rate of return on assets since their first review. At that time it used net operating assets of the airport (on a historical cost basis). From the third review to date, however, it used indexed historical costs, or current cost accounting. This involves adjusting historical to current costs (using the retail price index as the indicator of inflation) for an opening asset base, and then adding or subtracting according to planned additions and retirements or disposals over the future five-year period. Table 6.2 gives a worked example of the adjustment to the RAB for London Stansted Airport.

Capital expenditure has to be limited to what is necessary for airline operations, as with the opening RAB. Clearly airports are keen to inflate assets so as to be allowed a higher monetary return and profit. Conversely, airlines object to any unnecessary projects being included. Depreciation is the actual amount based on airport policy, while the inflation rate is from government statistics.

Additional land might be acquired for future expansion, especially for an additional runway. The cost of this is generally accrued until such expanded facilities are brought into operation, at which point it is added to fixed

Table 6.2 Regulatory asset base calculation for Stansted Airport, 2006/07–2008/09 (£m)

£m	*Actual*	*Projected*	*Projected*
	2006/07	2007/08	2008/09
Opening basic RAB value	912.1	1,028.3	1,134.0
Capital expenditure	111.4	118.2	131.8
Proceeds from disposals	0.0	0.0	0.0
Depreciation charge	–40.5	–45.8	–41.7
Inflation (RPI) adjustment	45.4	33.3	27.9
Closing basic RAB value	1,028.4	1,134.0	1,252.0

Source: CAA (2007).

assets. Thus airlines are not charged until the land and associated assets are operational.

6.4 DCF models

This method estimates the value of airport assets based on their expected future cash flows, which are discounted to their present value. This concept of discounting future money is commonly known as the time value of money. This means that cash generated sooner is worth more than cash generated at a later date. For example the cash that an airport generates today is more valuable than that generated in, say, 20 years' time. This is because cash can be reinvested to earn a return and if payments are delayed this value is not available. The size of the discount is based on an opportunity cost of capital and it is expressed as a percentage or discount rate. Reinvestment and discount rates dropped to very low levels in the years following the banking crisis of 2008, but the discounting process is still required. Chapter 4 describes how to calculate an airport's discount rate and gives typical levels that are being applied to valuation and capital appraisal modelling.

The starting point for calculation of each year's cash flow is EBITDA, which is usually published in historical income (or profit and loss) statements. It is essentially before-tax profits, with depreciation and amortisation (which do not involve any cash movement) added back. Unlevered free cash flow is EBITDA less capital expenditures in the year less taxes (actual expected cash payments) less working capital. This is the cash flow that is uncommitted. Levered free cash flow is an alternative measure that takes into account the interest on actual debt, which is deducted from unlevered free cash flow (remembering that EBITDA is before any interest payments).

For a valuation using the DCF method, one first estimates the future cash flows that are forecast to be generated by an investment or company (airport). This involves deciding the number of years that the airport will remain 'economic'; shorter periods than its economic life could be considered but need to reflect the terminal value of the airport at the end of the discounting period (and the terminal value itself will also be discounted). Finally, the discount rate needs to be chosen after considering the riskiness of those cash flows and interest rates in the capital markets. The discounting process then produces the present value of the future cash flows, which can be compared with the schedule of capital investments.

There are two ways to calculate the terminal value: the 'Gordon Growth Model' and the 'Exit multiplier (ratio)'. The first takes the last year of explicit forecasts of an airport's profits or cash flows and assumes that they will continue to grow at the long-term average growth in perpetuity. Thus if the final forecast year was, say, year 20 when cash flow was projected to be \$50m and the long-term cash-flow growth is estimated to be 2 per cent a year, a terminal value is calculated by multiplying \$50m by $1.02/(0.07 - 0.02)$. This formula uses the decimal form of growth and discount rates, with the discount rate in this example assumed to be 7 per cent or 0.07. The resulting terminal value is $1,020m, treated as a cash inflow at the end of year 20, and discounted to its present value in the same way as the cash flows in each of the 20 annual periods.

Terminal Value = [Final Projected Year Cash Flow x (1+Long-Term Cash-Flow Growth Rate)] divided by [Discount Rate – Long-Term Cash-Flow Growth Rate]

The second way of estimating the airport's terminal value is to find a suitable multiplier or ratio of price/value to earnings or cash flow and apply that to the last year of forecast earnings or cash flow ($50m in the simple example above). A commonly used ratio would be EV/EBITDA, which could be estimated by looking at similar airports that already have a market capitalisation. In the above example this method would give a terminal value, assuming an EV/EBITDA ratio of 20, of $1,000m, close to the estimate using the Gordon Growth model.

This method of determining an airport's value is often described as a 'three-phase DCF'. The first phase is the initial period over which detailed forecasts for the airport are prepared. This would be at least three years into the future, and probably not more than five. The second phase is characterised by investment opportunities and the potential for expansion over the next, say, 5–10 years, while in the third phase the return on capital is expected to gradually fall towards the company's cost of capital. The maximum for all three phases would be 40 years. Cash flows are forecast over each of the three periods and discounted to present values using the airport's weighted average cost of capital (WACC). Total Enterprise Value is then the addition of the opening invested capital, the DCF value and the present value of any terminal value at the end of the period. This may be adjusted by the addition of any non-airport assets and minorities to give an equity value, which, divided by the number of shares issued, gives a value per share of the equity.

Fraport's share price averaged €33 per share during May 2010, with 91.9 million shares issued. This would give a market capitalisation or total equity value of €3,033m, somewhat less than the DCF valuation in Table 6.3.

A major advantage of the DCF method is it allows the forecasting of separate airport businesses, e.g. aeronautical, ground handling, parking, shopping. The net present values can be calculated for various economic and

Table 6.3 Fraport valuation, May 2010, WACC 7.02%

Present value of cash flows, 2010 to 2015:	–€889.7m
Present value of cash flows, 2016 to 2035:	€2,986.0m
Present value of cash flows, 2036 to 2049:	€1,223.5m
Terminal value:	€1,826.2m
Total enterprise value:	€5,146.0m
Deducting net debt, leases and various adjustments gives equity value: €3,600m	
Dividing equity value by total shares issued gives value per share: €39	

Source: Lobbenberg (2010).

aviation scenarios, and the sensitivity of the project to external 'shocks' estimated. The model of forecast cash flows will also be able to take into account local and regional factors and constraints and competition from other airports. It can also take into account likely future capital investment. Another advantage is the ability to assess the impact of economic regulation, especially where price caps are imposed (see Chapter 10). The DCF model allows the estimation of the value of the airport with and without such regulation, or for example the effect of subsidies that some airports might enjoy (Jorge-Calderon, 2013).

The disadvantages of this method are the difficulties in forecasting 30–40 or even 20 years into the future. For example in the early to mid-1990s few foresaw the success of the low-cost airlines in Europe, even though they had established themselves as a major force in the US by then.

6.5 Market-based models: ratio methods

6.5.1 Airport and related businesses

In the previous section, ratios were used in one method of determining terminal value as an input to DCF modelling. However, they can also be used to estimate EV or equity values based only on current levels of earnings or cash flow (i.e. the latest actual year's reported earnings or estimates for the coming year). This alternative method that is commonly used by financial advisers is the application of price-earnings and related ratios (discussed in Chapter 3). It is also called 'transaction comparables'. It avoids more detailed forecasting of cash flows and terminal values, and is generally simpler to apply. In this section it will be applied to the airport (or airport group) as a whole, followed by the valuation of separate businesses in the following section. The steps taken to price shares using price-earnings ratios would be as follows:

- Estimate the airport's earnings or net profits for the current year and at least one future year.
- Estimate the historical or projected P/E ratio for the airport, based on a comparison of P/E ratios of similar (peer group) airports, and perhaps with reference to the relationship of the P/E of airports quoted in the market to the P/E ratio of the market as a whole.
- Calculate the airport's market capitalisation (earnings multiplied by the P/E ratio).
- Decide on the number of shares to be issued and the price per share.

Instead of P/E ratios, the more common ratio to use in this method is EV/ EBITDA. The main problem with the above procedure is the estimation of the P/E or EV/EBITDA ratio. The selection of the appropriate ratio is usually determined by finding a number of similarly sized airports which already have a stock market listing and thus have ratios that are published or can be calculated using stock prices (and debt amounts) and current earnings. There are a number of distortions that could be introduced to the valuation by these comparisons, such as variations in depreciation policies, off-balance sheet financing and operating leases. Tax policies might also differ, and local markets introduce added bias to the comparisons.

Sometimes, attempts are made to remove some of these by computing, for example, the cash P/E ratio. This is broadly the P/E ratio with depreciation (and any other non-cash items in the profit and loss statement) added back. But this favours those airports operating new facilities. Alternatively, depreciation could be adjusted so that the same policy is applied to all airports, but the other distortions still remain.

An alternative technique that is now used by a number of financial advisers in support of valuations is 'Enterprise Value' (EV), also known as 'Firm Value'. This takes as a starting point the company's market capitalisation and adds the book value of its net debt (long-term and current portion of debt less cash and marketable securities). This is supposed to value both the equity and debt sources of finance, and is thus free of any gearing distortion. The market rather than book value of debt finance cannot normally be used, since the majority of airport long-term debt is not issued against a tradable security.

EV improves the denominator of the traditional P/E ratio; for the numerator, earnings are adjusted to take into account the other distortions described above. This measure provides smaller fluctuations over the business cycle, but has the downside of 'concealment of the considerable depreciation effects on accounted earnings' (Vogel and Graham, 2010, p. 29). Thus earnings are considered before deduction of interest, tax, depreciation and amortisation (EBITDA). An alternative formulation subtracts also lease rental payments (EBITDAR or EBDRIT). The ratio of EV to EBITDA or EV to EBDRIT is then used for valuation purposes, and compared with other airports. Some analysts also use EV/Sales, usually expressed as a percentage.

Figure 6.1 examines the ratios supporting various airport valuations over the past 15 years. Some have been acquisitions, with minority and majority positions included; others, such as the Brazilian airport privatisations, were long-term concessions (see also Chapter 8 for a fuller discussion of the privatisation process). Leaving aside the difference in nature of the deals, EV/EBITDAs ranged from around 12 to 18 between 2000 and 2004, to between 20 and 30 over 2005 to 2008, and came back down to 10–13 from 2008 to 2010. Most recently they have settled at around x15.

Ratio techniques are very dependent on the peer group of comparable airports that is used to provide a range of ratios to apply. This inherently loses the airport-specific factors, many of which are impossible to replicate across the peer group. The following should be considered:

- Airport maturity
- Potential for improving non-aeronautical revenue

- Economic regulatory environment
- Air traffic mix
- Airline dependence
- Capacity constraints
- Catchment area potential
- Environmental constraints.

The factors listed could restrict future traffic and earnings growth or introduce additional risk. They could also boost growth and earnings. Catchment area potential could be significantly improved by the construction of rail or even high-speed train connections, invested in and operated by an enterprise that is entirely unrelated to the airport. The airport's neighbouring city may have high growth potential (e.g. many Chinese cities) or be faced with maturity or even decline (e.g. Detroit).

The economic regulatory environment varies considerably, with the single till preferred by airlines and dual till by airports. Other airports have less complex price controls (see Chapter 10). Price caps can be incorporated into DCF modelling as well as sum of the parts techniques. They are less easy to take into account using ratios, for example with Heathrow, Aéroports de Paris and Fraport (an obvious peer group) all having different regulatory approaches.

Environmental constraints could take the form of noise limits to landing and take-offs, or compensating those living in noise-sensitive areas. The

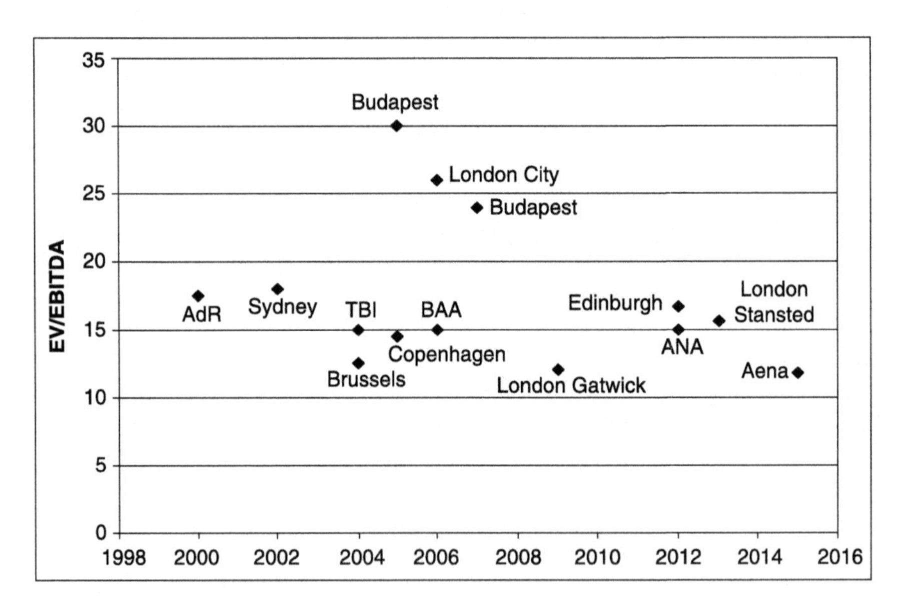

Figure 6.1 Ratios underlying airport transaction values 1985–2015

Source: Aviation Strategy (2015a, 2015b, 2015c).
Note: Transaction values in excess of €1 billion.

latter could be financed by noise charges. Engine emissions could also be the subject of charges, often revenue neutral. They could play a crucial role in expansion plans, for example London Heathrow's third runway proposals might all be subject to EU limits on NOx (for both aircraft and ground vehicle emissions).

Finally, another factor that cannot easily be incorporated into the possible valuation approaches is dependence on one airline. This could be a positive or negative impact: dependence on one very large network carrier might be beneficial in that it would find it hard to relocate at another hub airport; on the other hand it would have strong negotiating power, and it could divert connecting traffic to another of its hubs (e.g. Lufthansa from Frankfurt to Munich, or IAG from Heathrow to Madrid). However, being dependent on a large low-cost carrier has a greater downside risk, in that aircraft can easily be moved to other base airports.

6.5.2 Sum of the parts valuation

Another approach to valuation considers each of the separate businesses that are combined under the airport group. These are valued separately using the ratio technique described in the previous section, and based on the premise that the value in each part could be realised through a sale (for example by selling an airport's ground handling operations). For a small regional airport that is limited largely to airport operations and a collection of concessions, only a valuation of the whole airport makes sense. It should be noted that the sum of the parts may add up to less than the value of the whole.

Table 6.4 gives a worked example for the Fraport Group. It has four distinct businesses: its main Frankfurt aviation hub, its retail and property activities, its ground handling operations (which many airports now outsource under concession agreements), and its other activities. These were largely its majority holdings it had in Lima and Ljubljana airports and Twin Star. HSBC valued its Frankfurt aviation at the regulated asset base, since this effectively restricts its return and thus value. EV/EBITDA ratios of

Table 6.4 Sum of the parts valuation: Fraport, 2015 projection

	EBITDA FY2015 end (€m)	*Target EV/ EBITDA*	*Implied value 2015 end (€m)*
Aviation	237.6	9.7	2,300
Retail and properties	362.1	8.2	2,969
Ground handling	51.6	6.0	310
External activities	173.0	various	1,142
Group	824.3	8.2	6,721

Source: Lobbenberg (2014b).

8.2 and 6.0 were applied to the retail/property and handling businesses respectively, and its airport holdings assumed multiples of between x10 and x21 (applied to each airport's EBITDA, taking into account the stake that Fraport had in each airport).

Table 6.4 shows the calculation of EV; in order to arrive at equity value minority holdings need to be added to the group EV (at their book or market values), minority interests and debt need deducting. This example produced an equity value per share of €45, compared with the average share price of €47.8 in November 2014 (Lobbenberg, 2014b).

6.6 Summary

This chapter has described the various valuation techniques available to analysts, and the different occasions on which valuations are needed. In general, investment bank equity analysts tend to use DCF modelling since their main focus is in assessing current market share prices. On the other hand IPO advisers tend to prefer ratios or transaction multiples which are simpler and provide them with a range of market valuations and prices per share.

Balance sheet based valuations are the easiest to use since historic and pro forma balance sheets will already have been prepared for statutory and budgeting purposes (see Chapter 4). The main problem here is the use of historical cost less accumulated depreciation to value the assets: firstly, the assets may have been acquired many years ago and land value may not be included at all; secondly, updating values to current costs or replacement values may not be easy. Some do this by using national price indices, others by using more economic concepts such as opportunity costs. Where an airport is subject to rate of return or price cap regulation, present-day values are generally used for establishing a Regulatory Asset Base (RAB).

DCF models are the most expensive technique but once built they can be used for sensitivity tests. They allow airport-specific factors to be easily incorporated, as well as regulatory controls such as price caps. They can also be reversed by using the current market share price to determine equity value and thus EV, and then using the model to recalculate growth rates in earnings.

The major problem with the ratios or transaction comparables technique is in the selection of the peer group of airports, which *already have* stock market listings or at least a recent trade sale or share placement. The second problem is the choice of ratio, especially in cases when a company has not achieved profitability. In these cases EBITDA would be better than earnings, but 'revenues' may have to be selected for the denominator of the ratio.[3] On the other hand, it is relatively easy to apply, needing no complex and time-consuming forecasting (apart from one year ahead).

In conclusion, as more and more airports are privatised and listed on stock exchanges, more and more airports can be considered for peer groups or transaction comparables and ratio analysis. This would make these techniques more attractive, with DCF methods used for larger IPOs.

Enterprise value was seen to be an important concept in airport valuation. The next chapter looks at the provision of debt and equity that are crucial to EV and financing the asset base and expansion projects.

Notes

1 For example, the Thai Ministry of Finance holds 70% of the shares of the quoted company Airports of Thailand.
2 Brussels Airport provides a not very successful exception to this: for a time it was operated as two separate concessions, one for the passenger terminal and the other for all the remaining (mostly) airside assets.
3 As for Amazon and a number of high-tech company IPOs.

7 Financing of airports

7.1 Introduction

Airports have traditionally been relatively profitable, especially those with an annual passenger throughput exceeding 1 million, and generally able to cover their operating costs (as was discussed in section 1.5). This has been true regardless of the fact that the majority were owned by national or local governments and, at least until more recently, run as public utilities. The implication of this for financing new investments is that, for many airports, a large proportion of funds used to finance capital investment can be generated from internally generated cash flow.

In addition to using internally generated cash flow, which at least in the past has not been a costly method of financing development,[1] airports have also used alternative sources of finance, the majority of which are as follows:

- Internal funds or retained profits (cash flows)
- Loans or grants from local or national governments
- Commercial bank loans (debt financing)
- Bonds or loan notes
- Loans or grants from EU or other governmental institutions
- Equity finance, part or full privatisation
- Joint ventures
- Leasing/franchising
- Build-own-operate-transfer (particularly in emerging markets where a short-term skills shortage prevails).

Each of these will be examined in turn, together with their relative importance in total financing. It should be stated that finance is often required for reasons other than airport capital investment. This might include financing the start-up or initial years of operation of an airport, the restructuring of the stakeholder shares, rescue finance in hard times, and management buy-outs.

The following sections will largely apply to international airports outside the US. Finance for US airports will be discussed in the last section of this chapter (7.8). Private financing has played an increasing role in Europe where more and more airports have been privatised or at least operate as separate commercially run subsidiary companies. Europe accounted for more than half of airport private equity investment between 2011 and 2015 compared to only 15 per cent in Asia, 14 per cent in Australasia and 9 per cent in America (The Economist, 2015).

7.2 Internal funds

Financing airport investments out of internal funds has been the principal source of finance for major airports. This is usually the cheapest and most efficient means of financing development. For smaller, unprofitable airports, where cash-flow levels are insufficient to meet capital expenditure requirements, there are significant benefits to being owned by multi-airport authorities, where expenditure needs can be financed from cash flows generated from larger, more profitable airports in the group. Examples include AENA in Spain, the former BAA in the UK, ANA in Portugal and Avinor in Norway.

The level of revenue from operations depends on the pricing policies adopted in relation to both aeronautical and non-aeronautical activities. Airport expenditure includes staff, outsourced activities, depreciation, maintenance, materials, and cost of sales and energy consumption (utilities). The difference between the two provides the cash available for financing. One question that frequently arises is how far current charges are allowed to pre-finance future investments. Policies on this vary and regulators will also need to take a position (see more on this in section 10.5).

An appropriate measure of the volume of funds available from internal sources can be obtained from calculating the level of cash operating profits. This is obtained from calculating the level of operating profit before major expense items not involving a movement of funds. Depreciation is likely to be the only significant such item, and is added to operating profit to obtain cash flow. Net interest payments would need to be deducted from this to arrive at cash flow available for financing investments and/or payment of dividends. More airports tend to pay dividends than airlines. For example Malaysia Airports paid a dividend in every year from 2006 to 2013, ranging from 10 to 20 sen per share. It also had a dividend reinvestment plan which allowed investors to convert their dividend into shares. On the other hand Malaysian Airlines last paid a dividend in FY2004.

Airports ranging from the smaller Billund to the medium-sized Hamburg and the larger Copenhagen Airport have financed all investments from cash flow. For example, the latter's 2014 cash flow from operating activities of DKK1,806m was almost sufficient to cover dividend payments of DKK957m and investments of DKK922m, with new loans taken out about equal to loan repayments. Airports that operate as a government department or civil aviation authority, such as those in Luxembourg, Iceland or Greece, are financed through a mixture of general tax revenue and airport user charges, the distinction between the two often being blurred. Norway and Sweden are operated by a separate authority, and have a much greater degree of financial autonomy.

Depending on internally generated cash and the degree to which it is returned to shareholders, interest payment costs vary considerably by airport, both absolutely and as a percentage of operating expenses. Those airports that return a large share of profits to shareholders tend to need to borrow more at times of heavy capital expenditure (for example Heathrow as shown in Chapter 3). Copenhagen Airport does not always generate sufficient cash for investments, and its interest payments reflect past borrowings to cover periods of high investment. Airports such as Vienna, which has financed a large part of investments out of cash flow, have little borrowing and interest expenses are relatively low.

Very few airports that are operated as public corporations pay dividends to shareholders. Düsseldorf and Manchester airports, as well as the Airport Authority of India, are a few of the rare exceptions. Private or part-privately owned corporations, however, do generally pay dividends to satisfy certain investors that require some income on their investments (e.g. pension funds) as opposed to all capital gain. Of the part or wholly privately owned companies, Vienna currently distributes just under 40 per cent of its net profit to shareholders, and Aéroports de Paris has a policy, applied over the past few years, to distribute 60 per cent of net profits. Fraport had paid a dividend of €1.25 per ordinary share in each of the five years up to the end of 2013; this amounted to 52 per cent of the group's net profit in 2013 (payout ratio), offering a dividend yield of 2.3 per cent based on the share price at the end of December 2013. Vienna Airport paid a dividend of €1.30 per share in 2013 with a slightly lower yield at the end of the year compared to Fraport (2.1 per cent), and a payout ratio of 37 per cent. In the Asia-Pacific region, Auckland Airport moved to distribute 100 per cent of underlying after-tax profits to shareholders.

Airport investments tend to be very large and sporadic, rather than spread evenly. This is because of the minimum size of new passenger or cargo terminals and runways. It is often not possible to add capacity in small amounts, for example adding a second runway or even a terminal extension. To do so would cause greater disruption and not take into account the interlinked nature of the airport system.

Thus, the timing and extent of capital expenditure are judged to be critical. Too early and the airport has an underused asset; too late and traffic (revenue) will have been lost due to capacity constraints and/or delays imposed on airline customers. This often means that internal funds need to be supplemented by other sources of finance at certain times of heavy investment activities, even where cash reserves have been built up: for example, Frankfurt Airport's second terminal and Brussels Airport's new terminal both involved substantial borrowing from banks. It also means that examining the relationship between internal funds and investments even over the past five years will not necessarily give a very true or fair picture of airport finance. Nevertheless, the airport sector appears to be able to raise debt (loans) on a reasonably long-term basis with debt maturities often in excess of 25 years.

7.3 Short-term finance

Most companies have bank or overdraft facilities with one or more banks. Airports are no exception, and larger airports or airport groups tend to have facilities with more than one bank. For example Auckland International Airport had facilities with three commercial banks at the end of 2013: NZ$135,000 and A$47,270 with the Commonwealth Bank of Australia; N$150,000 with Bank of Tokyo-Mitsubishi; and a N$/A$ multicurrency facility of N$80,000 with the Bank of New Zealand. These can be drawn up to the stated amounts, and one of these was undrawn at the end of 2013. They all had a short-term maturity date but some run until terminated by either side. Rates of interest ranged from 3 per cent to 3.6 per cent, such short-term borrowing not necessarily being relatively cheap (and subject to short-term fluctuation in rates) but offering the ability to access the cash at very short notice. The purpose of these facilities or short-term loans is usually to meet unpredictable spikes in expenditure.

7.4 Equity finance and stock exchange listing

Equity finance in terms of issuing new share capital has not been very common except for new projects and privatisation (discussed in Chapter 8). There may be a mixture of straight equity and convertible loans available. This can alter the required rate of return depending on the conversion options. Preference share capital is also used but this is less popular than in other industries. Often sovereignty issues dictate that part privatisation and/or foreign ownership limits prevail. High-profile examples include BAA, Vienna, Copenhagen (see below) and Aer Rianta taking an equity stake in Birmingham Airport in the post-Eurohub era. The Australian airport equity route is, however, regarded in some quarters as being more of a trade sale.

Birmingham Airport's Eurohub passenger terminal was financed in part in this way from private sector equity investors. Similarly, 20 per cent of the new Brussels Airport passenger terminal was financed in straight equity and convertible loans. Just under 40 per cent of the cost of Munich's new airport was financed with new share capital, of which around three-quarters was in the form of preference shares on which no interest was paid.

The 25 per cent privatisation of Copenhagen Airport merely transferred the state's holding to private investors (and airport staff), rather than raising new equity. Thus the proceeds from the sale of just under DKK700 million went to the Danish government. A similar transfer occurred with the sale of the national and regional government's shares in Vienna Airport, with no new equity issued.

Equity finance is one of the two main forms of external long-term finance discussed in this chapter, the other being loan/bond finance. It consists of various classes of shares which are issued by the airport in return for a consideration or price. They may be subsequently listed and bought and sold, usually through a stock exchange, but often direct through a private placing or trade sale (sale to another airport operator).

A new issue of shares can either be offered to the public (and financial institutions) or placed solely with financial institutions. The first is called an 'Initial Public Offering' or IPO, often followed by secondary and subsequent offers. A prospectus will be issued, showing past financial performance and short-term prospects. The issue will need to be underwritten to ensure success, and this is done by obtaining commitments from several financial institutions to take a given number of shares at a substantial discount in return, and for a fee. The second also requires a prospectus but in this case the shares are marketed direct to financial institutions without inviting offers by the general public, and sometimes without obtaining a stock market listing.

7.4.1 Share issues

Various classes of share may be issued by a company in order to raise money for the business. The holder of the share has various rights, the main usually being:

- The right to a dividend, if one has been declared
- The right to vote at various meetings and by post
- The right to a share of the assets if and when a liquidation takes place (although they would only be paid after all the other classes with claims on the assets had first been paid).

The rights of shareholders are normally described in the Articles of Association reflected in the company laws of the country in which the company is based. In some countries (such as China and Russia), company law is less well developed and shareholders need to rely on government agencies to enforce their rights, rather than the law courts.

The airport's balance sheet will show the nominal or par value of the shares issued, together with any premiums paid on subscription. The total number of shares that has been authorised by the shareholders is also shown. Heathrow Airport Ltd had issued (called-up, allotted and fully paid) a total of 857.6 million shares at the end of FY2011, each having a nominal value of one pound sterling.[2] The proceeds from any issue of shares at above nominal value are shown as part of reserves under shareholders' funds as 'share premium reserve'. Both of these will appear under shareholders' or stockholders' equity, which will also reveal any revaluation surpluses or deficits, other reserves and retained profits and losses from previous years. A less common case is Auckland Airport, its 12,000 issued shares having no nominal or par value, the balance sheet only showing paid-up capital.

Different classes of ordinary share are sometimes issued and these will be shown separately under shareholders' equity. For example, Beijing International Airport had issued a total of 4.33 million shares (all with RMB1 nominal value) at the end of FY2013, split into 1.88 million H-shares, which could be held by foreign nationals and traded on the Hong Kong Stock Exchange, and 2.45 million domestic shares for Chinese nationals. The domestic shares ranked *pari passu*, in all material respects, with H-shares except that all dividends in respect of H-shares are declared in RMB and paid in HK dollars. In addition, the transfer of domestic shares is subject to certain restrictions imposed by PRC law.

Where an airport is considered too strategic to be controlled by foreign interests, its government can retain a 'golden share' following transferring the airport to the private sector. This was the case for the UK's BAA airport group. The share gave the UK government the final say in major decisions such as selling a controlling stake to 'unsuitable' interests; in 2003, the EU ruled that such arrangements contravened EU law, and the BAA and other golden shares issued by EU companies were discontinued.

Capital can be raised from existing shareholders through a rights issue, where the owner of each share has the right but not obligation to subscribe to a given number of new shares in proportion to their existing holdings, on the basis of a given ratio, say, one new share for every three shares held. A rights issue will need to be priced at a discount to the current share price of up to 15 per cent, which is why the rights have a value in themselves even before they are fully paid up. New shares can also be issued in the form of a free distribution of the company's reserves (accumulated from previous years' profits) by a scrip or bonus issue, but this will not raise any new capital.

An example of a rights issue was Auckland Airport's issue of 1 new share for 16 existing ones in February 2010. The issue was 99.82 per cent subscribed at the offer price of NZ$1.65, raising NZ$126.4m for the airport.

7.4.2 Initial Public Offering (IPO)

An IPO is the sale of shares to the public for the first time, usually prior to a stock exchange listing. The shares could then be traded in the secondary market. The process is often a means for the controlling and possibly founding shareholders, which may be those who launched or developed the business such as a public or local authority together with any venture capital firms, to sell all or part of their stakes. New shares may also be issued at the same time to raise fresh capital for expansion. It could also be the method of privatisation of an airport or airport group, as was the case with the BAA (see Chapter 8). More recently, this was the approach by the Spanish government for the sale of its group of Spanish airports.

The IPO will normally be priced at a level that ensures that all the shares will be subscribed. If not, one or more investment bank will underwrite the issue: agree to take the shares that are not taken up at a preferential price or for a commission.[3] Sometimes, the price is adjusted downwards following feedback from the market via the lead manager of the issue (investment bank). This may be because of events that negatively affect the market in general or factors specific to the industry and company. An example of this was the IPO of the fast-expanding Indian airline, Air Deccan, in 2006. An initial price range for the shares of Rs300–325 was suggested by the airline, but their advisors eventually persuaded them that Rs150–175 was more realistic. The shares were finally offered at Rs148, but the shares dropped to Rs98 on the opening day of trading on the Mumbai Stock Exchange, largely because of factors affecting the Indian market in general. They drifted lower to Rs85 over the next month (Aviation Strategy, 2006). This is an example of both over-optimistic pricing (the airline was trading at a loss), and a severe change of market sentiment too late to withdraw the issue.

IPOs are often marketed to the general public and financial institutions separately, each being allocated a given number of shares. The price per share may be determined in advance and bids sought at that fixed price. However, the prospectus may indicate a price range with bids sought above the bottom of that range. The public are then asked to submit their bids in terms of a monetary amount, the number of shares they receive then depending on the final price. The final price is decided following the results of a 'book building' phase, involving the lead investment bank adviser consulting financial institutions about demand for the shares and bid price intentions. Once the book is closed, the price will be decided (there could be two prices: one for the institutions and one for the public). In cases where the issue is oversubscribed, bids will be scaled down pro rata, with public and institutional allocations often dealt with separately. Oversubscription may also trigger a 'greenshoe' option whereby additional shares may be sold for a short period after trading in the shares starts. Where a small number of founder shareholders retain a large stake after the IPO, they may sign an agreement not to sell any of their holding for a specified 'lock up' period, usually between six months and one year.

An IPO is one of the methods of selling government shares to the private sector (privatisation), with the proceeds helping to reduce the budget deficit. However, it would be possible to issue new shares in order to provide a cash injection for the airport (see Table 7.1). The proceeds might also be used to reduce the balance sheet debt of the airport, although that has often been done prior to privatisation.

Equity sources can include:

- individual investors
- venture capital companies, and private equity
- investment trusts, pension funds and insurance companies.

Table 7.1 Large international airports with stock market listings

Airport	*Share price*	*Market capitalisation*
	4 November 2015	
Europe/Africa:		
Fraport	€57.34	€5,287m
Aéroports de Paris	€113.50	€11,232m
AENA	€98.90	€14,835m
Zurich	CHF745	€4,241m
Vienna	€84.60	€1,777m
Asia-Pacific:		
Malaysia Airports	MYR8.00	€2,477m
Airports of Thailand	THB190.00	€6,072m
Auckland Airport	NZ$4.11	€3,084m

Source: Lobbenberg (2015b).

The major question (aside from the expected rate of return) is what level of control will be handed over to the equity investors, but many pension and other funds are happy to take a minority position. Pension funds have recently been a major source of capital for airports, often taking quite large holdings in individual airports, mainly in Europe: the Ontario Teachers' Pension Plan jointly controls Copenhagen Airport (together with Macquarie European Infrastructure Fund), 48.25 per cent of Birmingham Airport, 100 per cent of Bristol Airport (having bought 50 per cent from Macquarie) and 39 per cent of Brussels Airport; the UK universities pension fund owns 10 per cent of Heathrow Airport; and the Public Sector Pension Board of Canada acquired the Hochtief portfolio of minority holdings in the following airports: Athens, Budapest, Düsseldorf, Hamburg, Sydney and Tirana. Finally, Gatwick Airport has as minority owners the National Pension Service of Korea with 12.14 per cent of its equity, and the California State Pension Fund (CalPERS) with 12.78 per cent (see also Chapter 8). Pension funds as well as insurance companies see airports as having low risk with almost no bankruptcies, while at the same time yielding more than government bonds; they are able to match their long-term liabilities with an airport's long-term assets; and they have good growth prospects (Condie, 2016). These investors like reliable cash payments which depend on regular dividend payments which airports make.

Sovereign wealth funds are also investors in airports with the Abu Dhabi Investment Authority having 15.9 per cent of Gatwick Airport; Qatar Aviation Investments has 20 per cent and China Investment Corporation 10 per cent of Heathrow Airport.

7.4.3 Joint ventures

A joint venture (JV) is a specially set-up company that would typically be a mix of the airport and an outside investor. The advantage of this approach is that the outside JV investor will bring a blend of additional capital and management skills to the table. A common or consistent goal on the part of the various stakeholders is fundamental. Exit mechanisms should be agreed between the airport and investor as should dividend policies before the venture proceeds. One such joint venture has been Macquarie and the Ontario Teachers' Pension Fund (mentioned above), which together invested in a number of airports (see also in Chapter 8).

Some of the secondary placings in Table 7.2 were to joint ventures, for example an airport operator such as Fraport partnering with a major Greek conglomerate to increase its chances of winning the bidding competition. Others might be to one or more financial institutions such as pension funds. The airports involved in these deals may have been previously privatised through an IPO, as was the case with Vienna and the London airports.

Table 7.2 Full or partial secondary placing of airport shares

Airport(s)	*Type*	*Seller*	*Buyer*	*Year*	*Value of sale*
Greek regional airports (14)	Full	Greek government	Fraport and Copelouzos Group	2015	€1,234m
Vienna Airport	Partial 29.9%	Austrian government	Airports Group Europe	2014	€514.9m
Aberdeen, Glasgow, and Southamption	Full	Heathrow Airport Holdings	Macquarie and Ferrovial	2014	
Belfast International	Full	TBI/Abertis	ADC-HAS	2013	€297m
Athens Budapest Düsseldorf Hamburg Sydney Tirana	Partial	Hochtief AG	Public sector Pension Investment Board of Canada	2013	$2,000m
Cardiff (UK)	Full	Abertis	Welsh government	2013	£52m
London Stansted	Full	Heathrow Airport Holdings	Manchester Airport Group	2013	£1,500m
London Gatwick	Full	BAA	Global Infrastructure Partners (GIP)	2009	£1,500m

Airport(s)	*Type*	*Seller*	*Buyer*	*Year*	*Value of sale*
Edinburgh	Full	BAA	Global Infrastructure Partners (GIP)		£807m
Auckland (NZ)	Partial 7.6%	New Zealand Superannuation Fund	Various institutions		NZ$276m

Source: Tretheway and Markhvida (2013) and authors (from various press releases and airport websites).

7.5 Debt and bond financing

The previous section covered equity finance, describing it as 'perpetual' finance that does not have to be repaid as long as the company is trading. Investors can be reimbursed through dividends and share buy-backs and ultimately through profits from share sales. Debt and bond finance, on the other hand, generally has a due date or term by or over which it has to be repaid, with interest usually charged on the outstanding balances.

In order to cover debt and bond investors against the borrower defaulting on repaying the debts, a security or charge is often included in the agreement. This could be on any of the assets of the borrower, which would be transferred to the lenders in the event of default or bankruptcy. Finance for specific projects can also be secured on the cash flows generated by the assets financed through the project.

Fixed and floating charges are used to secure borrowing by a company. Such borrowing is often done under the terms of a debenture issued by the company. Charges on a company's assets must be registered at UK Companies House or a similar government facility and may also need to be registered in some other way, e.g. a charge on land and buildings must also be registered at the Land Registry.

A fixed charge is a charge or mortgage secured on particular property, e.g. for an airport this could include land and buildings, equipment, shares in other companies, etc. A floating charge is a particular type of security, available only to companies. It is an equitable charge on (usually) all the company's assets both present and future, on terms that the company may deal with the assets in the ordinary course of business. Very occasionally the charge is over just a class of the company's assets, such as its stocks.

The floating charge is useful for many companies, allowing them to borrow even though they have no specific assets, such as freehold premises, which they can use as security. A floating charge allows all the company's assets, such as stock in trade, plant and machinery, vehicles, and so on, to be charged.

The banking crisis that started in 2007/08 resulted in weaker commercial banks that became much more strictly regulated. This resulted in a cutting back of lending to airports or airport-related projects, with remaining loans both more expensive (higher risk premiums) and of shorter term. This in turn led to many companies seeking finance direct from savings institutions such as pension funds and investment trusts, thus bypassing the banking system. This was called 'disintermediation' or the more recent (and easier to say) 'shadow banking'. Airports already relied on bonds for some of their finance, but the trend between 2007 and 2014 was for less lending from commercial banks and more through the issue of bonds and direct loans from institutions, under the same terms as banking lending but often for longer periods.

7.5.1 Bank debt

Bank debt is a way of financing airports through loans made from a bank or consortium of banks. The bank acts as an intermediary, lending money that has been deposited with it, together with its borrowings, to industry. The term of the loan could be short- or long-term, but would be unlikely to extend much beyond 12 years. Interest will be fixed for the period of the loan or variable (adjusted periodically with reference to the market LIBOR or similar rates). Loans are usually in the airport's own currency, and both variable interest and foreign currency loans will often require hedging instruments to be acquired to cover these risks. Three major default events are included:

- Issuer fails to pay principal or interest or any other amounts due within 30 days after the relevant due date
- Issuer fails to meet all obligations within 30 days
- Cessation of payments or insolvency of the issuer.

Default might also be triggered if any of the following covenants are not complied with:

Information covenants: The provision of financial statements and other information within a given time period, typically 150 days after the end of the financial year.

Operational covenants: Maintaining its corporate and legal status, restricting the type of business or revenue stream that the airport can target.

Financial covenants: Credit rating downgrades (see section 7.6 below), cash flow to interest ratio maintained, say, at 1.5 or above, and debt/assets kept below, say, 0.7.

Breach of any of the above gives the lender the right to demand repayment and/or to cancel its obligation to make further advances. Another requirement in relation to debt could be the transfer of funds to a separate bank account, out of which debt servicing (payments of interest and capital) can be made. An example of this is Sydney Airport's cash balance of A$106.0

million in FY2013 in a separate bank account which could only be used for the repayment of its debt.

Commercial bank loans are widely used by airports in Germany, the Netherlands, Finland, France and Belgium. Rates of interest would be somewhat lower than for the same airport under private ownership, especially where government guarantees are available. Copenhagen started using these sources of finance after corporatisation in 1990, with a DKK1.2 billion loan from the Mortgage Bank of Denmark. A large part (57 per cent) of the new passenger terminal and associated facilities at Brussels Airport was financed by bank loans. Amsterdam Airport makes considerable use of loans, in addition to issuing bonds that are tradable and are awarded a high credit rating. Aéroports de Paris's bank borrowing at end December 2013 was mostly from the European Investment Bank (EIB), with €480m of 15-year debt, with a further €85m from CALYON and other banks. As discussed later, the airport relies more on issuing bonds.

Smaller airports tend to rely more on grants from public bodies and finance related to specific investment projects. One of these smaller airports that is still government owned, but has some shares listed and traded on an exchange, is Aeroporto di Firenze (AdF). In addition to owning Florence Airport it also owns smaller airports in the same Italian region at Siena and Pisa (with 1.9 million passengers in total in 2012).

With debt and bond financing it is important for repayments to be spread out and not experience peaking or spikes. This makes it easier for airport treasurers to meet commitments without additional short-term borrowing. Aéroports de Paris provides an example of an airport debt repayment schedule which contains some gaps without having any serious peaking (Figure 7.1).

The gaps identified in Figure 7.1 can be filled by issuing new debt that matures in 2018/19, 2024 to 2026 and 2028/29. The airports' average debt maturity was 7.5 years, relatively short-term for a company with long-term assets, but it was up from 6.4 years at the end of 2012. A large part was fixed rate debt with little need for interest rate swaps.

7.5.2 Bonds

Bonds are securities that are sold directly to investors without the intermediation of banks. Since 2008 commercial banks have been heavily regulated, resulting in the removal of riskier assets from their balance sheets and a reduction in riskier lending. This has made bonds a more attractive option, at least for larger airports. Bonds can be issued in foreign currencies in addition to the airport's own currency and can often be for a longer term than banks would contemplate. The world's largest market is in the US, but investors there clearly prefer US dollar issues.

Bonds are marketed mainly to financial institutions as a higher risk and higher return alternative to placing funds on deposit with commercial banks. The issuer generally acquires a credit rating for the bond to help in marketing.

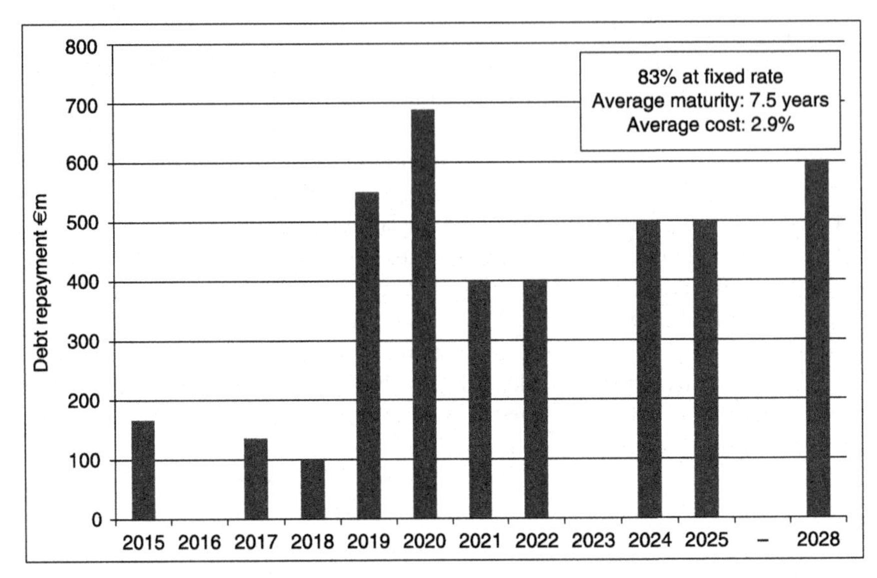

Figure 7.1 Aéroports de Paris debt maturity profile, end 2014

Source: Aéroports de Paris (2015).

Usually one or more banks will market the bonds and agree to take any securities that are not sold at a slightly more attractive price, in addition to their underwriting commission (say 0.35 per cent of the principal amount). There will also be a considerable amount of documentation that will be found in the prospectus for the sale. This will include the major default events and covenants that were discussed in the previous section. There are three types of bond, which depend on the method of calculating and paying interest:

Fixed rate bonds: a bond on which interest is calculated at a fixed rate and which is usually payable in arrears on a fixed date or fixed dates in a year.

Floating rate bonds: a bond on which interest is calculated at a floating rate and which is usually payable in arrears on a fixed date or fixed dates in a year; the floating rate is determined with reference to market interest rates as published on pre-specified dates (for example the six-month US dollar interbank rate on 1 April).

Zero coupon bonds: a bond on which no interest is payable; the bond is offered at a large discount to its par redemption value, enabling holders to be compensated for not receiving interest. Also known as 'accrual bonds'.

They can also be either 'registered bonds' whose holders are kept in a register, or *bearer bonds* which are not registered and interest can only be paid if the bond coupons are presented for payment. Bonds are usually issued in the currency of the issuing airport, with a small discount offered on the full price (issued at, say, around 1 per cent below par).

Attractive low interest rates in foreign currency can often be more than offset by exchange rate movements such that borrowing costs are higher. Most of an airport's revenues are denominated in its home currency, so it has little natural hedging capacity in other currencies. Hedging can be used to offset some of the exchange rate downside risk, but this has a cost. For example, Heathrow Airport Holdings Ltd took out cross-currency swaps to hedge currency risk on interest and principal payments on its foreign currency-denominated bond issues. This raised its cost of borrowing by just over 1 per cent. Most of Sydney Airport's A$7.3 billion borrowing was in Australian dollars, with some Canadian and US dollar debt.

In June 2003, Aéroports de Paris issued €600 million worth of bonds that carried an interest rate of 2.75 per cent and a term of 25 years (due on 5 June 2028). It was issued at a discount, or 98.841 per cent of par, giving it a yield to maturity of 2.78 per cent. The airport thus took the opportunity of securing long-term funding at an attractively low rate of interest. Interest was to be paid annually, and the bonds are quoted on the Euronext stock exchange (although not traded very frequently). The purpose of the issue was to finance the airport's continuing investment programme. The airport group had an A+ rating from Standard & Poor's (S&P) at that time.

Heathrow Airport Holdings Ltd (formerly BAA plc when it was the holding company for Heathrow, Stansted and three UK airports outside London) had just over £10 billion of secured bonds outstanding at the end of December 2012 (Table 7.3). These were due between 2013 and 2041, with interest rates ranging from 1.65 per cent to 12.45 per cent (average 4.4 per cent). Most of its finance was denominated in UK pounds. It issued bonds worth a further CAN$450m in June 2014 at a fixed interest rate that was only 1.17 per cent above the rate at which the Canadian government could borrow.

Table 7.3 Heathrow Airport Holdings Ltd bonds outstanding by currency, 31 December 2012

Currency	*£ million*	*% breakdown*
UK pounds	8,686	85.5
Euros	2,214	21.8
US dollars	959	9.4
Canadian dollars	245	2.4
Swiss francs	268	2.6
Total outstanding	10,158	100.0

Source: Heathrow Airport Holdings (2013) Ltd.

On the other hand Aéroports de Paris borrowed almost solely in euros, with only €163m out of €3.5 billion of bonds in foreign currency (Swiss francs).

7.5.3 Loans/grants from government

Airports owned by national or local government sometimes make use of grants or loans from these sources. In France, many airports are financed from grants from local or regional authorities. In Germany, some airports have borrowed from local authority shareholders, for example Düsseldorf, although these have recently been repaid. The new Munich Airport borrowed DM2.5 billion from its national, regional and local government shareholders in preference shares: this means that interest only had to be paid if the airport made a profit, and it was some years before this happened. Manchester Airport also made use of loans from local authority shareholders.

Italian airports such as Milan have also been given state grants of 20 per cent of total investment amounts. Similarly, state grants contributed towards 19 per cent of Turin Airport's development programme. Palermo's new passenger terminal was entirely financed by the regional government (60 per cent) and the state (40 per cent).

In the Netherlands, Maastricht Airport's investments have been 90 per cent financed from external sources, including regional development and provincial grants. For Swedish airports on the other hand the converse was true, with only 9 per cent of finance coming from government grants, the remainder from internal funds. To summarise the current status on government loans and grants:

- These can be from local or national government; this varies on a country by country basis.
- This form of financing was a critical factor in the early development of the airport industry in Europe.
- The requirement for payback and propensity for write-off can vary between countries.
- As a source of finance this is reducing in importance as governments try to put their airports on more of a commercial footing.

However, grants will continue to be a source of finance for regional airports that are thought to be in the public interest in terms of the wider economic benefits that they generate.

7.5.4 Loans/grants from EU institutions

Loans and grants tend to be more easily obtainable for airports in regional development areas in the EU, for example, in Spain, Portugal, Greece and

Ireland, and more recently Eastern European countries. EIB credit facility and loans have also been used by airports in the wealthier parts of the EU, principally Germany. Finance from EU sources can be categorised as grants (ERDF and the Cohesion Fund), guarantees (European Investment Fund) and loans (EIB).

European Regional Development Fund (ERDF)

Set up in 1975, the ERDF is one of four structural funds established by the European Commission to reduce the disparity in economic development between the EU regions. Since 1975, more than ECU (European Currency Units) 30 billion has been disbursed on projects in the least developed (Objective 1) regions. The fund provides financial assistance of up to 75 per cent of the cost for projects in Objective 1 regions, and up to 50 per cent of the cost for Objective 2 and 5b regions.

The following airport projects have been financed by the ERDF:

France: Ajaccio, Bastia, Calvi, Figari (all in Corsica) and various overseas territories
Greece: Athens, Heraklion, Thessaloniki and 26 other airports
Ireland: Dublin, Cork, Shannon and Connaught
Portugal: Madeira, Ponta Delgada, Covilhã, Figueira da Foz and Vi la Cha
Spain: Malaga, Almeria, La Coruña, Vigo, Santiago de Compostela, Alicante, and the Canary Islands (El Hierro, Lanzarote, Fuertaventura, Gran Canaria and Tenerife)
United Kingdom: Belfast International, Belfast City

A number of airport projects in Objective 2 regions were also financed in Belgium (Gosselies and Bierset), France (Metz–Nancy and Charleville-Mezières), Germany (Dortmund), the Netherlands (Twente), Spain (Barcelona) and the UK (Manchester, Humberside, Glasgow, Prestwick, Dundee, Newcastle, Teesside and Birmingham).

European Investment Fund

This fund was established at the December 1992 meeting of the European Council to promote economic growth and employment in the EU. It is to be aimed at small and medium-sized firms, and also the Trans-European Networks (TENs). The latter would include airport and air traffic control (ATC) funding. The fund provides guarantees for loans or bond issues. The intention is that, by assuming some of an airport's project risk, private finance will be more readily forthcoming. Since its establishment, the fund has provided guarantees of over €750 million, with €75 million for the development of Milan Malpensa Airport.

The Cohesion Fund

This was set up in December 1992 to promote social and economic cohesion in countries with GDP per capita of less than 90 per cent of the EU average (Greece, Spain, Portugal and Ireland). With the enlargement of the EU many Eastern European countries became eligible at the expense of countries such as Ireland. The Cohesion fund is used to finance environmental and transport-related projects in EU states. The fund supports transport infrastructure projects aimed at enhancing infrastructure provision within the framework of the Trans-European Transport Network (TEN-T). Airports at Athens, Corfu, Palma de Mallorca and Tenerife have benefited from this fund through grants of around €100 million.

European Investment Bank (EIB)

This was created by the Treaty of Rome to support certain capital investments that promote projects that meet EU priorities, especially regional development. In contrast to other EU finance, it is in the form of loans rather than grants. Such loans are usually for up to 20 years and cover up to 50 per cent of the total investment amount. The cost of borrowing is based on the rate at which the EIB can borrow plus an administrative charge of 0.15 per cent. The Triple A rating that the bank has means that it can offer attractive rates in comparison with commercial bank loans.

Loans were made for airport projects between 2005 and 2015. These totalled just over €5 billion, with a further €868m lending to non-EU countries. Thus the total lending to airports amounted to €5.9 billion, only 4.2 per cent of its total lending on all transport projects over the same period (Table 7.4).

It can be seen in Table 7.4 that Spain took the largest share with 34 per cent of total lending, followed by Germany with 30 per cent. The majority of non-EU lending went to China for its Beijing International Airport expansion project (€500m), with Oslo Airport Terminal 2 taking a further €200m.

European Bank for Reconstruction and Development (EBRD)

The EBRD started operations in April 1991 in response to the collapse of Communism in the East. Its shareholders are 64 countries, the EU and the EIB (described previously). It expanded from a Central and Eastern European focus to countries such as Mongolia, Turkey and Egypt, and most recently Greece and Cyprus. It provides loan and equity mostly on a project basis, and usually providing a catalyst for private sector finance. The basis for a loan is the expected cash flow of the project and the ability of the client to repay the loan over the agreed period. The credit risk can be taken entirely by the Bank or may be partly syndicated to the market. A loan may be

Table 7.4 European Investment Bank lending to EU airports 2005–2015

Project	*Country*	*Signature date*	*Amount (€m)*
Milan Airport III	Italy	2006 to 2014	344
Nice Airport development	France	Nov 2013	100
Amsterdam Airport – security	Netherlands	Jul 2010 & Sep 2013	550
Lyon Airport development	France	Aug 2013	30
Gdansk Airport modernisation	Poland	Jun 2013	36
Balearic Airports infrastructure	Spain	2010/11	300
Canary Island Airports infrastructure	Spain	Dec 2009	80
ANA Airport extension	Portugal	Jul 2009	72
Frankfurt Airport A380 extension	Germany	2008/09	460
Berlin Brandenburg Airport	Germany	2008/09	983
Malaga Airport infrastructure	Spain	Nov 2008	250
Dublin Airport development	Ireland	2008/09	460
Rome Airport II	Italy	May 2008	80
Vienna Airport expansion	Austria	Dec 2006	100
Leipzig–Halle Airport	Germany	Dec 2005	85
AENA V – Barcelona Airport	Spain	2006 to 2007	1,100
Total EU			5,030

Source: EIB (2015).

secured by a borrower's assets and/or it may be converted into shares or be equity-linked. Full details are negotiated with the client on a case-by-case basis, but the following gives some idea of the main parameters:

- Minimum €5–15 million, although this can be smaller in some cases
- Fixed or floating rate
- Senior, subordinated, mezzanine or convertible debt
- Denominated in major foreign or local currencies
- Short- to long-term maturities, from 5 to 20 years
- Project-specific grace periods may be incorporated.

The EBRD has provided loan finance to a number of airports in Russia and Eastern Europe, notably Pulkovo St Petersburg.

7.5.5 Loans/grants from international development banks

In addition to the EU funding institutions discussed in the previous section, development banks have been operating in other parts of the world for many years. The African Development Bank, the Asian Development Bank and the Inter-American Development Banks have all provided long-term loans to airports as well as provided technical assistant support for airport projects. These operate in a very similar way to the International Bank for Reconstruction and Development (IBDR), commonly known as the World Bank.

An example of a World Bank airport-related loan was US$50m to finance around half of a new airport at Shangrao in Jiangxi province, China, in 2013. The loan was repayable over 25 years with interest charged at the reference rate for the currency (US$) plus a variable margin. In 2010, the World Bank extended a US$280m loan to help finance a $436m rehabilitation and expansion of Cairo Airport's Terminal TB2. This was a 20-year loan at a margin over LIBOR.

7.6 The role of rating agencies

The role of rating agencies is essentially providing support to those investing in debt securities such as bonds and loan notes. Companies that issue such debt often pay a rating agency for providing investors with an in-depth analysis of the borrower and the likelihood of default. These firms earn their revenues from companies, including airlines and airports, which wish to issue securities (bonds, commercial paper or preferred stock), as well as from selling reports to investors. For example, both S&P and Moody's received US$30,000 for rating a $100m unsecured placement of Southwest Airlines' securities (Morrell, 2007).

The agencies' analysis aims to evaluate the likelihood of the timely repayment of principal and interest relating to debt securities, or dividends for preferred stock. The analysis covers both the aviation industry in general, and the particular circumstances and prospects for the airport or airport group concerned. The two major agencies together have over 100 analysts making detailed analyses of company financial statements, making any necessary adjustments for variations in accounting practice.

The two main agencies that publish ratings for quoted debt securities, including those issued by airports, are S&P and Moody's. A third is called Fitch. Together they rate just over 90 per cent of all the obligations of all industries. They have been criticised for not predicting collapses such as Enron and Parmalat, and more recently Lehman Brothers, but their defenders argue that in the first two cases they were supplied with fraudulent data. The rating agencies were not the only ones not to recognise and act on the acute situation of Lehman and many other banks. It can also be argued that competition is restricted by entry requirements, but this is being addressed in the US by Congress and the Securities Exchange Commission (SEC). However, since the banking collapse they have benefited from the growth in bond issues which need a rating for successful marketing. The following shows the grading system used by S&P, together with the corresponding one for Moody's, which might rank airports slightly differently:

Investment grade:

S&P: AAA, AA, A and BBB
(+ and – indicate relative standing within each grade)
All have capacity to pay interest and repay principal, with increased susceptibility to adverse economic conditions as grades fall.
Moody's: Aaa, Aa, A and Baa

Speculative grade:

S&P: BB, B, CCC
(+ and – indicate relative standing within each grade)
All have speculative characteristics regarding the payment of interest and repayment of principal, with increased vulnerability to default as grades fall. C is highly vulnerable to non-payment, while an obligation rated D is in default.
Moody's: Ba, B, Caa, Ca and C

Investment grade rating brings two considerable advantages to the issuer: firstly, it allows the security to be issued at a lower price than a speculative grade one, say with an interest rate a few percentage points lower. Second, some institutional investors can only buy investment-grade paper.

It is worth noting that ratings agencies such as S&P or Moody's offer airport bond ratings (long- and short-term) in the AA+ region for airports in North America and A+/– and even higher in other parts of the world (Table 7.5). However, where governments retain 100 per cent or majority control of airports the ratings are likely to reflect more on the government's financial record than that of the airport. There are not many airports that can match this, although it should be stressed that many airports still have substantial government shareholdings.

7.7 Leasing

Leasing is a form of finance more appropriate to airport equipment than to buildings, aprons or runways. While many airports may make use of leasing for smaller items of equipment, both Frankfurt and Stuttgart airports reported that this had been a significant form of financing for them. Some airports have been 'sold' on what is effectively a long-term lease (e.g. the Australian airports). An option for outright purchase is built into this quasi-finance lease structure. US airports lease land to airlines that subsequently build (terminals) on that land and then renegotiate terms after about 25 years.

Table 7.5 Examples of airport credit ratings

	S&P rating	*Date*	*Debt*
Europe:			
Aéroports de Paris	A+	Dec 2012	Bonds
Amsterdam Schiphol	A+	April 2014	Notes
Copenhagen	Baa2*	May 2015	
Manchester Airport Group	BBB+	Dec 2014	Bonds
Rome	BBB	Dec 2003	Senior unsecured
Zurich	A+	April 2015	Bonds
Asia-Pacific:			
Airport Authority Hong Kong	AAA	Sept 2013	Senior unsecured
Auckland Airport	A–	Feb 2015	Notes
Malaysia Airports	A3*	May 2015	
Sydney Airport	BBB	April 2014	Secured notes

* Moody's rating.

Source: S&P and airport websites.

7.8 Finance for US airports

Financing US airports is very different from in other countries. There is close federal involvement in setting user charges and providing grants for capital investment. Outside the US the approach first depends on whether the airport is run as a part of central or local government finances, or whether it has been 'corporatised' or privatised. In the first case financing airport investment is part of the national or local government budgetary process; in the second case, commercial sources can supplement internal cash (which may depend on economic regulation of user charges and rate of return on assets).

Table 7.6 shows that, excluding issuing tax-exempt bonds, internally generated funds were the largest single source for US airports, with both federal grants and passenger charges important sources. Large and medium-sized airports rely more on Passenger Facility Charges (PFCs) and less on Airport Improvement Program (AIP) grants (GAO, 2015).

Table 7.6 Funding sources* for US airports average 2009–2013

	US$m	*%*
Airport Improvement Program (AIP) grants	3,304	24.9
Passenger Facility Charges (PFCs)	2,744	20.7
State and local contributions	1,121	8.5
Airport revenues	6,083	45.9
Total	13,252	100.0

* excluding bond issues.

Source: GAO (2015).

Funds are made available by Congress from the Airport and Airway Trust Fund which receives revenues from taxes on domestic and international travel, domestic cargo transported by air, and aviation fuel (see Chapter 2). There is a complex system of allocating AIP funds to airports. Congress granted commercial airports the rights to raise money from passenger charges to finance airport development. Most of the money raised from these PFCs has been from large and medium-sized airports. An increase in the cap of $4.50 per flight segment and $18 per round trip was allowed in 2000. Nearly all states provide financial assistance to airports, mainly in the form of grants as matching funds for AIP grants. These grants are funded by means of a variety of sources, including aviation fuel and aircraft sales taxes.

After some recent initial interest in privatisation, US airports are still owned by local government and run as a public utility (this is discussed in Chapter 8). Private sector involvement has thus far been limited to concessions to operate terminals and commercial franchises. Financing remains dominated by tax-exempt bonds issued by the airport authority but often guaranteed by the incumbent airline lessee, for example where one airline dominates the passenger terminal whose expansion is the reason for raising funds (they are also called 'revenue bonds'). According to the GAO study cited above, bonds are issued by larger airports to pay for defined capital projects. Between 2009 and 2013 bonds raised an average of US$6.3 billion per year.

An example of a large US airport issuing revenue bonds is Chicago O'Hare. It does not publish financial statements for the airport as a separate entity, but details of airport revenues, expenses and balance sheet for O'Hare and Midway airports can be found in the City of Chicago annual reports and statements.

7.9 Summary

Airports tend to be consistently profitable and cash positive, but outside finance still tends to be used for major programmes of terminal or runway extension, which by its nature tends to be 'lumpy'. Some airports distribute more to shareholders in dividend payments and thus need to raise funds more often. The most common finance is bank debt and bonds, the latter requiring a credit rating to market successfully to financial institutions. Most airports still retain at least a minority of shares held by government and thus credit ratings are attractive and interest rates little above government bond rates. Terms vary from 5–15 years. Longer terms are available from government development banks such as the World Bank or European Investment Bank, especially where airport projects generate broader economic benefits.

The next chapter covers the airport privatisation process in depth, referring to and building on many of the financing techniques and types of investor introduced already.

Notes

1 Its cost is the opportunity cost in terms of interest or return forgone of investing in an alternative project or placed on deposit with a financial institution. It also avoids any restrictive conditions or covenants that external finance often imposes.
2 It had also issued 100,000 redeemable preference shares of £1 each, and just under 22 million non-redeemable preference shares of 1 pence.
3 Underwriting discounts and commissions totalled US$1.89 per share for the JetBlue IPO, or 7% of the issue price (from JetBlue Prospectus, 11 April 2002).

8 Airport privatisation

8.1 Introduction

This chapter covers privatisation, which has been a key trend in the airport industry for over 25 years. It can have a major influence on nearly every area of airport finance, including aeronautical and non-aeronautical revenue generation, cost control and efficiency, airport expansion and sources of investment.

Privatisation is sometimes defined as the sale of shares of a company on the stock exchange. However, this is too narrow a meaning for a concept which more generally tends to be interpreted as any movement away from government control of facilities and services towards private sector participation. In other words, privatisation can be considered as the transfer of economic activity from the public sector to the private sector. It certainly involves private sector management but may not always result in state ownership being given up. Within this context there are a number of different airport privatisation approaches, some more radical than others, and these are discussed in this chapter.

The chapter begins by covering the reasons for privatisation in the airport industry and its origins and development. The chapter then considers the key issues that need to be addressed when making privatisation decisions and explains the different types of privatisation that exist. This is followed by an assessment of the current situation as regards private participation in airports, how this involvement varies by global region and the financial consequences. The chapter concludes by discussing the major organisations involved in airport privatisation and the subsequent international airport operators and investors that have emerged.

8.2 The development of private participation in airports

8.2.1 Reasons for privatisation

In general economic terms, there are a number of arguments in favour of privatisation. An overarching reason is the belief that private firms, with clear profit maximisation motives, will have greater incentives to perform well by increasing economic efficiency. They can introduce commercially focused management which will be able to be innovative and exploit diversification opportunities. At the same time the private sector will have access to commercial markets for investment, whilst the risk and financial burden, and maybe also the political control, can be removed from the public sector which itself can benefit financially from the privatisation proceeds. The counter-arguments are that the profit maximisation objectives of private firms may lead to excessive prices, poor standards of service and inadequate investment. Moreover there may be insufficient consideration being given to externalities, such as controlling environmental impacts and maintaining social justice, as well as health and safety, and working conditions for employees.

Over the last 25 years or so, an increasing number of airports have been privatised. The specific reasons for these developments mirror very closely the general economic arguments discussed above. For example, Rikhy et al. (2014) summarised these as being: developing traffic demand or meeting such demand; providing broader economic development; receiving cash to deleverage the federal and municipal government's or airport's balance sheets; financing large-scale airport infrastructure; reducing or transferring risks; transferring technology and operational expertise; sharing best practices; and bringing efficiency to the design and operations.

A study of a large number of privatisations discussed in the academic literature identified the following six most significant objectives for airport privatisation, in order of importance (Graham, 2011):

1 Improving efficiency and performance
2 Providing new investment funds
3 Improving the quality of management and encouraging diversification
4 Improving service quality
5 Producing financial gains for the public sector
6 Lessening the public sector influence.

Historically airports were seen as relatively attractive investments, primarily because of strong growth prospects, commercial opportunities (which are often not existent with the privatisation of other infrastructure assets), and limited competition because of high barriers to entry and minimal threats of substitutes. Whilst these views still remain to a certain extent, as discussed in Chapter 9, the competitive forces for airports have increased significantly and the more footloose nature of airlines (notably the LCCs) and the poor performance of others have meant that the operating environment, particularly for smaller airports, is now much more challenging. Recent external shocks, poor economic conditions and stock market volatility have also increased uncertainty, and in some cases made private participation in airports less appealing. Moreover whilst the long-term nature of investment in airports can provide a stable environment for business growth, it can also be problematic with the large amounts of upfront investments that may be needed and the increased insecurity concerning the distant future, especially because of the multiple stakeholders involved and the need for a high level of regulation in many areas of operation. Nevertheless most airport privatisation projects continue to attract much attention from potential private sector operators and investors.

8.2.2 The movement towards airport privatisation

The airport industry has come a long way from being viewed primarily as a state-owned utility with public service obligations. As discussed in Chapter 1, as the airline industry started to mature and evolve with deregulation and ownership changes in the 1970s and 1980s, airports began to be considered more as commercial enterprises. This 'commercialisation' resulted in many airport operators becoming more autonomous by loosening their ties from the government (for example by becoming companies under government ownership), as well as treating their airports more as businesses by focusing much effort on generating non-aeronautical revenues and actively marketing themselves to their customers. In some ways airport privatisation can be viewed as a natural progression from this commercialisation movement. At the same time there was a steady need for new investment to keep up with traffic growth, and a greater reluctance by some governments to get involved with financing the sector, which had demonstrated itself to be capable of being self-sufficient, unlike other activities, such as health and education, which were considered to be more worthy of support.

The first ever airport privatisation took place in the UK in 1987. This involved the 100 per cent share flotation of the national government-owned British Airports Authority (BAA), which at that time owned the London airports of Heathrow, Gatwick and Stansted and the Scottish airports of Glasgow, Prestwick, Edinburgh and Aberdeen. It occurred at a time when the pro-privatisation Conservative government was privatising a number of nationalised industries. The share flotation was seen as highly successful in financial terms, as witnessed by rising share prices and improved financial performance, and so consequently this encouraged further debate as to whether other airports should be privatised. However, in the following few years only a handful of airports (Vienna, Copenhagen and in some UK regions) were actually privatised. A contributing factor to this unexpected inactivity was the first Gulf War of 1991, and the subsequent economic and political uncertainty which this brought.

By 1996, the economic climate was much more favourable, air traffic was growing steadily and there was a need for substantial investment at many airports. As a consequence there was an increased and renewed interest in airport privatisation in various parts of the world, primarily either as a means of providing much-needed investment, or as a way of improving airport management/efficiency, or both. In the next few years, examples of airport privatisation could be found in Europe (e.g. Düsseldorf, Naples, Rome and Birmingham), South and Central America (e.g. Argentina, Bolivia and Mexico), South Africa, Malaysia, Australia and New Zealand. This period is viewed as the 'gold-rush' days of airport privatisation, as the healthy airport environment, and the desire of many operators to get involved in what was seen as a lucrative and relatively stable investment opportunity, generated much interest.

However, most of this activity was temporarily halted by the events of 9/11, and the subsequent wars in Afghanistan and Iraq, as well as the outbreak of Severe Acute Respiratory Syndrome (SARS), which were accompanied by less favourable economic conditions and a much more uncertain future. Some proposed privatisations, such as at Brussels and Milan, were abandoned, and only a few (e.g. Sydney and Malta) took place. However, by 2004, with an improved overall outlook, privatisation came back onto the agenda of a number of airports. Examples included Brussels, Budapest, Larnaca/Paphos and the Paris airports, as well as the operator Airports of Thailand. India also experienced privatisation of New Delhi and Mumbai airports where strong economic and traffic growth had meant that there was an urgent need for modernisation and expansion. Much interest was generated amongst investors at this time, and the prices paid for airports grew steadily.

This second major wave of airport privatisation was subsequently slowed down by the onset of the global financial crisis and economic recession in 2008. As a consequence, investment funds were generally more difficult to access which, for example, meant the failure of the proposed Chicago Midway Airport privatisation in 2009. On the other hand, privatisation was also seen as a way to raise funds to support large sovereign debts, for instance, with the privatisation of the Portuguese airport company ANA in 2013, and with AENA the Spanish airport operator and the 14 regional airports in Greece in 2015. Compared with the pre-financial crisis days, recent privatisation activity has generally been more limited but nevertheless in the last two years (2014–2015) there have been a number of new developments for a diverse collection of airports including Toulouse in France, Kansai in Japan, Mactan Cebu in the Philippines, Santiago in Chile, the new Istanbul airport in Turkey and the operator Airports Corporation of Vietnam.

8.3 Privatisation concepts

8.3.1 Issues to be considered

As the popularity of privatisation has grown, so too have the variety of privatisation options on offer. Ultimately the choice of privatisation will depend very largely on the government's objectives in seeking privatisation, for example, as to whether the key purpose is to improve performance, bring in new investment funding, or enhance the quality of management. One of the most important and complex considerations is the degree of government influence following privatisation (Brutsch, 2013). Many governments favour retaining at least some control, because of the strategic role that airports play as national and regional assets, their ability to facilitate trade and tourism, and the very significant externalities that they can cause. As a result many privatisations are 'partial' in that airport control is shared between the public and private sectors, although this can be challenging given that the two sectors are likely to have different overall objectives. An alternative may be to seek finance from the private sector, as in a typical public–private partnership (PPP), and transfer management, but not ownership or total control, over to the private sector. If little state influence remains, and if the airport or airports in question appear to have substantial market power, it is often feared that they will act like a private monopoly. In this case they may not always operate with the best interests of the airport users in mind by raising charges, reducing the service quality, or underinvesting in infrastructure. For these reasons privatisation often goes hand in hand with a new economic regulatory environment, which is discussed in detail in Chapter 10.

Another choice that has to be made is whether a group (or 'network' or 'system') of state-run airports should be privatised as one entity, or split up as separate airport privatisation projects. As discussed in Chapter 2, often within an airport group there will be a few large international airports that are profitable, and a larger number of smaller regional or local airports that are loss-makers. As a consequence the profits from the large airports may cross-subsidise the loss-making airports and so the smaller airports on their own may appear very unattractive for privatisation. Moreover, it can be argued that there are other potential benefits of group operations, such as the ability to share resources and expertise, reduce costs due to scale effects, and adopt a strategic and co-ordinated approach to airport development. However, on the other hand, group operations may inhibit competition, discourage investment at certain airports (if there is spare capacity elsewhere) and lessen the ability of management to innovate and specialise in certain types of airport business models. As a consequence, as further discussed in Chapter 9, some airport groups have been privatised as a single entity (e.g. BAA, Argentina, AENA) whilst others have been split up (e.g. Australia, Brazil) depending on the government's weighting of the relative importance of these influencing factors. The total transaction costs for group privatisation are likely to be significantly less than for individual privatisation.

There are numerous other issues that need to be considered during the complex process of deciding what type of privatisation is the most appropriate – ICAO (2012b) has produced a manual on airport privatisation to aid such decisions. These include the size of airport, time period, health of the capital markets, investment needs and many other factors that are summarised in Figure 8.1.

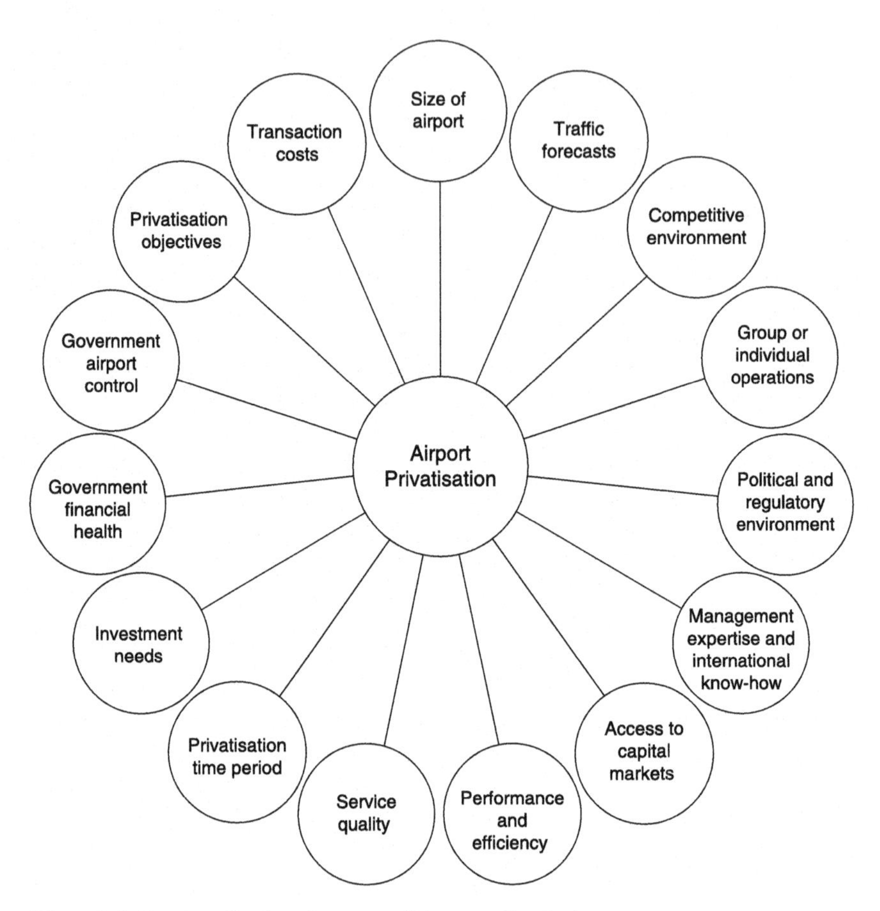

Figure 8.1 Factors affecting the type of airport privatisation

8.3.2 Privatisation approaches

There are a number of different privatisation and private participation approaches which can be used for any economic activity. These have been developed and moulded to suit the specific needs of the airport industry. Four common approaches have emerged which are summarised in Table 8.1 although hybrids of these also exist. For each of these options, the private involvement could be total or partial.

The first approach, share flotations or equity market issues, has been discussed in Chapter 7 in relation to one way of financing airports. Typically with this option, the proceeds will go directly to the government owner, for example as with the recent Initial Public Offering (IPO) of the Spanish operator AENA in 2015 which was used to help reduce Spain's substantial budget deficit. With this privatisation, 21 per cent of the equity went to

Table 8.1 Main characteristics of airport privatisation models

	Share flotation	*Trade sale*	*Concession*	*Build-Operate-Transfer (BOT)*
Main features	Airport operator shares are sold on the stock exchange through an initial public offering (IPO) or secondary offering	Airport is sold to one or more strategic investors through a public tender	Airport operating concession is granted for a fixed time period	Airport build and operating concession is granted for a fixed period of time
Ownership	Shareholders	Investors	Government	Government
Risk	Shareholders	Investors	Government and concessionaire	Government and concessionaire
Management expertise	Initially unchanged	New	New	New
Time period	Permanent	Permanent	Temporary (typically 20–30 years)	Temporary (typically 20–30 years)
Other issues	Management and employees can be incentivised through share ownership	Restrictions on the maximum stake held by (a) individual owners or (b) overseas interests or (c) owners of competing airports can be imposed	Upfront and/ or annual fee paid. Concession agreement may contain service quality or investment requirements	New build may relate to certain facilities or the whole terminal. Can be considered as a special type of concession agreement

three pre-agreed consortia (Ferrovial Aeropuertos; Corporacion Financiera Alba; and the UK-based Children's Investment Fund) with an IPO for a further 28 per cent. The government retained 51 per cent ownership of AENA. On the other hand, the money from the IPO may be used for the financing of future airport investment as with the case of the partial IPO of the Airports Corporation of Vietnam in 2015. It may also be used for paying off balance sheet debt in cases when it is too high relative to equity.

With a 100 per cent share flotation, airports face little in the way of state control other than that encountered by any commercial company, although a degree of government influence can still be maintained by issuing a golden share which gives right of veto over undesirable takeovers deemed to be against national interests. This was the situation with the BAA privatisation until 2003 when golden shares were no longer allowed under EU legislation. Moreover, with the exception of this BAA privatisation, all of the airport share flotations have only been on a partial basis. An important feature of this type of privatisation is that it is likely that there will be less immediate changes to the management approach and structure of the airport operator, due to typically there being a fairly large number of small, passive investors. Overall, whilst this approach was quite a popular option in the early days of privatisation, there are only very few recent examples, as can be seen from Table 8.2.

A trade or freehold sale has generally been a more popular option. This is when the airport is sold, again either in its entirety or only partially (often called a 'minority sale'), to a single, or more commonly a consortium of investors. Historically these were called trade sales as such strategic partners may have been drawn from established airport operators, or engineering, construction, utility or infrastructure companies, who together were not only capable of bringing in additional funding but they also possessed various

Table 8.2 Examples of partial and full airport privatisations since 2000

Share flotation	*Trade sale*	*Concession*	*Build-Operate-Transfer (BOT)*
China (2000): BCIA	Germany (2000): Hamburg	Peru (2000): Lima	Turkey (2003): Ankara
Switzerland (2000): Flughafen Zurich	Italy (2000): Turin	Jamaica (2003): Montego Bay	India (2004): Hyderabad, Bengaluru
Germany (2001): Fraport	UK (2001): Newcastle	India (2006): Delhi, Mumbai	Albania (2005): Tirana
China (2002): Hainan Meilan	Malta (2002)	Turkey (2007): Antalya	Cyprus (2005): Larnaca and Paphos
Thailand (2004): AOT	Australia (2002): Sydney	Kosovo (2010): Pristina	Bulgaria (2006): Varna and Burgas
Italy (2004): Venice	Hungary (2005): Budapest	Russia (2010): St Petersburg	Georgia (2007): Tbilisi, Batumi
France (2005): AdP	UK (2007): Leeds Bradford	Croatia (2012): Zagreb	Tunisia (2007): Monastir, Enfidha
Italy (2006): Pisa	China (2007): Xi'an	Brazil (2012): Brasilia, São Paulo (Guarulhos, Viracopos Campinas)	Saudi Arabia (2012): Madinah
Spain (2015): AENA	UK (2013): Manchester	Portugal (2013): ANA	Turkey (2014): Istanbul
Airports Corporation of Vietnam (2015)	France (2014): Toulouse	Japan (2015): Kansai	Myanmar (2015): Yangon

Source: Compiled by the authors from various sources.

Note: The table only shows the first privatisation. There may have been subsequent changes or more sales.

technical, operational, financial and commercial skills and know-how to deal with the complexities of the airport business. However, increasingly such sales are being dominated by the involvement of the global fund management industry. For instance a sale took place with the Manchester Airport Group (MAP) in the UK in 2013 where 35.5 per cent of the group was sold to the Australian fund manager Industry Funds Management (IFM), primarily to enable MAG to buy Stansted airport. Another recent example of a sale of this type included the privatisation of the first major regional French airport, namely Toulouse, in 2014 where a 49.9 per cent stake went to a consortium consisting of a Hong Kong infrastructure investment company (Friedmann Pacific Asset Management) and a Chinese company (Shandong Hi-Speed Group) that specialises in investment, construction and highway operations. Eight more major regional airport trade sales are expected, the next being Nice and Lyon.

It is essential with this privatisation approach that effective due diligence is used by analysing and validating all the financial, commercial, operational and strategic assumptions that have been made for the sale. In this way the risks of the investments can be assessed accurately and fully addressed in advance. Even with such safeguards there has been a certain amount of flux with airports privatised in this manner, with partners being replaced quite frequently as airports' and/or investors' circumstances change. However, some of the secondary sales of airports have been merely motivated by refinancing needs or the end of the financing cycle which tends to be relatively short-term for infrastructure funds. The UK has experienced more individual airport trade sales than anywhere else in the world, and it may be seen from Table 8.3 that very few airports have kept their original privatisation partners, with a significant number of secondary sales taking place.

The third privatisation approach involves a concession arrangement. The difference here with the IPO or trade sale is that the government maintains ownership and the privatisation model only lasts for a set number of years, typically between 20 and 30 years. Some types of leasing arrangements can also be considered under this definition, although if the lease is of a longer period, for example 50 years (with an option for another 49 years) for Australian airports, the privatisation tends to get viewed more as a 'trade' sale. The key features of such leasing agreements will also tend to be different.

A concession approach typically involves an upfront payment with an annual fee, based on a percentage of gross revenue. There may be additional conditions related to service quality and investment requirements. The fixed-term nature provides greater flexibility for the government but may inhibit operator investment or motivation at end of contract. It is also quite a complex model to introduce because there needs to be agreement on the allocation of all risks between the airport operator and government. This in turn means that the transaction costs will be relatively high. The risks associated with operating and financing the airport and traffic will usually be handed over to the concessionaire who will generally be best able to assess

Table 8.3 Privatisation at UK airports

Airport	*Ownership (December 2015)*	*Private interest (December 2015) (%)*	*Original privatisation date*	*Original private ownership*
Aberdeen	Ferrovial/Macquarie Group	100	1987	BAA
Belfast International	Airports Worldwide	100	1994	TBI
Birmingham	Local authorities/Ontario Teachers' Pension Plan/Employee share trust	51	1997	Local authorities/Aer Rianta/NatWest Ventures/Employee share trust
Bournemouth	Manchester Airport Group (MAG)	35.5 (100% MAG)	1995	National Express Group
Bristol	Ontario Teachers' Pension Plan	100	1997	Cintra/Macquarie Bank
Cardiff	Welsh Government	100	1995	TBI
Durham Tees Valley	Local authorities/Peel Group	89	2003	Local authorities/Peel Group
East Midlands	MAG	35.5 (100% MAG)	1993	MAG
Edinburgh	Global Infrastructure Partners (GIP)	100	1987	BAA
Exeter	Rigby Group	100	2007	Balfour Beatty
Glasgow	Ferrovial/Macquarie Group	100	1987	BAA
Leeds Bradford	Bridgepoint	100	2007	Bridgepoint
Liverpool	Peel Group	100	1990	Local authorities/British Aerospace
London Gatwick	GIP/Abu Dhabi Investment Authority/California Public Employees' Retirement System/National Pension Service of Korea/Future Fund Board of Guardians	100	1987	BAA

London Heathrow	Ferrovial/Qatar Holding LLC/Caisse de Dépôt et Placement du Québec/ Government of Singapore Investment Corporation/Alinda Capital Partners/China Investment Corporation/Universities Superannuation Scheme	100	1987	BAA
London Luton	Ardian/AENA	100	1998	TBI/Bechtel
London Stansted	MAG	100	1987	BAA
Manchester	MAG (Local authorities/Industry Funds Management (IFM))	35.5	2013	MAG (Local authorities/IFM)
Newcastle	Local authorities/AMP Capital	49	2001	Local authorities/Copenhagen Airport
Norwich	Local authorities/Rigby Group	80.1	2004	Local authorities/Omniport
Prestwick	Scottish Government	100	1987	BAA
Southampton	Ferrovial/Macquarie Group	100	1961	Nat Somers

Sources: Compiled by the authors from various sources.

Note: Luton is a concession so only operations but not ownership has been transferred to the private sector.

and manage these risks, whilst other risks, such as those arising from planning delays, terrorism, force majeure, or changes in externally imposed safety or security regulations, may be retained by the government. As with trade sales it is essential for the concessionaire to carry out due diligence but also to ensure that there is a good balance of risks shared with the government. A recent example is the 44-year concession contract starting in 2016 for the New Kansai International Airport Company which will operate Kansai and Osaka airports in Japan. The concessionaires are ORIX Corporation, a local Japanese financial services group and the French operator Vinci Airports.

A similar approach to a concession is adopted with a Build-Operate-Transfer (BOT) privatisation model, which is a generic term which is applied to a number of related options such as Build-Lease-Transfer (BLT), Build-Own-Operate-Transfer (BOOT) or Build-Transfer-Operate (BTO). The key difference between a BOT and concession type of privatisation (although actually a BOT agreement is often just considered as a special type of concession arrangement) is that major investment is needed for a BOT, frequently for a totally new airport, or perhaps for a new passenger terminal or other facility. An example here is the new Hanthawaddy Airport which will serve Yangon in Myanmar. The BOT arrangement was agreed in 2014 and it will run for 30 years. The contract was awarded to a Singapore–Japan consortium which includes a subsidiary of Changi Airport Group. Table 8.4 shows some more examples of concession/BOT agreements.

Not mentioned so far are management contracts, which some argue should not be defined as true 'privatisation' because of their short-term nature – typically 5–10 years. With these, the contractors take over control of day-to-day decisions but have only very limited strategic responsibility or investment commitment. There will normally be no equity involvement. These are often used in areas of high risk, or where other privatisation models are not possible because of regulatory or financial constraints, or where governments are opposed to more radical privatisation models. The contractor will usually receive a fee for the management of part, or all, of the airport. Some of the many examples of recent management contracts include the Schiphol Group's contract with Aruba Airport, Aéroports de Paris with Algiers Airport and Fraport's involvement with the airports of Cairo and Jeddah Airport.

8.4 The current situation

Overall, according to ACI (2015b) 70.8 per cent of world airports are under public ownership, 13.8 per cent under private ownership and the remaining 15.4 per cent under mixed ownership. The corresponding figures by passenger traffic (66.7 per cent, 15.4 per cent, 17.9 per cent) show a slightly higher share of total or partial privatised airports because it tends to be the largest airports that are privatised. Indeed a study of European airports found that the 78 per cent of airports publicly owned handled only 52 per cent of

Table 8.4 Examples of concession/BOT privatisation

Airport	*Date of agreement*	*Length of concession*	*Annual revenue payment*	*Investment conditions*
Peru: Lima	2001	30 years	47%	US$1.3m investment required in first 180 days and US$110m by 2005
India: New Delhi	2006	30 years	46%	US$2bn investment required (first stage of development)
India: Mumbai	2006	30 years	39%	US$1.6bn investment required (first stage of development)
Jordan: Amman	2007	25 years	54%	US$750m investment required
Kosovo: Pristina	2010	30 months: terminal construction+ 20 years: operation	Rising from 18% to 55%	US $140m investment required
Russia: St Petersburg	2010	30 years	Fixed annual payment US$ m and a variable 11.5% revenue fee	Up to 2013, mandatory investment of US$1.0bn, then investment linked to traffic growth
Brazil: São Paulo (Guarulhos)	2012	20 years	10%	US$2.7bn investment required
Brazil: São Paulo (Viracopos Campinas)	2012	30 years	5%	US$5.05bn investment required
Brazil: Brasilia	2012	25 years	2%	US$1.6bn investment required

Sources: Compiled by the authors from various sources.

the European traffic, whereas the remaining 22 per cent of airports that were partially and fully private airports handled 48 per cent of traffic – again indicating that privatisation is more characteristic of larger airports (ACI-Europe, 2010).

Table 8.5 shows the top 20 airport operators with private sector involvement by revenue in 2014. All of these are positioned within the top 45 airport operators in the world. Moreover the revenue of the top 40 private airport companies accounted for half of the revenue of the top 100 airport operators (CAPA, 2015c). Some of these private airport firms are

Table 8.5 Ownership structure of top 20 airport operators with private sector involvement by revenue 2014

World airport operator ranking	*Airport company*	*Country*	*Revenues ($USm)*	*Private share*
1	Heathrow Airport Holdings	UK	4,425	Full
2	AENA Aeropuertos	Spain	4,172	Partial
3	Aéroports de Paris	France	3,679	Partial
4	Fraport	Germany	3,156	Partial
13	Japan Airport Terminal	Japan	1,566	Full
17	TAV Airports	Turkey	1,296	Full
19	Beijing Capital International Airport Group	China	1,241	Partial
20	Airports of Thailand	Thailand	1,230	Partial
21	Manchester Airports Group	UK	1,185	Partial
22	Aéroportsi di Roma	Italy	1,061	Full
23	Flughafen Zürich AG	Switzerland	1,048	Partial
24	Southern Cross Airports Corporation Holdings	Australia	1,043	Full
27	Gatwick Airport Limited	UK	1,024	Full
28	Malaysia Airports Holdings Berhad	Malaysia	1,018	Partial
30	Shanghai Airport Authority	China	932	Partial
32	Guangzhou Baiyun International Airport	China	896	Partial
33	GMR Airports	India	892	Full
36	Flughafen Wien AG	Austria	831	Partial
42	Airports Company South Africa	South Africa	698	Partial
44	Copenhagen Airports A/S	Denmark	684	Partial

Source: Airline Business (2015).

listed on domestic or international stock exchanges either as a result of privatisation through an IPO (e.g. AENA, Paris, Fraport, Zurich) or because they have always been a private company (e.g. Japan Airport Terminal, TAV Airports and GMR Airports).

In total in 2013, ACI (2015b) stated that there were 555 airports in the world with private sector participation. Overall, it may be seen from Figure 8.2 that concessions contracts are the most popular. As regards listed companies, China has the most listed airports, either on the domestic (Xiamen, Shenzhen, Shanghai Hongqiao, Beijing, Mielan Haikou and Guangzhou) or Hong Kong stock exchanges, whilst the UK has experienced the most individual trade sales, as can be seen from Table 8.3. In Europe, actually concession and BOT projects have been relatively rare with the airports of Luton, Pristina, Zagreb, Athens, Larnaca/Paphos and a number in Turkey being exceptions. By contrast in emerging economies, the concession type of

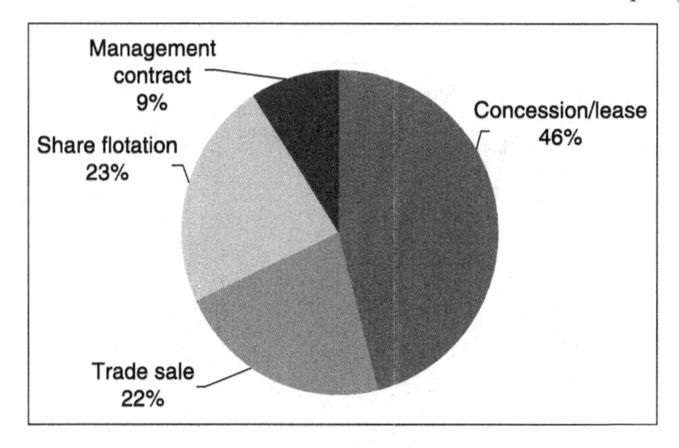

Figure 8.2 Distribution of airports by privatisation model 2013

Source: ACI (2015b).

privatisation is by far the most common. Indeed according to the World Bank (2015), concessions in low- and middle-income countries accounted for 51 per cent of airport contracts and 62 per cent of investment commitment between 1990 and 2015.

Figure 8.3 shows that Europe, the continent that first witnessed privatisation, has the most private sector involvement followed by Latin America-Caribbean and Asia-Pacific. However, in recent years there has been a trend towards more privatisation in emerging markets which, as discussed in Chapter 1, are forecast to experience much higher growth rates than in the mature markets of North America and Western Europe. With the exception of a few airports (e.g. Athens and the French regional airports), most future activity seems likely to take place outside of these regions, mostly within emerging economies but also possibly in Japan. This country is one of the world's largest aviation markets but as yet, except for the recent concession agreements for Sendai Airport and the New Kansai International Airport Company (NKIAC), has not witnessed privatisation and there remain significant obstacles to overcome (Graham et al., 2014; Miyoshi, 2015).

There is little private sector involvement with airports in North America. This is partly because in Canada for the major airports there is a unique governance model where the airports are owned by the national government but managed under long-term leases by 'not-for-profit' local airport authorities. Moreover in the US, nearly all airports remain under local public ownership although as discussed in Chapter 7 a notable feature is that the airports have always had considerable access to the capital markets with tax-free bonds as a source of funding and so arguably the case for privatisation, in that it allows the injection of new sources of finance, is less convincing. Moreover there are other unique factors of the US system such as the legally

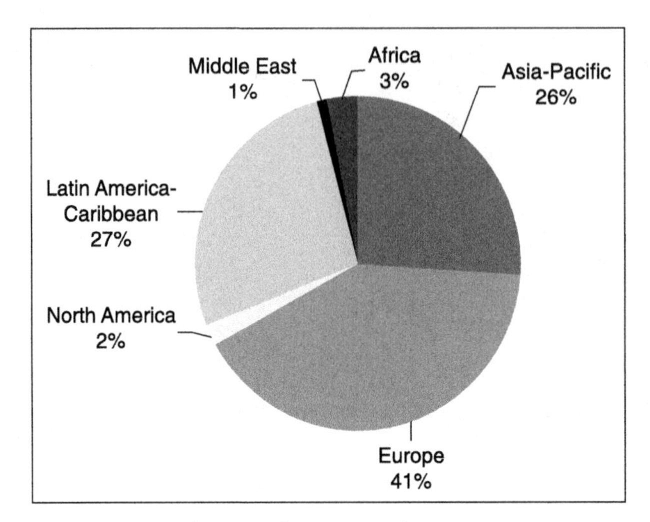

Figure 8.3 Distribution of airports with private sector involvement by region 2013

Source: ACI (2015b).

binding contracts with their airline customers and grant funding through the Airport Improvement Program (AIP) (see Chapter 2) which make any moves towards privatisation that much more challenging. In addition there are other major legal obstacles, most notably prohibiting airport revenues (including sale proceeds) to be used for non-airport purposes (so-called 'revenue diversion laws').

However, increasing pressures on the AIP funding because of federal budget cuts, and other factors such as poor financial health of a number of local government owners, have meant that there has been increased interest in airport privatisation (for example see Enrico et al., 2012). In fact way back in 1996 the federal government introduced their Airport Privatization Pilot Program which made provision for five airports to be exempted from some of the legal requirements that impede their sale to private entities – in 2012 this was increased to ten airports (Federal Aviation Authority (FAA), 2013). However, even though a number of airports have been interested in the program, including Chicago Midway which has had two unsuccessful attempts at being privatised, only one airport, namely that at San Juan in Puerto Rico, has been privatised (Poole, 2015). In spite of there being a need for significant new investment in the US, there appears to be little likelihood of any major airport privatisation developments in the near future. The only likely viable alternative seems to be the possibility of private–public partnerships in construction and operation of new terminals as has occurred with Terminal 4 at New York's JFK Airport, the domestic and international terminals at Orlando Sanford Airport, and is planned for the Central Terminal Building at New York's La Guardia Airport (CAPA, 2015d).

8.5 Financial consequences of privatisation

Given that there is now private participation at over 550 airports, a key question must be, what has been the impact of this and have the stated objectives for privatisation been achieved? In terms of improving performance and efficiency, ACI (2015b) observed that the partial and fully privatised airports on average generated more revenue per passenger in both the aeronautical and non-aeronautical areas. However, they also had higher costs per passenger, which is not in line with the assumption that such airports are more effective in cost control. Overall the highest EBITDA margins were achieved with the totally private airports (56 per cent), followed by the public airports (54 per cent) and then the mixed-ownership airports (45 per cent). The evidence is also rather inconclusive in the academic literature. For example Vasigh and Gorjidooz (2006) found no significant relationship between efficiency and airport ownership when a sample of 22, both public and private US/European airports, was examined. Moreover, when Oum et al. (2003) looked at a large sample of major Asia-Pacific, European and North American airports they again observed that ownership had no significant impact. However, Vogel (2006) found that partially and fully privatised European airports operated more efficiently than public ones. Also Oum et al. (2006) concluded that airports with government majority ownership were significantly less efficient than airports with a private majority ownership, although there was no statistically significant evidence that fully state-owned airports were less efficient. Likewise Oum et al. (2008) concluded that there was a high probability that airports owned/operated by a majority private firm achieved higher efficiency than those owned/operated by a mixed enterprise with a government majority. More recently Vasigh et al. (2014) observed that privatised airports in the UK outperformed the partially privatised, government-owned airports in Latin America; however, the public US airports outperformed both of these groups of airports.

There is overwhelming evidence that in many cases privatisation has enabled new injections of investment. Nevertheless, for a variety of reasons, such as conflicts that have arisen between governments and the new private operator and the enforcement of the terms of privatisation agreements, problems related to the selection of the most suitable investor, or inappropriate/unrealistic estimations of passenger airline demand and the financial situation, a few airport privatisations have not worked. For example there have been the unilateral cancellation of the agreements by the government (e.g. at Budapest, Manila and Male airports), sales back to the airport (e.g. Toronto, Stewart and Costa Rica) or the renegotiation of existing agreements (e.g. Quito, Argentina).

In recent more challenging economic times, smaller airports have been viewed in a less attractive light and considered to be more risky. As already discussed this is partly because of their inherent financial disadvantages and also because of their dependence quite often on a few dominant airlines, increasingly LCCs, which can be very footloose. In a few cases this has meant that airports have been temporarily or permanently sold back to the government as with Frankfurt Hahn and Luebeck in Germany, and Prestwick and Cardiff in the UK.

As discussed in Chapter 6, potential investors in airports will consider the price of the airport (enterprise value, EV) in relation to profit, typically using the EV/EBITDA ratio or multiples, when deciding whether to invest (see Figure 6.1). For earlier IPOs, such as those of BAA, Copenhagen and Vienna, the multiples were in the region of five to ten. This rose to between x10 and x20 for some of the early partial and total trade sales of airports such as Bristol, Cardiff, Wellington, Hamburg and the major airports in Australia and South Africa before 9/11. With the subsequent partial IPOs of Fraport and Aéroports de Paris the multiples fell back to around x10–11 but with the revival of interest in airport privatisation in the mid-2000s, and the emergence of international fund managers as major investors, the values rose rapidly to around an all-time high of x30 for the airport privatisations of Budapest and Leeds Bradford (Aviation Strategy, 2015a).

However, the financial crisis of 2008 onwards put a halt to these high values with the exception of the Brazilian privatisations (LeighFisher, 2012) (which were considered to be very attractive to local infrastructure firms new to the airport business especially because of the high forecast growth rates). Recent transactions have risen up again to around x15 but not as high as the over-heated values prior to the financial crisis. The multiple for the AENA IPO in 2015 was around x12. However, it must be noted that generally trade sales enable the airport to be sold at a higher price than with an IPO. This is because with a trade sale there will be more control over the financial, operational and management structures post-privatisation and the detailed due diligence process will help reduce the risks. Indeed in 2015 the multiples for the listed European airport groups were around x11, compared with the recent trade and private transactions of other airports at the x15–18 level (Aviation Strategy, 2015b).

8.6 Participants in airport privatisation

A large range of different investors and companies have been involved with airport privatisation projects. This includes some of the traditional airport operators such as AENA, Fraport, Malaysia Airports, Aéroports de Paris (AdP), Flughafen Zurich, Vancouver and Changi Singapore who have been able to expand beyond their previously well-defined national barriers (Table 8.6). There are also newer specialist airport operators such as TAV Airports and others, originally from related sectors such as property, utilities, infrastructure and construction, which saw some possible opportunities and potential synergies with airport operations. These include Ferrovial, Vinci, Hochtief (now AviAlliance), and the Indian companies GMR and GVK (Table 8.7). Interestingly there are a couple of examples of equity partnerships

Table 8.6 International airport operators/investors connected to established airport operators

Operator/investor	*Main airport/airport connection*	*Airport participation (excluding management contracts)*
Aéroports de Paris Management (AdPM)	Wholly owned subsidiary of Aéroports de Paris (AdP)	Chile: Santiago Croatia: Zagreb Jordan: Amman Mauritius Belgium: Liege Mexico: OMA Guinea: Conakry Saudi Arabia: Jeddah (Hajj terminal) AdP has 38% share of TAV Airports, 8% share of Schiphol Group
AENA Internacional	Wholly owned subsidiary of AENA	UK: London Luton Mexico: Grupo Aeropuertos Mexicanos del Pacifico (GAP) Columbia: Cali, Cartangena de Indias
Airports Worldwide	Affliated with Houston Airport System	UK: Belfast International Costa Rica: San José, Liberia Sweden: Stockholm Skavsta US: Orlando Sanford
Changi Airports International	Wholly owned subsidiary of Changi Airport Group	Brazil: Tom Jobim Rio de Janeiro Russia: Krasnodar region airports India: Bengal Aerotropolis Myanmar: Hanthawaddy (Yangon)
Flughafen Zurich	Zurich	Brazil: Tancredo Neves (Belo Horizonte) Chile: Iquique, Antofagasta Curacao India: Bengaluru
Fraport	Frankfurt	Bulgaria: Burgas, Varna, Pulkova Germany: Hannover Slovenia: Ljubijana Turkey: Antalya India: Delhi China: Xi'an Xianyang Peru: Lima Greece: 14 regional airports Russia: St Petersburg Senegal: Dakar
Malaysia Airports Holding Berhad (MAHB)	Malaysian airports	Turkey: Sabiha Gokcen Istanbul India: Hyderabad
Schiphol Group	Amsterdam	The Netherlands: Rotterdam, The Hague, Lelystad, Eindhoven Airport Australia: Brisbane US: JFK Terminal 4 8% share in AdP
Vantage Airport Group	50% owned by Vancouver Airport Authority	Canada: Hamilton Jamaica: Montego Bay Cyprus: Larnaca and Paphos

Source: Compiled by the authors from various sources.

with these operators, such as a cross-shareholding of 8 per cent between AdP and the Schiphol Group, AdP having a 38 per cent share of TAV Airports, and Vinci having an 8 per cent share of AdP.

Financial institutions (e.g. investment banks, pensions, private equity) have always played a major role in supporting airport privatisation consortia but in more recent years have started investing directly in airports and have become major players in these developments (Rikty et al., 2014; CAPA, 2015e; Condie, 2016). As a result airport privatisation is increasingly being dominated by international funds such as infrastructure funds, pension funds, insurance funds and sovereign wealth funds. These types of funds are

Table 8.7 Other international airport operators/investors

Operator/investor	*Headquarters*	*Airport participation (excluding management contracts)*
AviAlliance (previously Hochtief AirPort)	Germany	Greece: Athens Hungary: Budapest Germany: Düsseldorf, Hamburg Albania: Tirana
Ferrovial	Spain	UK: London Heathrow, Southampton, Glasgow, Aberdeen Spain: AENA
Global Infrastructure Partners (GIP)	US	UK: London City, Gatwick, Edinburgh
GMR Group	India	India: Delhi, Hyderabad Philippines: Mactan Cebu
GVK	India	India: Mumbai, Bengaluru
Industry Funds Management (IFM)	Australia	UK: Manchester Airport Group (MAG) Austria: Vienna Australia: Brisbane, Melbourne, Adelaide
Ontario Teachers' Pension Plan	Canada	UK: Birmingham, Bristol Belgium: Brussels Denmark: Copenhagen
TAV Airports Holding	Turkey	Turkey: Izmir, Ankara, Alanya Gazipasa, Istanbul Ataturk, Bodrum Georgia: Tblisi, Batumi Macedonia: Skopje, Obrid Croatia: Zagreb Tunisia: Enfidha, Monastir Saudi Arabia: Medinah
Vinci Airports	France	Dominican Republic: Dominican AERODOM France: Nantes, Toulon Japan: Kansai Cambodia: Phnom Penh, Siem Reap, Sihanoukville Portugal: ANA Portuguese airports Chile: Santiago 8% share in AdP

Source: Compiled by the authors from various sources.

discussed in Chapter 7. Macquarie funds and Global Infrastructure Funds (GIP) are examples of infrastructure funds involved with airports. UK examples may be seen in Table 8.3 – Macquarie is involved with Glasgow, Aberdeen and Southampton airports, whilst GIP is involved with London Gatwick, London City and Edinburgh airports. Relevant pension funds in the UK include Industry Funds Management (MAG), the Ontario Teachers' Pension Plan (Birmingham and Bristol airports) and the UK Universities Superannuation Scheme or USS (London Heathrow) whilst Ardian is an insurance fund involved with the Luton Airport concession. There are sovereign wealth funds associated with both London Heathrow (China Investment Corporation, Qatar Investment Authority, Government of Singapore Investment Corporation) and London Gatwick (Abu Dhabi Investment Authority, the National Pension Service of Korea and the Future Fund investors).

Most of these funds are interested not just in airports but in most types of infrastructure assets, and so tend not to have the same degree of allegiance to the airport business as with some of the previous airport privatisation investors. As a result they are very much focused on the airport's financial returns. Consequently it is the major airports that they are primarily interested in, the smaller regional airports being less attractive and more risky. It needs noting that the sovereign wealth funds are a rather special case and tend only to be interested in minority shares at large high-quality airports (Condie, 2016).

Whilst this dominance of the international funds has been increasing, at the same time some of the original investors have left the sector or have scaled down their involvement. This includes a number of established airport operators such as Heathrow (formerly as part of BAA) and Copenhagen, who are focusing on their core business. Likewise the Spanish infrastructure company Abertis has pulled out of all its involvement with airports to refocus on its toll roads and other surface transport interests. The German construction company Hochtief also sold its airport division (now called AviAlliance) in 2013 to Canada's Public Sector Pension Investment Board (PSP).

A quite popular structure for an investor in other airports seems to be one which has operational expertise and a funding provider, such as MAG and IFM, Airports Worldwide with Ontario Municipal Employees Retirement System (OMERS) and Houston Aviation System (HAS) and AviAlliance, which combines the former expertise of Hochtief Airports with PSP. Moreover it is usual practice with trade sales and concession agreements to have a consortium of a couple of different partners who can bring in different expertise and financing ability, and share the risk (Feldman, 2008). When there is some major capital investment needed, typically with BOT projects, often a construction company partner may be an advantage, for example Vinci, which is one of the world's largest construction companies. Furthermore having a local partner can help the consortium understand local circumstances and conditions (and may well be politically essential) whereas having an international partner may bring with it knowledge and experience of global customers, suppliers and the financial markets. The privatisation tender may well stipulate what types of partners are required.

8.7 Summary

This chapter has described the origins and development of airport privatisation. It has identified the different privatisation models that exist, namely share flotation, trade sale and concession/BOT, and the different types of operators and investors. Increasingly airport privatisation is being dominated by international funds such as sovereign wealth funds, infrastructure funds and pension funds. Whilst in the early years in countries such as the UK, some of the arguments for privatisation were voiced in ideological terms related to reducing state control and increasing airport efficiency, the rationale today for airport privatisation seems also entirely focused on more practical considerations such as the need for investment, the acquisition of management and operational expertise or the use of sale proceeds as a means to reduce large government budget deficits.

It is evident that most large aviation markets have experienced at least some airport privatisation, with the exception of Japan and the US where major obstacles to full-scale privatisation exist, even though at least in Japan there appears to be some changes on the way. In the future it is likely to be emerging markets, which are forecast to have the greatest traffic growth, which witness the most privatisation. This may well include more developments in major countries such as India and Brazil, even though growth in the areas has slowed down somewhat. As discussed in Chapter 1, China will also be expanding its air services, building many new airports, but privatisation experience here to date has been relatively unsuccessful with operators such as AdP, Vinci and Copenhagen ceasing to have involvement, leaving Fraport as the only international airport operator with a major interest at one airport.

Meanwhile in a number of other emerging markets, the political and economic risks are currently too much of a hindrance for attracting private sector interest in airports. Elsewhere in Europe and in other areas that already have significant private involvement, most of the privatisation activity is likely to be with secondary sales. Regional and small airports, with limited markets and inherent economic disadvantages, are likely to be the least attractive to present-day investors unless they are privatised as a group as with the recent Greek regional airports' privatisation.

Having investigated many of the complex issues associated with airport privatisation, the last two chapters will now cover airport competition and airport economic regulation. A knowledge of these two areas is not only fundamental in order to fully understand all the challenges associated with privatising airports, but also to appreciate in detail the major impact that both can have on airport finances.

9 Airport competition

9.1 Introduction

Chapter 1 has already described how the nature of airports has been transformed very substantially in the last few decades. One area where there has been a dramatic change is in the level of airport competition that exists. When airports were considered to be solely suppliers of transport infrastructure, they were often viewed as monopoly providers. Passenger demand was determined by the catchment area and the airlines' choice of airport was severely limited by the system of restrictive bilateral agreements. However, with airline deregulation and liberalisation spreading to many parts of the world, markets have been opened up to much more potential or actual competition between airlines and, as a result, between airports as well. This has allowed different types of airline developments, such as the formation of global alliances and the emergence of the low-cost sector, which rely on the use of certain airport business models as part of their competitive strategy. Moreover the move towards commercialisation and privatisation of the airport industry (see Chapter 8) has meant that airport operators have a much more competitive and businesslike outlook in seeking new, or retaining existing, customers.

The degree of airport competition can have a very significant impact on airport finance and investment. Competitive pressures can drive down airport charges, promote more flexibility in pricing and encourage airports to become more efficient. Undoubtedly a more competitive environment is one of the key reasons for the increased interest in airport benchmarking which was discussed in Chapter 5. On the other hand, the absence of competition can also have major consequences and may result in the need for government intervention to correct for market failures. This may include the controversial area of state aid or subsidies. It may also cover economic regulation which has the primary aim of controlling the potential abuse of market power. This latter area of government policy can be crucial for the financial management of airports and so the next chapter (Chapter 10) is largely devoted to discussing the many complicated issues related to airport economic regulation.

This chapter focuses on airport competition, which itself is very complex because of the different levels of competition that can exist (Figure 9.1). At the broadest level, airports can compete with other services and facilities. For example on the aeronautical side this can be high-speed rail, and on the non-aeronautical side this can be shopping malls or Internet shopping. Video-conferencing, and destination competition for holidays and short breaks, are also factors affecting an airport's competitive position. Then there is potential competition between airports, both when they are operated as individual entities and when they are under common or group ownership. The next section considers this in detail and also looks at the related issue of airport expansion and competition. In addition there is competition within airports, such as the competition for the provision of a certain service or between airport terminals. This is examined in the following section. Finally the chapter concludes by expanding the discussion to include state aid and subsidies because of the potential role that these can play in distorting competition.

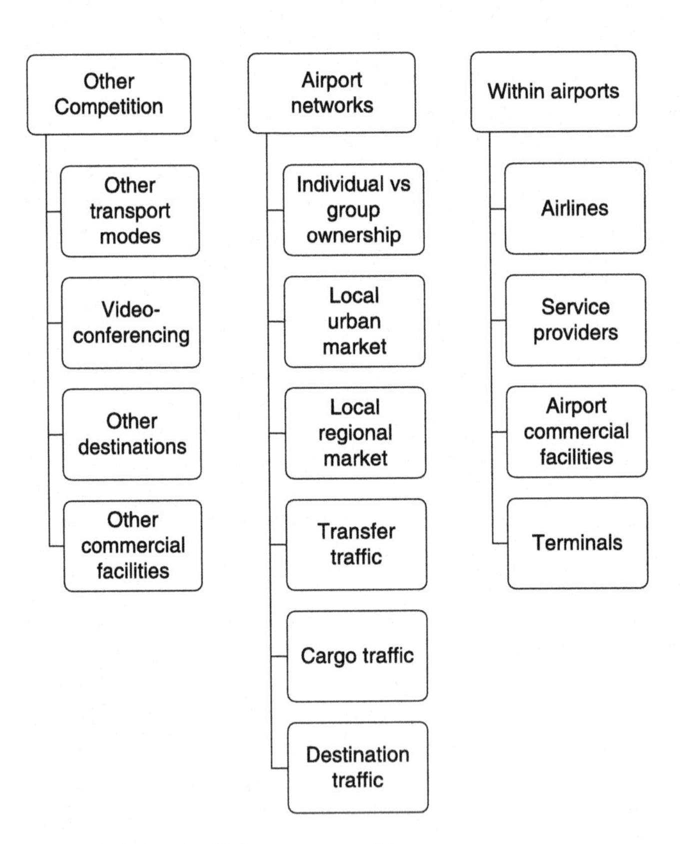

Figure 9.1 Levels of airport competition

9.2 Competition between airports

9.2.1 The nature of competition between airports

Whilst the extent of competition that exists between airports in any specific circumstance can be, and in many cases has been, fiercely debated, often there are some common arguments that emerge. Firstly, it is very difficult to disentangle airport competition from airline competition at airports when the passenger viewpoint is being considered (Morrell, 2010). Frequently, apparently strong competitive forces between airports will be caused by their airlines themselves being in intense competition. Indeed there is much evidence to show that once locational and accessibility factors have been taken into account, the passengers' choice of airport is largely driven by the nature of the airlines which serve the airport in terms of fares, destinations and services on offer. For example for the three major airports in the Washington, DC region in 2013 (Baltimore, Dulles and Reagan National), the primary stated reasons for passengers using the airport were accessibility (60, 49 and 70 per cent, respectively) followed by the quality/price of the air services (37, 48 and 27 per cent, respectively) (Mohammed and Roisman, 2014).

The second factor to consider is whether or not airports have overlapping catchment areas. The weakest competition tends to exist when airports possess a unique catchment area, particularly if they are based on an island or in a remote location. Destination airports, as defined in Chapter 1, can be similar if there is just one airport providing access to a distinct destination, such as Alice Springs, Sharm El-Sheikh or Las Vegas. However, in other cases, there may be more than one airport serving a major tourist attraction such as Barcelona (Barcelona, Girona or Reus) or Venice (Marco Polo or Treviso), resulting in much stronger competitive forces.

Overlapping catchment areas may exist in an urban or city situation as in London (Heathrow, Gatwick, Stansted, City and Luton), Paris (Charles de Gaulle and Orly), Washington (Dulles, Reagan National and Baltimore), New York (JFK, La Guardia and Newark), Moscow (Domodedovo and Sheremetyevo) and Shanghai (Pudong and Hongqiao). It may well be that when there is more than one airport serving an urban area they will take on different roles. Chapter 1 identified six different types of airport models, namely hub airports, destination airports, business airports, low-cost airports, cargo airports and airport networks. In a city context, business airports, low-cost airports and cargo airports often play a more secondary, specialised role. They can nevertheless compete directly to a certain extent for the city's traffic. Airports that have marketed themselves as low-cost alternatives have arguably been the most successful in this role. For example in Europe there are a large number of such airports, sometimes having been developed from former military use, for instance Hahn (Frankfurt), Bergamo (Milan) and Weeze (Düsseldorf). In North America there are also a number of secondary airports primarily serving LCC traffic such as Providence and Manchester (Boston), Burbank and Ontario (Los Angeles), Sanford (Orlando), Atlantic City (Philadelphia) and Hamilton (Toronto). Elsewhere there are fewer secondary airports, with some notable exceptions such as Sharjah (Dubai) and Avalon (Melbourne).

When more than one airport serves a major city or urban area this is commonly called a multi-airport system (MAS). Bonnefoy et al. (2008) identified 59 MASs worldwide, observing that the comparative number in each global region reflected the relative maturity of air transport there. They listed 25 in Europe, 18 in North America and fewer in Asia-Pacific (8), Latin America (5) and the Middle East (3) – although this may have changed slightly in recent years with the steady traffic growth in these latter three regions. The most frequent type of MAS is composed of a primary and secondary airport (e.g. Chicago, Frankfurt and Melbourne) but there are also cases of two primary airports (e.g. Miami and Shanghai). The London, Los Angeles and New York MASs were identified as some of the most complex.

Overlapping catchment areas may also occur with regional airports, especially when regional or local governments have been or are responsible for these. This ownership structure can lead to overinvestment resulting in overcapacity, because the objectives for airport expansion can be political or driven by economic development reasons, rather than just steered by commercial or financial considerations. Japan is one such example where there are over 100 airports in total. If such regional airports are relatively free to compete, as they are for instance in Europe, this can produce a very challenging situation for the airport operators as they struggle to cope with underutilised facilities, a small critical traffic mass for their non-aeronautical facilities and downward pressure on their aeronautical charges from their airline customers who can play one airport off with another.

When catchment areas do not overlap directly, and if a country possesses a major airport which has a high concentration of both short-haul and long-haul services, it will be difficult for other airports in the same country to compete. However, such major airports may compete internationally as primary or mega hubs aiming to provide good global flight connectivity and efficient passenger transfers. As discussed in Chapter 1, within Europe airports such as London Heathrow, Paris CDG, Frankfurt and Amsterdam have traditionally competed in this way, although arguably the list of competitors could now be extended to include airports such as Istanbul Ataturk and those in the Middle East. Figure 9.2 shows very clearly how the relative connectivity of these latter airports (measured in terms of a weighted number of weekly connections) has changed. In Asia there are also a number of notable primary airport hubs such as Seoul Incheon, Hong Kong and Singapore and there are major cargo hubs such as Hong Kong and Dubai. In addition, there are secondary hubs which compete to a more limited degree such as Jakarta Soekarno–Hatta, Copenhagen or Abu Dhabi. Ultimately most of these hub airports will be very much dependent on the

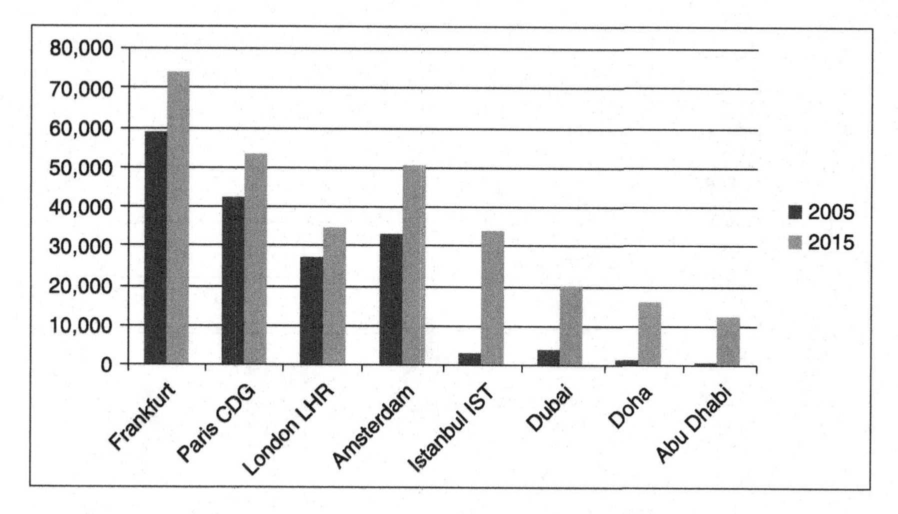

Figure 9.2 Hub connectivity for major European and Middle Eastern hubs 2005 and 2015

Source: ACI Europe (2015d).
Note: Hub connectivity is measured in weighted weekly schedules.

operating strategies and network plans of airlines and global alliance developments but undoubtedly financial strategies, such as reduced charges for transfer traffic and other support, can help. For example in 2015, Singapore Changi Airport extended its initiatives to strengthen the competitiveness of the Singapore hub, which included reductions to transfer passenger fees, to landing fees for larger aircraft types, and to franchise fees for flight catering and ground handling services, as well as strategic support measures to encourage the efficiency of airline and ground handling operations (Changi Airport Group, 2015).

In spite of the degree of competition varying between different types of airports as a result of a complicated mix of factors related to issues such as market share, pricing, quality of service, capacity provision and substitution possibilities, there is a broad consensus that the competitive forces have increased and that this is having a major impact on many aspects of the airport business, including airport finance and marketing (Forsyth et al., 2010; Halpern and Graham, 2013). Indeed Copenhagen Economics (2012) found that in Europe airlines had become more footloose, being able and willing to switch away from airports if the conditions were not right. It found that many routes were opening and closing as the result of the high degree of switching taking place with the airlines. For example, in 2011 around 2,500 new routes were opened whereas 2,000 were closed and every year around 20 per cent of the total routes were openings and 15 per cent were closures. Copenhagen Economics also found that passengers had more

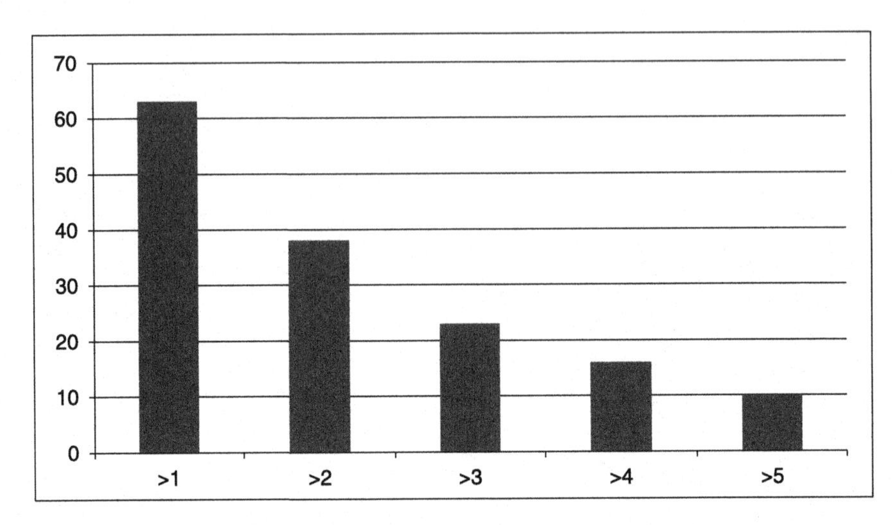

Figure 9.3 Number of European airports (handling more than 1 million annual passengers in 2011) within a radius of a two-hour drive

Source: Copenhagen Economics (2012).

choice and there was more than one airport accessible for nearly two-thirds of Europeans within a two-hour drive (Figure 9.3). The evidence suggested there was increasing choice for both local departing and transfer passengers.

However a counter-study to the Copenhagen Economics report (which was prepared for ACI Europe) was published by IATA (2013), which argued that network airlines had limited switching ability compared to point-to-point traffic, which it claimed had been overlooked in the previous research. In a further response by ACI Europe (2014), it was contended that European airports would become increasingly reliant on origin and destination traffic for future growth. Moreover, IATA (2013) argued that passengers strongly prefer to use their closest airport rather than to exercise the choice available to them. It therefore reasoned that this limited the extent of airport competition for origin-destination passengers although this point was refuted in the further response of ACI Europe (2014). This lively debate between these two leading industry bodies indicates the complex nature of airport competition and the existence of quite divergent views.

9.2.2 Competition within airport groups

As previously discussed in Chapter 1, a number of airports are operated as an airport network or group under common ownership. Arguably such a model could inhibit competition as well as hindering local management innovation but this has to be balanced against the potential benefits of network operations, such as the ability to share resources and expertise, reduce costs due to scale effects, and adopt a strategic and co-ordinated approach to airport development. With common ownership, financial cross-subsidisation can occur between airports, which may help the airport operator but may not be popular with all users.

As mentioned in Chapter 8, group ownership has been a particular issue when airport privatisation has occurred and experience in this area has varied considerably. For example in the Americas, just over 30 Argentine airports were privatised as a group, whereas in Brazil the major airports were privatised individually. Meanwhile in Mexico the airports were divided into four different groups with a mixture of small and large airports in each group. Elsewhere, in Australia, the government decided on individual privatisations for the major international airports when the airports were privatised. In Ireland for many years the three main airports, Dublin, Shannon and Cork, were run as a network by the state company Aer Rianta. In 2004, with the objective of achieving more choice and competition, the still government-owned Dublin Airport Authority (DAA) was established to replace Aer Rianta and to give Shannon and Cork more autonomy with separate boards of directors. However, it was not until the end of 2012, after a considerable amount of debate, that Shannon Airport was separated from DAA and free to compete as a separate state entity called Shannon Airport Authority.

By contrast, in a few cases proposed airport privatisations have not actually gone ahead because of anti-competitive fears. For example, in the UK this was an issue with the possible joint ownership of Belfast International and Belfast City airports, and also with Bristol and nearby Exeter Airport. Likewise Vienna Airport was not allowed to take over the operations of nearby Bratislava Airport. In other cases common ownership is viewed as a way to exert some influence over the type of traffic which is attracted to each airport. For example up until 2009, Fraport owned both Frankfurt and the low-cost airport Frankfurt Hahn and was able to direct the LCCs to Hahn. Similarly the Schiphol Group not only owns Amsterdam but also Rotterdam and Lelystad airports and holds a majority share in Eindhoven Airport. It views this as a way to supplement capacity for certain airline operations, for example general aviation and regional, charter and LCC traffic. Aeroporti di Roma also owns both Fiumicino and Ciampino, with the latter specializing in low-cost and general aviation operations.

Arguably the most contentious and long-running debate has occurred with the London airports. The three major airports (Heathrow, Gatwick and Stansted) were privatised through an IPO of the BAA group in 1987 (see Chapter 8). At that time proponents in favour of group operations argued that there were only limited competitive pressures between the three airports because they served distinct markets and Heathrow was very dominant. Meanwhile opponents argued that Gatwick and Stansted could compete for charter traffic and that the former was developing into a credible alternative airport to Heathrow. However, these possible benefits of competition were dismissed in favour of the other strategic, financial and operational gains that group operations was seen to bring. Subsequently in the next couple of decades as the more liberal and competitive aviation environment spread through Europe, a number of high-level reviews revisited the possibility of splitting up BAA but it was not until 2009, over 20 years after the initial privatisation, that finally the structure of BAA was required to change. This came after a lengthy review by the UK's former competition authority (the Competition Commission), who concluded that common ownership of airports in the London area gave rise to adverse effects on competition (although it also identified a number of other inhibiting factors such as Heathrow's position as the only significant hub airport in the south-east of the UK, the economic regulatory system and the planning regime) (Competition Commission, 2009). Gatwick and Stansted were required to be sold. Gatwick had actually been sold in 2009 before the final decision was made and Stansted was sold to the Manchester Airport Group (MAG) in 2013. The Competition Commission also found that BAA's common ownership of Glasgow and Edinburgh airports in Scotland hindered competition and so it was required to dispose of one airport. Consequently BAA sold Edinburgh in 2012.

9.2.3 Competition and airport expansion

A key issue regarding airport competition and finance is the impact of providing new capacity. At a very basic level, there will typically be three options for airport expansion which may be used in isolation or in combination with each other (Figure 9.4). These are expanding the existing airport,

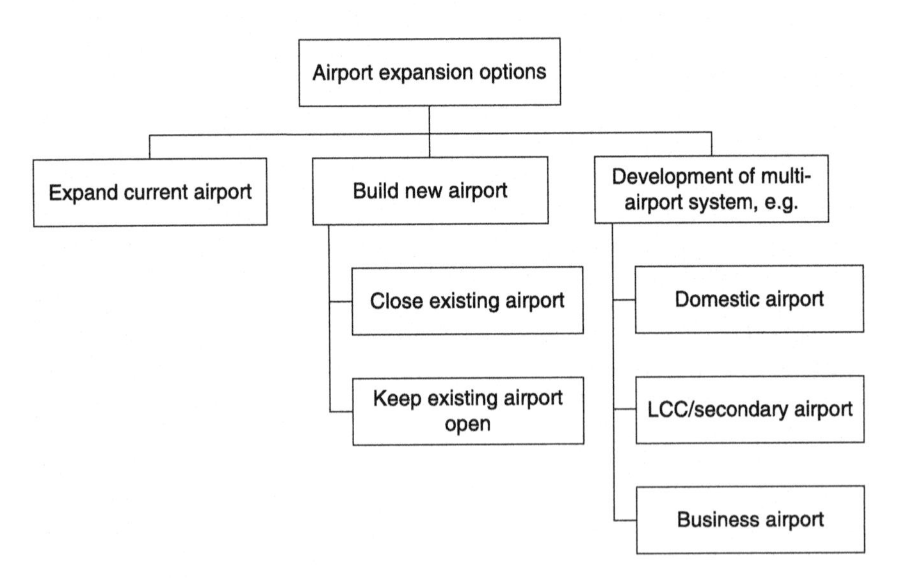

Figure 9.4 Airport expansion options

building a new airport or spreading the traffic around a MAS. There are many global examples where a single primary airport has been expanded to cope with the increasing demand (e.g. Atlanta, Delhi, Lima). Clearly in these cases there must be sufficient land and other physical conditions to allow this to happen, and the likely increased environmental impacts on the surrounding area must be considered an acceptable trade-off. This in itself will not necessarily produce any increased airport competition, although clearly it may enhance the airline competition at the airport if the increased number of slots gives access to more airlines. Moreover passenger accessibility to the airport will remain the same in this case, unless there are major parallel improvements to the road or public transport system when the airport is expanded. From a financial viewpoint, however, this may very well be the cheapest investment option, and by becoming larger the airport may be able to take advantage of scale economies.

By contrast, building a new airport will very often be the most costly option, particularly if new surface transport infrastructure has to be considered and there is a long and complex planning process to navigate. There are currently a number of very large new airports under construction, such as the second airports at Beijing and Dubai. This may be the only option when land is not available, or the greater environmental impacts are not acceptable at the existing airport. The new location may be more reachable to certain new passenger groups, but may also be less accessible for some existing passengers.

There are usually two scenarios for the existing airport in this situation. Firstly, the existing airport can be closed down. Examples here include Munich (1992), Denver (1995), Hong Kong (1998), Oslo (1998), Athens (2001) and Doha (2014). Clearly this may result in a loss of jobs and income at the existing airport, but this may be balanced by new opportunities at the new site. There may also be the potential for redevelopment of the existing land. For example the site of Fornebu, the former Oslo Airport, has witnessed a mixed development of offices and light industry, housing and parkland. There will be no long-term problem with traffic allocation as all airlines will be required to shift, albeit there will be the expense of moving and the inconvenience. This will also not create any new opportunities for airport competition and may even hinder such development, for example as with the Athens 'new' airport where no additional airport development within the same catchment area is allowed.

An interesting case is Istanbul. There are currently two airports, both managed by private operators. The largest airport, Istanbul Atatürk, is run by TAV, the Turkish airport operator, and it handled 57 million passengers in 2014, predominately travelling on full service airlines. The other airport, Sabiha Gökçen, is operated by the Malaysian airport operator Malaysia Airport Holding Berhad (MAHB) and has grown from just being a secondary LCC airport (particularly the base for the Turkish airline Pegasus) to offering a wider range of services, including some shifted by Turkish airlines from the congested Atatürk Airport. In 2014 the airport handled 24 million passengers. With no feasible possibility of significantly developing these two airports, a new third airport is being built with the contract being awarded to the Turkish joint venture consortium of Cengiz-Kolin-Limak-Mapa-Kalyon. Its opening, with a capacity of 90 million passengers, is currently planned for 2017 when Atatürk Airport will be closed. However, TAV has a contract to run Atatürk Airport until 2021 and so will have to be compensated, in some as yet undisclosed manner.

The other scenario is to keep open the existing airport. Examples here include Montreal: Trudeau/Mirabel (1975), Tokyo: Haneda/Narita (1978), Osaka: Itami/Kansai (1994), Milan: Linate/Malpensa (1998), Seoul: Gimpo/Incheon (2001) and Bangkok: Don Mueang/Suvarnabhumi (2006). Often the original airport may handle domestic/short-haul traffic or become a LCC airport (e.g. in the US with Chicago Midway, Dallas Love Field and Houston Hobby airports). With this option the airports may be operated by the same or different operators, and clearly the latter may provide opportunities for airport competition. However, the new airport may be perceived as less attractive as it is often situated in a less convenient location, which will make it difficult to encourage the airlines to switch unless they are legally required to move. Convenient connectivity may also be lost if transfer passengers are forced to move from one airport to the other. As a result the role of a number of the original airports that stayed open has now changed from being solely domestic airports. For instance Gimpo, Don Mueang and Haneda airports all now serve some international routes. This raises general issues as to whether a dual-hub system can be successful or whether splitting a hub will always be damaging. Evidence from Europe, where BA abandoned a second hub concept at Gatwick Airport and likewise with Iberia at Barcelona, suggests that this is a challenging strategy.

The third option in addition to, or instead of, developing the primary airport or building a new one is to spread the traffic around a MAS or a network of secondary airports that can grow niche markets (such as domestic, LCC or business traffic) that serve different needs. This will be very dependent on the availability of existing infrastructure and in recent years, as discussed above, secondary airport development has often been driven by LCC traffic.

In choosing between these options, clearly there are many complex issues to be considered, only some of which will be concerned with the competitive forces between airports. Typically in the US and Europe, the expansion of existing airport infrastructure will be favoured because of barriers to new airports (in terms of land availability and high costs) as well as fierce environmental opposition. Indeed in relation to airport expansion in London, it was estimated that a new airport in the Thames estuary would cost in the region of £70–90 billion, which was considerably higher than the estimated costs for expanding Heathrow or Gatwick (Airports Commission, 2014). Elsewhere where currently there tends to be fewer airports, the high perceived benefits of strong growth and weaker opposition have often favoured new airport development. If traffic is going to be spread around more than one airport, either by keeping open an existing airport or by operating a MAS, there is also the important issue as to whether such traffic allocation should be done through regulation or left to market forces.

9.3 Competition within airports

9.3.1 Competition for airport services

As discussed in Chapter 2, many airport services, such as air traffic control, security, ground handling and the provision of commercial facilities, can be provided by the airport operator or a third party. Not only does this have a direct effect on the airport's financial performance, but the way in which they are offered, and whether there are competing services, can have a major impact on an airport's competitive situation in both price and service quality terms.

Arguably the area where there is most competition is for commercial facilities and services related to retail, food and beverage (F&B), car hire and bureaux de change. At some airports there may also be competition for other facilities such as hotels and car parks. However, one of the most controversial areas is ground handling. Basically these services can be provided by the airport operator, an independent handling agent such as Swissport or Menzies, or the airline itself (self-handling) or another airline. Practice varies throughout the world but there are many cases where the national airline of a country, or the airport operator, has a monopoly or near monopoly in providing these services. As a result this practice of not offering such services on a competitive basis can lead to excessive charges or poor service quality.

Sometimes there may be legal or regulatory requirements which will influence how airport operators provide ground handling services and the extent of competition between providers. For example, within the EU, directive EC/96/67 which was passed in 1996 provided for the phased liberalisation of ground handling services (EC, 1996). The long-term aim was to end all ground handling monopolies and duopolies by opening up the market to third-party handlers, recognising the right of airlines to self-handle, and guaranteeing at least some choice for airlines in the provision of ground handling services. As regards self-handling at all airports, airlines are allowed to self-handle for passenger services but at airports with more than 1 million passengers or 25,000 tonnes of cargo and for certain restricted services (such as baggage handling, ramp handling, fuel and oil handling, freight and mail handling) there can be a limit of no fewer than two suppliers. For airports larger than 2 million passengers or 50,000 tonnes of cargo, there is free access to third-party handlers although for the restricted categories of services, there must be a minimum of two handlers, with one of these suppliers being independent of the airport, or the dominant airlines that handle over 25 per cent of the traffic (Figure 9.5).

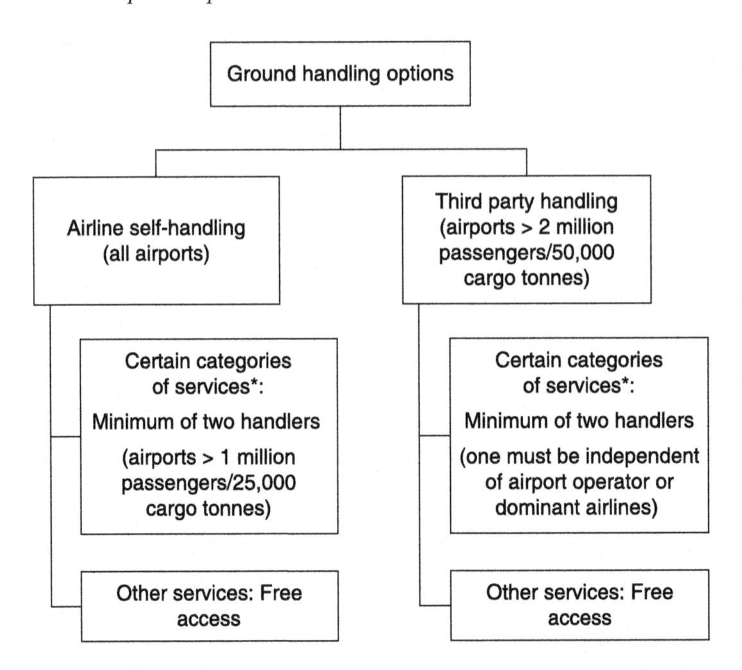

Figure 9.5 Key features of the EU Ground Handling Directive

*Certain categories = baggage handling, ramp handling, fuel and oil handling, freight and mail handling.

Source: EC (1996).

From the directive's introduction in 1996 until 2007, Airport Research Center (2009) found that the number of self-handlers and third-party handlers had increased significantly. Similarly, between 1996 and 2010, ACI Europe (2011) found that the airport operators had decreased their market share in ground handling from 25 per cent to 16 per cent, the airlines had reduced their share from 68 per cent to 39 per cent and the independent handlers had increased their share from 7 per cent to 45 per cent. However, whilst competition seems to have increased, research has also indicated that there could be improvements made to the efficiency and quality of the services offered (Airport Research Center, 2009; Steer Davies Gleave, 2010). The EC had planned to introduce some reform in this area under the so-called 'Better Airport Package' reform of 2011. These proposals were withdrawn in 2015 because of lack of agreement but the EC has stated that it remains committed to discussing how the functioning of the market and the application of the directive could be improved.

9.3.2 Competition between terminals

Arguably the greatest competition within airports could be achieved by having competing terminals which offer different prices and/or service quality. There could be varying quality standards and facilities to appeal to different airline segments (e.g. LCC vs alliance members) or passenger segments (e.g. long-haul vs short-haul, leisure vs business), albeit the more specialised the terminal, the less scope there may be for inter-terminal competition. Also if airlines have control of certain terminals, they could act anti-competitively and limit access to rival airlines. In addition, there are the issues that economies of scale may be lost with such a situation, capacity may not be optimally utilised, and strategic planning may become more complex with more than one operator.

However, in practice there is very little experience of competing terminals. Whilst some differentiation can often exist between the prices and service levels provided in alternative terminals, they are nearly always run by the airport operator – a prime example being LCC terminals. For the few historic examples of different operations, notably Terminal 3 at Toronto Airport or the Eurohub at Birmingham Airport, this strategy was not successful in the long-term and the terminals were brought back to common operation with the rest of the airport. It is in the US where there is the most experience of terminals run by different operators, in this case airlines, for instance at JFK Airport in New York. There has also been more limited similar practice in Australia. However, such independently run terminals have not really provided competition in terms of offering choice to the airport users, instead they have merely provided the airlines with more control over their own facilities.

Elsewhere competing terminals have been discussed, for example in the UK when the structure of BAA was being reviewed by the Competition Commission (2009) who recognised that terminal competition had the potential to benefit airlines and customers. However, they concluded there was considerable uncertainty related to these benefits and that additional costs would almost certainly be incurred with such a situation. In Ireland in 2002 the Irish government asked for expressions of interest from organisations which might wish to develop an independent/competing terminal at Dublin Airport (McLay and Reynolds-Feighan, 2006). Thirteen companies responded including international airport groups and airlines. The government appointed an independent panel to scrutinise these proposals and advise on the feasibility of the concept and in 2003 this panel decided in favour of an independent terminal. It concluded that this could bring effective competition at Dublin through increased capacity and quality of service (Department of Transport, 2003). However in 2005 it was decided that the DAA would be commissioned to build the terminal and that there would be a tender process to select the new operator, but in 2010 the government chose the DAA to run the terminal. So in the end there was no independent terminal.

9.4 Competition and state aid

As already discussed in Chapter 3, throughout the world there are many loss-making publicly owned airports, which rely on direct state subsidies to remain operational or to expand. Moreover, in some cases certain services, such as maintenance, may be provided by the government free of charge, or at less than cost. This may be especially the situation at smaller airports, where there is a greater proportion of state-owned airports which lack the critical mass to return large profits, but are also considered vital for the economic viability of the surrounding area. However, such direct or indirect subsidies can potentially have a major impact on distorting the competitive forces between airports in so far as they strengthen the financial position of the subsidised airport. For example, state funding granted to an airport could be used to maintain airport charges at an artificially low level in order to attract airlines.

Particularly in the EU, the use of public funds for the development of airports has been increasingly contested both by competing airports and by the airlines flying to these airports. In spite of the positive impacts on regional development and accessibility, state funding of airport infrastructure can produce a duplication of airports in the same catchment area and potentially create an overcapacity situation where traffic is split between a number of underutilised airports. Alternatively subsidies may be used to cover operating losses and/or to attract price-sensitive airlines, such as LCCs, with price incentives, marketing support or long-term contracts with differentiated tariffs.

In 2005 the EC issued guidelines to clarify how the EU competition rules applied to the public financing of airports and the start-up aid granted to airlines and regional airports by the state (EC, 2005). These guidelines specified the conditions under which certain categories of state aid to airports and airlines could be declared comparable with the internal market and confirmed the principles underlying the EC decision of 2004 concerning the case of Ryanair and Brussels South Charleroi Airport (EC, 2004) (which was in fact annulled in 2008). However, these guidelines failed to provide a clear legal framework for EU airports and resulted in many complaints involving illegal state aid, triggering around 100 investigations by the EC. In particular there was no clear guidance on the investment in/public funding of infrastructure. In fact it was not even clear as to whether public funding of airport infrastructure should be subject to EU State Aid rules in general, which was illustrated by lengthy debates related to the state financing of the southern runway at Leipzig–Halle Airport (EC, 2011). Moreover the guidelines in general were considered to be too complex and not adequate to ensure a level playing field for airlines and airports irrespective of their business models.

As a result, new guidelines were introduced in 2014. They take into account the EC's current view on how small airports can cover both their operating and capital costs, which were introduced in Chapter 1 and are detailed in Table 9.1.

To overcome the inadequacy of the previous investment aid guidelines, the new rules are linked to airport size and the aid is not allowed to exceed

Table 9.1 The EC's view on profitability of small airports

Airport size (Annual passengers)	*Airport cost coverage*
< 200,000	Might not be able to cover to a large extent their capital and operating costs
200,000–1 million	Usually not able to cover to a large extent their capital costs, but should be able to cover partially their operating costs
1–3 million	Be able to cover the majority of their operating costs and to cover partially their capital costs
3–5 million	Be able to cover to a large extent all their costs
> 5 million	Usually profitable and are able to cover all of their costs

Source: EC (2014a).

certain ceilings, the maximum being 75 per cent for the smallest airports (Table 9.2). There are exceptions for airports in remote and peripheral regions of the EU where there is more flexibility. In addition, with the aim of having more targeted investment, such funding will only be allowed when there is a genuine transport need and when there are clear positive impacts, such as regional development, less traffic development at major airports or improved accessibility. Public sector investment which will encourage duplication and unused capacity is not suitable. For airports larger than 5 million passengers, investment aid is not allowed except in exceptional circumstances where there is clear market failure.

As regards operating aid, the new guidelines offer a transition period for small airports of less than 3 million passengers, during which a maximum of

Table 9.2 Summary of the 2014 guidelines on state aid to airports and airlines

Type of aid	*Details*
Investment aid	• 3–5 million passengers up to 25% • 1–3 million passengers up to 50% • < 1 million passengers up to 75%
Operating aid	• 10-year transitional period for airports to wean them off operating aid and produce a self-sustaining business model – 50% of operating funding gap allowed for airports < 3 million passengers • Airports below 700,000 to be 80% reassessed again in 4 years
Incentive aid	Airports < 3 million passengers can receive start-up aid covering 50% of airport charges for 3 years
Airline–airport agreements	Market economy operator principle applies

Source: EC (2014a).

Note: Some exceptions apply especially to airports in remote and peripheral regions.

50–80 per cent of the initial funding gap (the difference between costs and revenues in 2009–2013) can be covered by aid. After this the airports need to cover their own costs and be profitable – although it was agreed that for airports with less than 700,000 passengers this will be reassessed after five years as a result of fierce opposition from the airport industry. The transition period is designed to provide small airports with enough time to adjust to new market developments and to improve their financial performance, for example by differentiating their business models, attracting new customers, introducing rationalisation measures, raising airport charges and diversifying their revenue sources. In terms of the other guidelines, as regards the rules for start-up aid for new airlines, these have been simplified so that airports with less than 3 million annual passengers will be able to receive aid covering 50 per cent of charges for new destinations during a three-year period. Again, more flexible conditions exist for remote airports and such incentives are only allowed for airports between 3 and 5 million passengers in exceptional circumstances.

As will be discussed in Chapter 10, a number of airport operators have now negotiated long-term contracts with airlines in Europe. These contracts agree the level of airport charges and other conditions, such as service targets, in return for an airline-guaranteed number of aircraft or traffic volume operating out of the airport. As such these ensure that the airport can plan for the long-term without fear of the airline disappearing, whilst the airline benefits from knowing that its long-term costs will be fixed. The 2005 guidelines did not really adequately consider such agreements, but the 2014 rules stipulate that these are considered free of aid if private investors operating under normal market conditions would have behaved in the same way. In other words if the airport total revenues from both the aeronautical and non-aeronautical areas at least cover the incremental costs imposed by the airline. If this is not the case, the agreement is considered as state aid.

The EC undertook an impact assessment of the new guidelines and concluded that no airport handling over 500,000 annual passengers would close, although some smaller ones would have to if they could not improve their financial performance. Figure 9.6 shows how the EC expected efficiency gains and increases in non-aeronautical revenue would compensate for an increase in costs due to the removal of state aid.

Since the guidelines were introduced in 2014 the EC has considered a number of cases. By October of that year it ruled that Zweibrucken Airport in Germany and Charleroi in Belgium had received state aid which was incompatible with the EU rules and had to be recovered. It was also found that certain airline agreements concluded by the managers of Zweibrucken and Alghero airports gave the airlines undue economic advantage which needed to be paid back. By contrast other agreements at airports such as Västerås, Frankfurt-Hahn, Angouleme and Nimes were not considered to give the airlines undue advantage (EC, 2014c, 2014d). Certain countries, such as the UK, have set up 'start up aid' called the Regional Air Connectivity

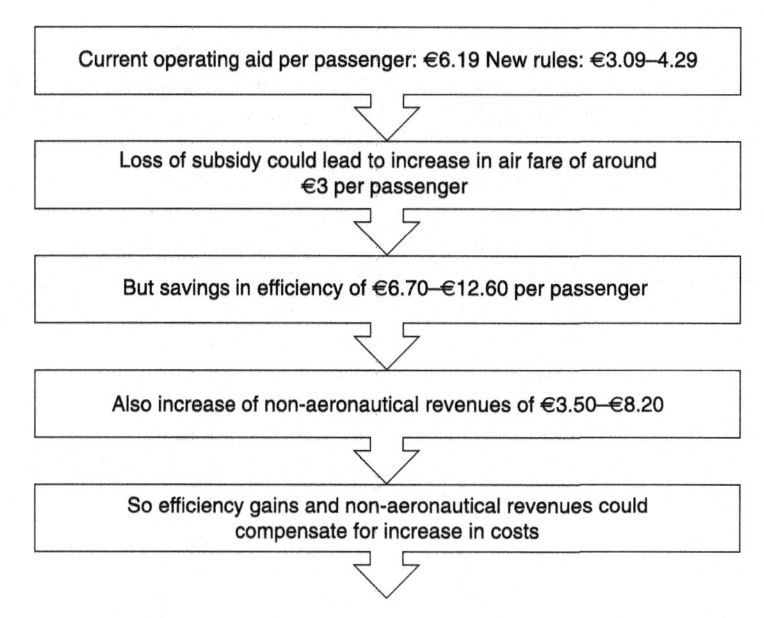

Figure 9.6 Financial impact of the 2014 state aid rules

Source: EC (2014b).

Fund where there is £56 million available between 2015 and 2018 to small airports of less than 5 million annual passengers. This aid has to be compliant with the EU guidelines. In December 2015 it was announced that Carlisle, Derry, Newquay, Norwich, Oxford and Southampton airports had been awarded aid from the fund to start services in 2016 (Department for Transport, 2015).

In other parts of the world, airport incentives may also be subject to government regulation. For example in the US, a subsidy (which is defined as a direct payment of airport revenue to an airline or to any provider of goods or services to that airline, in exchange for additional service by the airline) is not permitted. However, an incentive (defined as any fee reduction, fee waiver, or use of airport revenue for acceptable promotional costs, where the purpose is to encourage the airline to increase service at the airport) is allowed. Moreover, the airport revenue incentives are allowed to be used to enhance airline services at an airport and create an opportunity to increase traffic but not to contribute to a destination marketing programme that promotes a region, attraction, or business with the focus being on increasing regional revenue, not just that related to the airport's services or facilities (FAA, 2010).

9.5 Summary

This chapter has discussed the very complex and frequently debated area of airport competition. It is complex because competition between airports can vary quite considerably depending on what type of airport is considered. The level of competition will clearly have a major impact on an airport's ability to generate both aeronautical and non-aeronautical revenues and on the pressure that it feels to control its costs and operate in the most efficient manner possible. There is also the issue of competition within airport groups that can have major implications for the financial well-being of an airport operator and for any privatisation or expansion plans. Finally, competitive factors need to be considered within the context of the internal management of an airport, such as whether there should be effective competition with certain services that are provided or whether whole terminals should compete – the latter being a concept yet to be really seen in practice.

As the aviation industry moves towards even greater deregulation, it is likely that the competitive forces between airports will grow even stronger. However, there are still policy issues that will need to be addressed at a governmental level, most notably those related to airport subsidies. In addition, when competitive markets do not fully exist and subsequently there is the potential for market failure, there may be a need for economic regulation. This is discussed in detail in the next chapter.

10 Airport economic regulation and slot allocation

10.1 Introduction

The first and major part of this chapter considers the increasingly important topic of economic regulation. Airports are subject to other types of regulation, for example related to safety, security and the environment, but the focus here is just on the economic aspects of regulation. Also this does not cover state aid regulation, which within the EU context has been considered in Chapter 9. The chapter begins by assessing the rationale for airport regulation, linking this to airport competition issues which have been discussed in Chapter 9. The regulatory framework, which exists at various levels, is then introduced. This leads on to a discussion of the main types of economic regulation and the mechanisms related to these. This is then related to actual experience of regulation in different parts of the world.

The second and remaining part of the chapter examines the regulation of slots or slot allocation which is another economic issue of major significance to many airports. It examines why there is a need for slot allocation processes. A critical assessment of the current situation is provided which leads on to an examination of possible alternative slot allocation systems.

10.2 Rationale for economic regulation

In economic theoretical terms, when competitive markets exist with a large number of suppliers and consumers, no single supplier or consumer can influence the price or any other aspects of the market, resulting in no one having any market control. In this case the competitive markets produce an efficient resource allocation through the pricing mechanism. The price is set by the interaction of market supply and demand and if there is excess demand or supply at the market price, the suppliers and consumers will respond and change their behaviour.

However, this will not always be the situation and instead market failure may occur when markets may produce undesirable outcomes such as inefficient resource allocation. Market failure can occur for a number of reasons such as missing, incomplete or unstable markets, the existence of demerit or public goods or negative externalities, imperfect information, resource immobility or inequalities. However, one of the major causes of market failure is the wrong market structure and the existence of market power where a supplier can influence its own price and service levels, rather than these being dictated by market forces. In this case excessive prices may be charged which are much higher than the costs.

Government intervention can be used to correct market failures arising from an inefficient resource allocation. This can include using indirect taxation, subsidies or pollution permits. Governments may also get involved with direct control by being the supplier owner and operator. However, another popular method, especially for the control of market power, is economic regulation. This can be introduced instead of, or in addition to, general competition policy which may prohibit the abuse of a dominant position in a market and anti-competitive agreement between suppliers.

In economic terms, regulation attempts to maximise economic welfare by allocating resources in the most effective way. In other words, economic regulation has the ultimate aim of achieving economic efficiency. As discussed in Chapter 5, there are three key types of economic efficiency, namely technical/productive efficiency, allocation efficiency and dynamic efficiency. Ideally economic regulation should be designed to address all these areas by having incentives for cost efficiency, encouraging optimal demand and supply allocation and investment, and promoting improved production and innovation.

However, economic regulation may not necessarily be effective in improving economic efficiency. Regulation will bring with it direct administrative costs. These will be incurred by the regulatory agency, the regulated entities and other interested stakeholders. The costs, which can be very substantial, particularly if outside expertise is sought or if decisions are challenged, can be viewed as an opportunity cost in devoting scarce resources to the process of regulation. There may also be indirect costs associated with the distortion (or removal altogether) of normal market incentives. This may result in, for example, misleading incentives for investment, the lack of innovation, and too much focus and resources on the regulatory aspects of the business to the detriment of other important management areas. In this case government failure may occur when government intervention imposes a cost greater than the benefits sought through regulation and ultimately a net loss of economic welfare. Therefore airport economic regulation should only be imposed if the benefits to users outweigh the costs and when there is not already sufficient competition law to protect consumers from any market power abuse.

It can also be argued that, even when there is evidence of a natural monopoly, this is not necessarily a justification for economic regulation. A key point here, according to contestable markets theory and when there is a lack of entry barriers, is that the monopoly may not be motivated to abuse its market power. This is because it is the threat of competition, rather than actual competition, which will influence behaviour. Moreover other factors such as the price elasticity of demand, the countervailing power of the consumers and the extent to which the supply is constrained need to be taken into account. Therefore suppliers may appear to have substantial market power but may not actually seek to exploit this.

10.3 The airport economic regulatory framework

10.3.1 The global level

Having identified the general rationale for economic regulation, the concepts are now related to the airport industry. There is in fact a regulatory framework that exists at different levels ranging from global principles determined by ICAO to national or even local specific conditions.

The 1944 Chicago Convention, which was fundamental in laying the foundations of the international air transport regulatory system, established the basis for airport charging. Through successive editions of a policy document relating the charges for airports and air navigation services (the latest is the ninth edition), ICAO (2012a) has outlined its four charging principles of non-discrimination, cost-relatedness, transparency and consultation with users. As regards economic regulation (or in other words economic oversight), ICAO views the main purpose of this being balancing the interests of airports and public policy objectives by minimising the risk of airports abusing any dominant position they may have; ensuring non-discrimination and transparency; encouraging appropriate investment in a cost-effective manner; and protecting the interests of passengers and other end-users.

However, these principles of ICAO are only guidelines and have, over the years, been subject to many different interpretations. Moreover, ICAO does not recommend a specific system of regulation and nor does it state that airports should necessarily be subject to economic regulation. It says that this should depend on the specific circumstances of each country including the degree of competition, the costs and benefits of the different regulatory systems, and the institutional and governance frameworks. Furthermore it says that a regional or network approach could be considered if individual states do not have the capacity to perform economic regulation responsibilities themselves.

10.3.2 The regional level

Within the EU there is another level of regulation related to the European Charges Directive of 2009 (which became applicable from 2011) (EC, 2009). This applies to all airports with annual passenger numbers in excess of 5 million or, if a country has no airport of that size, the airport which has the highest volume. The directive adopted the ICAO principles of non-discrimination (although charges can be modulated for the public and general interest, including environmental issues), transparency and consultation between users. Airport operators have to provide details of the basis for charging and users are required to submit forecasts and development plans. However, airport charges can be varied if there is a difference in quality and scope of services. There must be user consultation, at least once a year, concerning the level of charges and quality of service, and airport operators must also consult with users before plans for new infrastructure are finalised.

However, as regards the ICAO principle of cost-relatedness there is more limited reference to this and arguably there is some contradiction since it allows airport networks to have a common charging system involving cross-subsidisation. In relation to service quality, the directive allows service-level agreements between airports and users but this is not a specific requirement. Finally, to ensure compliance with these conditions, countries are required to have an independent supervisory authority that will oversee the consultation, deal with any disputes or appeals, and determine or approve charges – although where possible the directive states that charges should be agreed directly by the airport operator and users.

It is not the EC's aim to impose a common regulatory system on all countries but rather to establish shared principles that are the same for the EU members. Moreover, since the legislation is a directive rather than a regulation, individual countries have more flexibility in its interpretation and implementation. Importantly it does not require for the airport competitive situation or the existence of market power to be assessed and instead uses a simpler and more basic airport size criterion to determine whether the conditions of the directive need to be applied. A review of the directive in 2013 (Steer Davies Gleave, 2013) found this inflexible size threshold to be a significant weakness but identified practical difficulties in changing this. The review also concluded that the consultation processes had improved since the directive had been introduced and that there was greater transparency of information, but there had been little impact on the structure and level of airport charges. Moreover it was found that the directive had not been applied consistently at all airports and so overall these initial impacts had been mixed.

10.3.3 The national level

Whilst such international and regional regulations are important in establishing principles for airport charging policies and frameworks, as already identified they do not seek to impose a common regulatory framework. Such decisions are made at a national level (Figure 10.1). Hence the focus of the rest of the discussion on economic regulation is on national policies and practice.

As discussed in Chapter 8, up until the 1980s virtually all airports were owned and operated directly by state-owned entities. At the same time most

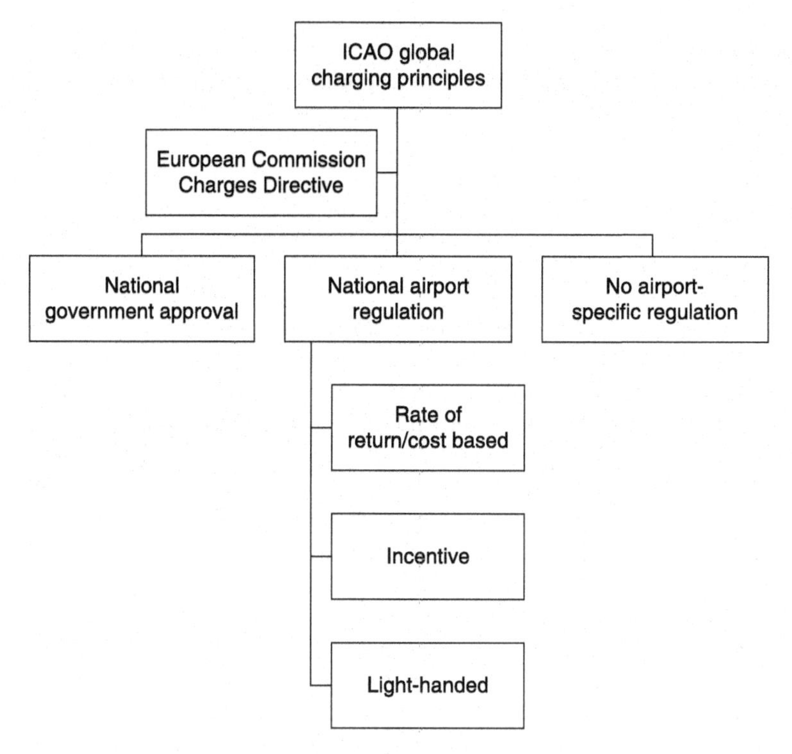

Figure 10.1 Levels of airport regulation

Note: For some countries there may be a regional/local level as well.

airlines outside the US were also under public ownership. The result of this meant that economic regulation was generally considered unnecessary because any issues related to market failure could be dealt with directly by governments in their role as suppliers within the industry. However, 1987 saw the first privatisation of a major airport group (BAA) and at the same time a new formal economic regulatory system was introduced. Subsequently privatisation became a popular trend within the airport industry at the same time as many of the world's airlines changed to total, or at least partial, private ownership. Hence the traditional supplier–consumer relationship which was previously closely controlled by governments was fundamentally transformed. As a result, in some cases governments have felt the need to intervene to correct market failure by using economic regulation. However, the types of regulation have varied considerably and this has generated considerable debate concerning the advantages and disadvantages of these different systems.

10.4 Types of economic regulation

There are a number of different types of regulatory regimes (ACI, 2013; Niemeier, 2009) but they can be broadly categorised into the following three:

1. rate of return (ROR) or cost based regulation;
2. incentive or price cap regulation;
3. price monitoring or light-handed regulation.

10.4.1 ROR and cost-based regulation

ROR regulation permits an airport operator to earn enough revenue to cover its costs and make a profit which provides a reasonable rate of return on the asset base. Thus the operator cannot set prices which are very high above the actual costs as the rate of return will be too high and unacceptable. Therefore in theory an airport cannot exploit any market power that it possesses. This type of mechanism guarantees a rate of return regardless of other developments and can encourage airports to adequately invest, as larger profits can be made if the capital investment is higher while producing the same overall return. However, whilst this method can ensure that prices are related to costs, it provides no incentives to encourage technical efficiency or reduce costs, and cost inefficiencies can be passed on to users through increases in prices. It can also provide an incentive to overinvestment (the so-called gold-plating problem or Averch–Johnson effect) in order to achieve returns on a higher asset base, with the risk of asset investment (as well as the increased costs) resting with the users.

In practice this regime is cumbersome and can be problematic to implement because of the difficulty in reaching agreement as to what assets should be included in the asset base and what rate of return is 'reasonable'. Also to prevent cost inefficiency and overinvestment, financial data has to be scrutinised at a very detailed and intrusive level, and every time there are changes to the financial situation or to other factors, these have to be considered – which can be to the detriment of innovation and encouragement of dynamic efficiency. Therefore, although this mechanism was the traditional approach that was used extensively, for example, in the US and Australia to regulate natural monopolies, it is not that common with airports nowadays. There is another similar regime called cost based regulation (or cost of service/cost recovery regulation). In this case the focus is primarily on the cost or providing the service (rather than investment) and so it is a simpler method but still provides no incentives to reduce costs, passes all cost risks to the users and is burdensome to implement.

10.4.2 Incentive or pricecap regulation

To overcome the shortcomings associated with these ROR or cost-based methods, alternative regulatory systems were sought. An important development was the use of a price cap which is the most widely used type of 'incentive' regulation, which was introduced in the 1980s as a consequence of privatisation of state utilities such as gas and electricity. The aim of this mechanism is to provide incentives to reduce costs and increase productivity while simultaneously controlling price increases. It uses a formula which allows for a maximum price increase after taking account of inflation. The difference between the inflation rate and the maximum price increase is the efficiency factor (often called the 'X' factor), which will take into account all the factors that the regulator considers will affect the airport's costs. If the airport operator manages to achieve greater productivity gains or has lower costs than expected, the additional profits can be kept as it is the prices rather than the profits that are regulated. Hence this method can encourage technical efficiency and is the reason why it is called a type of 'incentive' regulation.

The price cap is usually written as RPI +/− X (where RPI is the retail price index) or CPI +/− X (where CPI is the consumer price index). The 'price' value usually relates to a revenue per passenger figure or a weighted average price (see section 10.5). In addition, costs beyond the control of the airport (e.g. security costs) can be excluded from the regulation with the following formula: RPI +/− X + Y (where Y is the external cost). The X factor can be negative, for example to take account of productivity gains, or positive, if for instance prices need to be raised to cover new capital investment. Typically a 'building block' method is applied beginning with the definition and valuation of the regulated asset base (RAB) at the start of the price control or regulatory period. This is subsequently enlarged to take account of projected capital spending, the weighted average cost of capital (WACC) and the depreciation allowance. This is added to the projected level of operating costs (taking into consideration likely cost and productivity changes) to produce the total revenue needed which, when considered with traffic forecasts, can be used to determine the price cap.

An advantage of pricecap regulation over ROR regulation is that the airport's operating costs, asset base and rate of return only need to be reviewed periodically, typically every three–five years, to set the price formula. Also no consideration of inflation within this time period is needed. Moreover, the method is simpler to administer as airports can change their level or structure of prices as long as they still conform to the price cap without any justification needed by the regulator, which is not usually allowed with the ROR system. In the end, airports can keep the benefits of unpredicted cost efficiencies within the regulatory time periods, albeit this will be passed on to the users in the next period by resetting the pricecap.

In economic theory, a 'pure' price cap mechanism should use an X factor that is independent of an airport's RAB, capital investment and operating costs and more focused on potential productivity gains. However, in practice this has not been the case with airports (nor with most other industries) and so instead there is usually the building block regulatory process which is time-consuming, costly and involves the participation of a large number of stakeholders. The RAB valuations and WACC assumptions become very important in determining the price cap and hence the regulatory process can become more complex than envisaged. Consequently, it can be argued that in practice this type of regulation is not that different from ROR regulation and the problems of detailed and lengthy review processes and potential distorted investment decisions related to gold-plating.

However, on the other hand, it can be reasoned that pricecap regulation may actually give inadequate incentives to investment since it focuses on short-term operational efficiency gains within each price control period, whilst airport investment involves long-term decisions. Moreover, since long-term infrastructure investments will be relevant beyond a single regulatory period, decisions on investment will be dependent on the airport operator's understanding of how the regulator will take this into account in the future. Thus this may reduce the incentives to invest and lead to insufficient capacity and to congestion problems. Hence it is a subject of much debate as to whether price cap regulation within the airport industry has led to under- or over-investment. There is very little empirical evidence to support either argument although Starkie (2006) concluded that it is more probable overinvestment occurs, based on an analysis of UK and Irish airports.

10.4.3 Light-handed regulation

Both ROR and price cap regulation are generally defined as 'heavy-handed' models because of the intrusive nature of the information-gathering process and the rigidity in the regulation requirements. An alternative is a more light-handed approach. There are a number of different mechanisms in this case such as 'trigger', 'reserve', 'shadow', 'conduct' and 'fall back' regulation or price monitoring. Although the technical definitions of these vary somewhat, the general principle is that the market power of the airport operator is constrained by the threat of regulation, rather than actual regulation. Hence this threat is used to provide an effective safeguard against anti-competitive practices and discipline the airport's behaviour.

With this regime, the light-handed approach needs to be formally defined as with the other methods. For the threat to be credible there need to be trigger criteria related to the abuse of market power so that it is clear when the regulator has to become directly involved. If the criteria are not met, the regulator's powers are not exercised. In order for this system to work, the power to introduce regulation must be readily available and the consequences of any introduction must be unknown, so that any interested party is not incentivised to start political lobbying for the regulation.

It has been argued, for example by ACI Europe (2014), that this is a more proportionate approach for dealing with the modern-day, more competitive, airport industry. The light-handed approach will tend to be far less invasive, less costly and far less likely to be influenced by complex politicised arguments. Instead it should bring more flexibility to innovate and react to change and unforeseen developments within the industry. Nevertheless, there will be costs involved with the monitoring process of prices, and other areas such as service quality, depending on what the requirement is for a specific airport. Moreover, the establishment of the appropriate trigger criteria can be challenging.

Rather than adopting any kind of economic regulation, either heavy-handed or light-handed, another alternative is to just apply general competition law to airports, which will aim to foster or maintain competition in markets by prohibiting anti-competitive practices. This may also be accompanied by some kind of negotiated commercial contract between the airlines and the airport operator. These contracts can be used with price monitoring or trigger regulation. Traditionally it has not been common airport practice to have such a formalised relationship which identifies the rights and obligations of both parties, and instead airports published 'conditions of use' which merely described the services provided in exchange for the airport charges. However, it can be argued that, if there is a legally enforceable contract which is detailed in its coverage of the charges and how these are set, this can replace formal economic regulation and be more effective at considerably lower costs. Another advantage of commercial contracts is that they can be tailored towards the different needs of individual airlines, in terms of either the airport charges or the associated terms and conditions. It can also be reasoned that such contracts provide a distribution of risk between the airlines and airport operator – a feature formalised if there is an arrangement guaranteeing a reduction in charges in return for a promise of traffic growth. They can also support a common agreement on the levels of service quality needed and potentially encourage innovation without any unnecessary distortions associated with some of the other regulatory models. All of these features can provide incentives for improving technical and dynamic efficiency.

An important difference with this type of framework, and with the absence of a formal regulation, is that the contracts themselves can provide the way and means of resolving disputes, such as with arbitration or mediation, rather than having to use the expensive and potentially politicised appeal processes of regulation. Moreover, with the absence of a regulator and with no need to play regulatory games to achieve the best output, the airlines and airport operator should be in a better position to deliver a good working relationship which will benefit them both. This type of contract works best when there are a small number of airlines but it has also been used when some airlines have joined together to reach agreement such as at Copenhagen Airport. Overall the effectiveness will very much depend on the relative bargaining powers of the airport operator and its airlines. Moreover, there can be some concerns regarding allocative efficiency if the contracts have the potential to increase the market power of the existing airlines at the expense of new airlines, and hence allow the self-interests of these existing airlines to influence airport policies too much.

It is worth noting that in a growing number of cases airline–airport agreements have been reached at airports, particularly with LCCs (Starkie, 2012), that are not likely to be regulated because of market power issues. Due to the commercial sensitivity of the agreements, it is difficult to access details but in general terms the charges will tend to be linked to a price inflation index and there may be volume discounts. Other airport obligations may relate to service quality (such as a minimum turnaround time), the provision of marketing assistance and planned investment. In return the airline will guarantee to base a certain number of aircraft at the airport (which may increase in future years) and also perhaps guarantee a minimum number of passengers. In this case there is no 'fall-back' position if the agreement is not part of an official light-handed regulatory approach although there can be breach of contract issues needing investigation.

In summary, as industry structures have changed and market dynamics evolved, a number of different regulatory systems have been used. However it is important to note that many government-owned airports still have no formal mechanism. In these cases the airports will usually seek government approval before changing the level or structure of charges. In some cases this may be just a formality whereas elsewhere the government may have considerable influence. Overall, according to ACI (2015b), at 66 per cent of airports (representing 55 per cent of passengers) there is no formal regulatory system but instead charges are subject to government approval. Rate of return or cost recovery is practised at 15 per cent of airports (21 per cent of passengers) and price or revenue cap regulation exists at 12 per cent of airports (15 per cent of passengers). At a further 8 per cent of airports (9 per cent of passengers) there is no specific regulation or instead light-handed regulation exists.

10.5 Mechanics of airport regulation

10.5.1 Regulatory till

Once decisions have been made concerning the overall type of regulation, the precise mechanics of the chosen framework have to be established. One of the most important and controversial choices relates to the regulatory till that is to be used. This concerns what airport facilities and services are considered when the aeronautical charges are set. There are two basic methods, namely the single or dual till, and in between there are a number of hybrid approaches.

With the single till all revenues, both aeronautical and non-aeronautical, are taken into account when setting the airport charges. In reality this means that the profits from commercial activities are usually used to reduce the aeronautical revenues and therefore some cross-subsidisation takes place.

The main rationale for the single till is that without the aeronautical activities, there would be very little market for the commercial operations and hence it is appropriate to offset the airport charges in this manner and for the airlines to benefit (although increasingly there are a number of non-aeronautical streams generated from airport land which are not specifically related to aeronautical activities). Such an approach is normally favoured by the airlines as it is likely to bring the lowest level of actual charges for them but may be less popular with airport investors as it may limit the airport operator's ability to benefit from exploiting new commercial ventures.

The single till has a number of advantages but has also been subject to a considerable amount of criticism (e.g. see Starkie, 2008b). A key issue is that growing and busy airports may be in the best position to expand commercial revenues and use single-till principles to pull down airport charges. However, this makes no economic sense as the airport gets more congested and will have more difficulties in managing its scarce resources. Moreover the benefits are only short-term as it is only within each regulatory period that airports have the opportunity to reap the benefits of more profitable than expected commercial operations. In the long run the offsetting of aeronautical fees may provide less incentive to develop the non-aeronautical revenues further or undertake management innovation in this area.

By contrast, with the dual till aeronautical and non-aeronautical areas are treated as separate entities. Clearly one of the major problems with this is in allocating the many common and joint costs between these two areas – in this respect the single till is a much more straightforward concept. However, the dual-till approach allows airports with incentives to freely develop commercial facilities, which it can be argued makes more logical sense as these are not monopoly services (unlike the aeronautical side), because of competition both within the airport and elsewhere (e.g. the airlines, the high street, the Internet), which need to be controlled by regulation. Additionally as regards investment, it can be reasoned that the dual till can provide better incentives for the aeronautical area since as well as producing additional airport fees with more investment, the extra traffic volume can generate more unregulated commercial revenues. On the other hand, this approach may instead just focus airport investment on commercial facilities, perhaps to the detriment of the aeronautical services.

It can also be argued that the dual till will incentivise airports to keep the airport charges low in order to attract the traffic to maximise the commercial revenues, in line with the concept of airports as a two-sided market as discussed in Chapter 1. Thus the airport may be less likely to exploit any market power that it possesses (Starkie, 2001). In practice, for some airports with a single till (notably Heathrow and Dublin) there has been some debate as to whether there should be a shift from single to dual till, but the benefits of this have been fiercely challenged, particularly by the airlines, and so no changes have occurred.

However, a number of airports have adopted a hybrid till which falls in between the single- and dual-till approaches, where only certain non-aeronautical revenues or only a specified fraction of the revenues are used to cross-subsidise aeronautical revenues (Sharp, 2012). For example at Delhi and Mumbai airports, 30 per cent of non-aeronautical revenues are included in the aeronautical till, whilst Brussels and Paris airports are moving away from a pure single till – the latter by leaving retail and non-aeronautical real estate revenues unregulated. Overall, according to ACI (2015b), 45 per cent of airports (45 per cent of passengers) use a single till and in contrast 37 per cent of airports (40 per cent of passengers) have adopted a dual till. The remaining 18 per cent of airports have a hybrid till.

10.5.2. Definition of price and the basis for charging

Another detail that needs to be agreed is the definition of 'price', particularly when incentive regulation is being considered. The two most common approaches use either a tariff basket or a revenue yield value. The tariff basket price is a weighted average price of a specified basket of tariffs or charges, whilst the revenue yield price is defined as the revenue per unit of output, which is normally a passenger. The tariff basket approach is more complex to some extent because it requires information about all the charges and needs to be changed if charges are added or removed. However, in other ways it is simpler since it operates directly on charges and does not depend on other variables, such as passenger numbers which need to be forecast to calculate future revenue yield values. The tariff basket method may encourage airport operators to be creative in increasing charges which do not bear a heavy weight in the basket, whilst the revenue yield approach may encourage an airport to focus on increasing its passenger output (at the expense of cargo for example) so as to inflate the denominator and reduce the yield overall. Moreover, it can be argued that the tariff approach provides better incentives for service quality as there can be various prices for different aspects of service, whereas the yield system is purely driven by traffic volume. In reality practice varies, and according to a study (albeit of a few years ago) 59 per cent of European airports used a tariff basket method as opposed to 41 per cent with a revenue yield approach (SH&E, 2006).

A further very important regulatory aspect that needs to be considered is the evidence base that will be used to set the profit, cost or most commonly price conditions which are set by the regulator. Typically much of this will be based on the airport's average costs, which will include consideration of any proposed investment programme and the cost of capital, potential efficiency gains and costs related to service quality improvement. In some cases, for example increasingly in the UK, the regulator has compared performance in specific areas with other airports or similar organisations. Taking this comparative benchmarking approach to its limit ultimately leads to regulatory benchmarking or 'yardstick' regulation where industry best practice replaces the assessment of actual accounting costs for the setting of regulation conditions, resulting in the regulatory control being independent of any internal airport action influencing the key variables. However, data problems and the heterogeneous characteristics of airports have meant that as yet there is no example of yardstick regulation within the airport industry (see Chapter 5).

A range of other issues may need to be considered when setting the regulatory regime (Figure 10.2), including the overall basis for charging (e.g. whether a licence is needed). It is important to note that strict regulatory control on costs or prices could merely encourage airports to drop service standards and as a consequence a number of airports have formally established service standards (e.g. London, Dublin, Paris, Delhi) or require an appropriate quality monitoring system within the regulatory framework (e.g. the Australian airports, Hamburg). The duration of the regulatory period needs

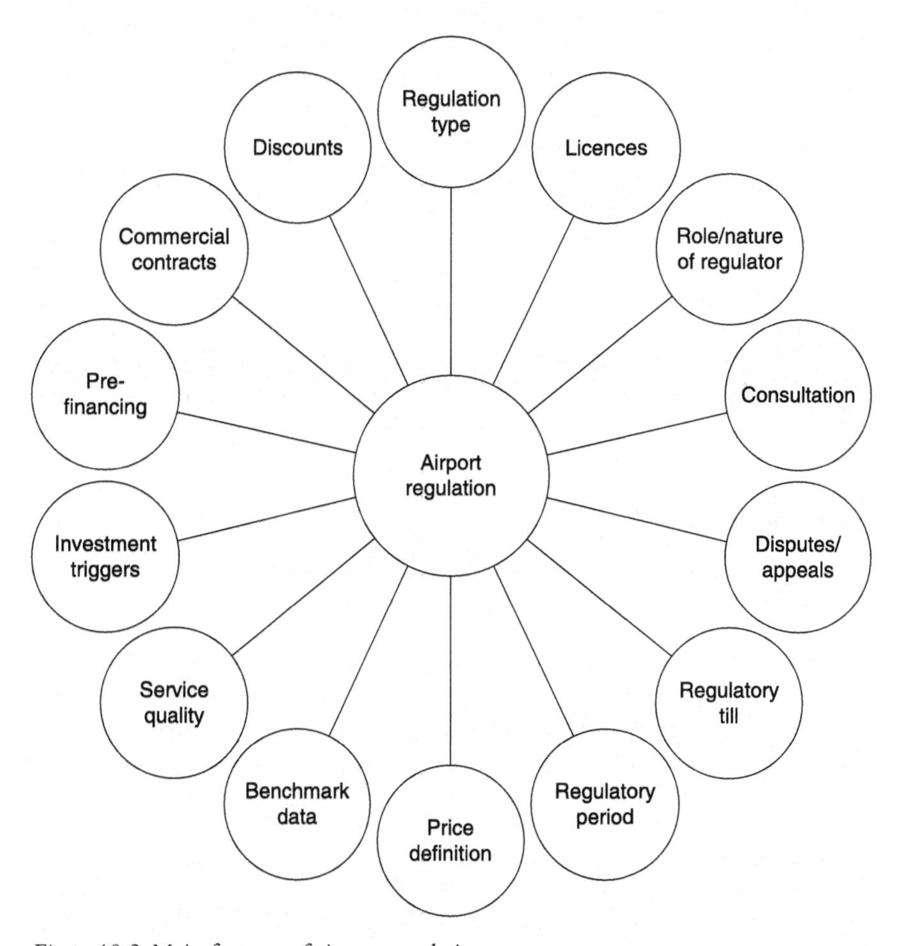

Figure 10.2 Main features of airport regulation

to be established which is typically three–five years. The requirement for, and the scope of, user consultation also need to be detailed as well as the amount of information disclosure. In addition, there may be financial incentives or penalties related to capital investment trigger points and conditions related to whether pre-financing is allowed.

10.5.3 Pre-financing

Pre-financing of future airport infrastructure through airport charges can be a particularly difficult issue. This is largely because there is no guarantee that the airlines paying the charges will actually be the airlines which will benefit from the new infrastructure and there may be no certainty that the airport charges will be efficiently spent to provide new facilities. The counter-arguments used by airports are that pre-financing in certain circumstances can provide a useful, cheaper source for funding investment in addition to loans and equity, which can also be used as security for raising extra finance, and that it avoids large increases in charges when the new infrastructure comes on stream. Arguably the most notable example of pre-financing is in the US where passenger facility charges (PFCs) go towards future development projects and a somewhat similar situation exists at Canadian airports. In the UK there has always been a certain degree of pre-funding but it is currently a highly controversial issue for Heathrow Airport, should approval for a third runway be granted, as there can be no guarantee that the airlines paying now will benefit from the future facilities; this is particularly the case as the EU slot allocation process (described later) favours new entrants when new slots become available (CAA, 2015; Humphreys, 2015). Another recent example is Dublin and the new Terminal 2, where the majority of investment was not pre-financed and an alternative approach was adopted.

10.5.4 Implementation

Finally, a key detail to be determined is actually how the regulatory system should be implemented. ICAO (2013) advises that, when the airport or airports in question are operated by the government entity, the regulation process should be functionally separated from the operation of airport services. It recommends that a country may wish to establish an independent economic oversight entity or regulator and also a third-party advisory commission (composed of air carriers, general aviation, the military, representatives of end-users and other principal parties) as a less formal tool to engage in meaningful dialogue with the airport management and review specific regulatory proposals. The European Charges Directive stipulates that there should be 'Independent Supervisory Authorities' but the practical situation in Europe is mixed (Steer Davies Gleave, 2013). Appeal and dispute procedures also need to be identified.

10.6 Experience of airport economic regulation

Having introduced the main features of airport economic regulation, this section now discusses experiences of regulation and the impact on airport performance. Table 10.1 provides two key details, namely the type of regulation and the regulatory till, for a number of selected international airports. Only a few airports in the table use a cost-based approach although this is a more popular approach when just government approval of charges is used rather than formal regulation. Germany is an interesting example because the government regulatory powers are devolved to the 16 German states and so there are a number of different regulatory approaches. Hamburg Airport has a dual-till price cap mechanism with a sliding scale based on traffic growth. By contrast at the airports of Frankfurt and Düsseldorf there is a more

Table 10.1 Regulatory regimes at selected airports

Country (airport)	*Type of regulation*	*Type of till*
Argentina (Aeropuertos Argentina 2000)	Price cap	Single till
Australia (Adelaide, Brisbane, Melbourne, Perth, Sydney)	Price monitoring	Dual till
Austria (Vienna)	Price cap	Dual till
Belgium (Brussels)	Airline contracts (cost based)	Hybrid
Brazil (São Paulo: Guarulhos and Viracopos, Brasilia, Rio: Galeão, Belo Horizonte)	Price cap	Hybrid
Denmark (Copenhagen)	Airline contracts (price cap)	Dual till
France (Aéroports de Paris)	Price cap	Hybrid
Germany (Frankfurt)	Airline contracts (cost based)	Dual till
Germany (Hamburg)	Price cap	Dual till
Hungary (Budapest)	Price cap	Dual till
India (Delhi and Mumbai)	Price cap	Hybrid
Ireland (Dublin)	Price cap	Single till
Netherlands (Amsterdam)	Cost based	Dual till
New Zealand (Auckland, Christchurch, Wellington)	Price monitoring	Dual till
Mexico (GAP, OMA, ASUR)	Price cap	Dual till
Peru (Lima)	Price cap	Dual till
Portugal (Lisbon)	Price cap	Hybrid
South Africa (ACSA)	Price cap	Single till
UK (London Gatwick)	Price monitoring (price cap)	Single till
UK (London Heathrow)	Price cap	Single till
US (all airports)	Cost based	Residual or compensatory till

Source: Compiled by the authors from various sources.

light-handed approach where there are long-term revenue sharing agreements – only when there is disagreement does the regulator fix charges on a cost based basis. Most other German airports are subject to cost-based dual-till regulation (Littlechild, 2012).

In the US, airport revenues are subject to a number of statutory requirements and policy statements, issued by the Federal Aviation Administration (FAA)/Department of Transportation, which are primarily concerned with ensuring that 'reasonable' fees are charged in relation to rate of return or cost based principles and that airport revenues are not used for non-airport purposes to cross-subsidise other municipal services. There are also conditions related to eligibility of the Airport Improvement Program (AIP) grants (see Chapter 7). There is no formal economic regulation and instead the legal system provides the means for enforcing and challenging the charging principles. Another unique US feature relates to legally binding contracts which are signed between the airlines and the airport operators. These 'Use and Lease Agreements' identify the fees and rentals to be paid, the method by which these are calculated and the conditions of use of the facilities (Faulhaber et al., 2010). These are a well-established feature of the airport–airline relationship in the US which influences major decisions and investment capabilities, unlike the other airline–airport contracts which are still evolving in other areas such as Europe.

Rather than having a single or dual till, US airports have a different cost allocation process with either a residual or compensatory approach (Richardson et al., 2014). The residual methodology guarantees that the airlines will pay the net costs of running the airport after taking account of the commercial and other non-airline sources of revenue. Therefore this is a somewhat extreme version of the single till where virtually all risks of running the airport are transferred to the airlines and other aeronautical users. By contrast, with the compensatory system the risks of running the airport are primarily left to the airport operator with the airlines just paying agreed charges based on recovery of the costs related to the facilities and services that they have used. This is more akin to dual-till principles. As with the single and dual tills, compromise US hybrid mechanisms have also been developed to suit increasingly diverse needs of airports and airlines.

The most popular approach for the airports in the table is a price cap. As already discussed, the first airports to be formally regulated with a price cap and single till in 1987 were in the UK with the BAA London airports (Heathrow, Gatwick and Stansted) and Manchester. This system was in operation until 2014 (although Manchester ceased to be regulated in 2009) when a new regime was introduced. This new framework provides for a more flexible licencing approach specific to each airport. As a result of a review of market power in 2013, only Heathrow and Gatwick have licences. Heathrow's licence involves a pricecap control whereas at Gatwick price monitoring has now been introduced for the first time (CAA, 2014b, 2014c; Cheong, 2015). This has partly been in response to Gatwick's

'Contracts and Commitments Initiative' which involved agreeing a series of commitments with its airlines on price, service conditions and investment. With a few key airlines (easyJet, Thomson, Monarch and Norwegian) it has integrated these commitments into bespoke formal contracts. Up until 2014, London Stansted was also subject to pricecap regulation but the regulator (the CAA) decided that the airport no longer possessed significant market power (CAA, 2014d). A key influencing factor was again long-term contracts agreed with the airport's three main airline customers, namely Ryanair, easyJet and Thomas Cook.

Other airports that have a pricecap regime include Dublin, and some in South Africa (Airports Company South Africa – ACSA, which operates the major airports of Johannesburg, Cape Town and Durban) and India (Delhi and Mumbai). Vienna Airport has a price cap based on a dual till which is applied directly to the charges with a tariff basket approach. This takes into account both inflation rates and traffic growth patterns with a sliding scale which protects revenues where there is slow growth, while requiring productivity gains to be made when traffic growth is high. Aéroports de Paris is also regulated by price, initially with a single till but this has now moved to a hybrid till. The three major privatised airport groups in Mexico (Grupo Aeroportuario del Pacífico – GAP; Central and Northern Airports Grupo Aeroportuario del Centro Norte – OMA; South Eastern Airports Group (Aeropuertos del Sureste de México) – ASUR) have price caps using the dual-till system. Price caps exist at other privatised South American airports in countries such as Brazil, Argentina (33 airports operated by Aeropuertos Argentina 2000) and Peru (Lima) although the type of till varies.

The major Australian airports (with the exception of Sydney) were previously regulated with a price cap based on a dual till when the airports were privatised in the late 1990s. However, there were a number of problems associated with this specific framework, such as weak investment incentives, profit volatility and cumbersome regulatory requirements. As a consequence this price cap regulation was replaced with a more light-handed price monitoring system (Arblaster, 2014). Subsequently several government reviews have considered the appropriateness of this newer system and have decided that it should stay (Productivity Commission, 2011). As a consequence many of the airports have entered into commercial contracts with their airlines. By contrast in New Zealand, where Auckland and Wellington were partially privatised in 1998, a light-handed approach for these airports (and the government-run Christchurch Airport) has always existed. Again periodic reviews of the situation have been undertaken but in spite of concern about the level of charges, particularly at Auckland Airport, this has remained the situation, although since 2011 these airports have been required to comply with more auditing, certification and verification standards and to disclose more information.

Copenhagen Airport is another airport which has had airport–airline agreements since the airport was privatised. Charge levels are decided on a price cap dual-till basis for a four-year period between the airport operator, Danish airports and IATA (representing the foreign airlines). This is approved by the regulator (the Danish Civil Aviation Administration) who only intervenes if an agreement is not reached. Brussels Airport also has five-year airline agreements, based on a hybrid till, which have to be ratified by the regulator.

In summary, there is considerable variation in the regulatory regimes used at airports and the most effective method and accompanying features remains a topic of hot debate from many different perspectives (e.g. see ACI, 2013; Biggar, 2012; Charlton, 2009; Forsyth et al., 2004; Niemeier, 2009; Oxera, 2013). ACI's core recommendations for economic regulation are (ACI, 2013, pp. 20–21):

- Seek competition rather than regulation
- The need for regulation should be determined on a case-by-case basis
- Intelligent regulation should seek consensus solutions
- Regulation should seek to be low cost and un-intrusive
- Regulation should be dynamic and flexible
- The regulator must be independent
- Regulation should recognize that airports are incented [sic] to expand traffic to maximise commercial revenues rather than to exploit any available market power
- If rigid price controls are applied, the format should be price cap.

In recent years, primarily because of the increasingly competitive environment, the arguments for a more light-handed approach, involving for example trigger regulation and airline contracts, have been given increased attention, particularly from an airport viewpoint (Copenhagen Economics, 2012; ACI Europe, 2014). Indeed Bush and Starkie (2014) have argued that more attention needs to be paid to the risks of economic regulation hampering the growth of competition and the development of commercial relationships between airports and airlines.

The airlines collectively are more cautious and have expressed different views (IATA, 2013, p. 29):

> Regulators need to be careful not to rely on airport competition delivering a good outcome for passengers and other airport users in terms of price and service quality. Effective and proportionate economic regulation is required in order to ensure a fair deal for consumers.

Engagement and commercial negotiations with airlines (usually accompanied by a reduction in regulatory intervention) have become a more significant part of many regulatory regimes and most commentators are in agreement that the traditional 'one-size-fits-all' system needs to make way for a more flexible case-by-case approach.

One of the problems in assessing the impact of different regulatory models is that only limited, and in some cases contradictory, evidence exists. These difficulties are compounded with the use of different analytical tools. A relatively early study by Oum et al. (2004) based on 60 global airports and an index number total factor productivity approach found better performance with a dual-till pricecap model as compared with single-till price cap or single-till rate of return. Adler and Liebert (2014) also found that dual-till pricecap regulation was the most efficient form of regulation in weak competitive conditions, but when airport competition was strong regulation was found to inhibit efficiency, when they undertook a Data Envelopment Analysis (DEA) with 51 European and Australian airports. Assaf and Gillen (2012) combined SFA and DEA approaches and using a sample of 73 global airports examined the combined effects of governance and regulation, which led them to conclude that fully private airports with price monitoring were the best performers. In terms of impacts on the actual level of charges, Bel and Fageda (2010) undertook a study of 100 European airports and found no significant variation with different regulation mechanisms, whereas Bilotkach et al. (2012) observed in a study of 61 European airports that lower charges were evident with both single-till regulation and light-handed regulation.

A final practical issue related to economic regulation relates to the measurement of market power. Whilst Chapter 9 introduced some of the key factors that determine the extent of airport competition, to measure the existence of market power requires an in-depth economic analysis of all the airport's relevant markets (e.g. passenger vs cargo, terminal vs transfer, aeronautical vs non-aeronautical), and the competitive constraints related to these. If these constraints are strong, the corresponding existence of market power will be weak. These constraints can be measured by assessing factors such as market share, switching costs, capacity and congestion, buyer power and the effects of pricing. Whilst these concepts are quite frequently discussed in theory there has been very limited developed application using empirical evidence – two notable exceptions being Bilotkach and Mueller (2012) who considered the market power of Amsterdam, and Polk and Bilotkach (2013) who assessed the market power of hub airports. Moreover there is no consensus of view concerning an appropriate detailed methodology, which led Maertens (2012) to develop a common approach which he used on a wide range of European airports. Even in countries where more detailed market power analysis has been undertaken, such as in the UK, parallel analyses undertaken in 2007–2008 by the CAA and Department for Transport resulted in the former concluding that Stansted did not possess significant market power and the latter reaching the opposite conclusion (CAA, 2007; Department for Transport, 2008).

10.7 The slot allocation process

10.7.1 Current practice

Whilst the previous chapter has argued that there are now greater opportunities for airport competition, and this chapter has discussed whether competitive constraints are such that the need for heavy economic regulation is diminishing, there still remain some significant obstacles that hamper an airport's ability to operate in a truly commercial and competitive manner. Undoubtedly one of the most challenging of these is the airport slot allocation process. Whereas in most commercial businesses the pricing mechanism (and any associated economic regulation) is used to balance supply and demand, this is not the case in the airport industry where there is an additional procedure to fulfil this role.

Slot allocation is a process that assigns airport arrival and departure time slots in advance to all airlines for planning and scheduling purposes. At some airports, when supply exceeds demand (so-called 'Level 1' airports) there is usually no problem with the airlines gaining their desired slots. At other 'Leve1 2' airports, demand may be approaching capacity at some peak periods but slot allocation can be resolved through voluntary schedule adjustments. However, for the remaining Level 3 airports, demand will outstrip supply and this is when formal procedures have to be used to allocate slots. Overall there are around 170 Level 3 airports worldwide and around an additional 120 Level 2 airports (IATA, 2015c). As can be seem from Figure 10.3, a

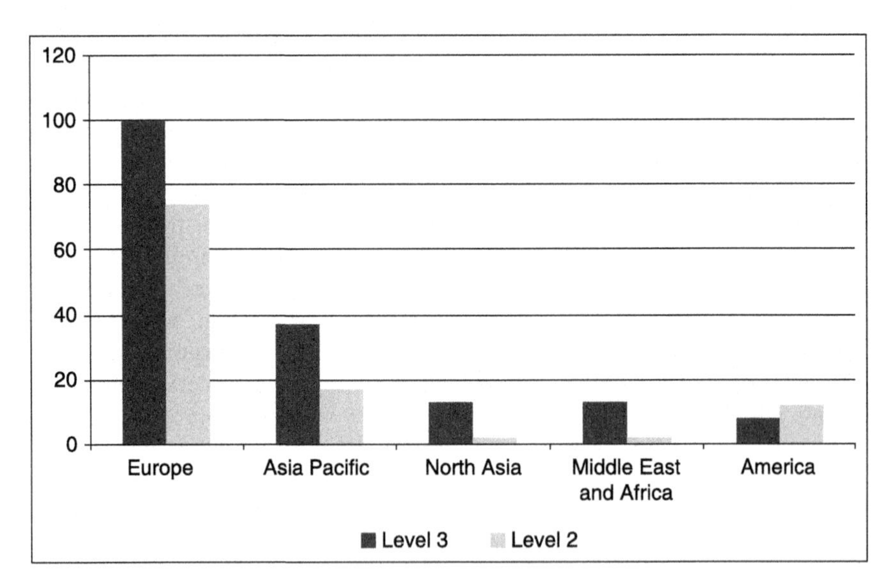

Figure 10.3 Number of Level 3 and 2 airports by world region 2015

Source: IATA (2015)

large majority of these airports are in Europe but this underestimates the capacity shortage situation in the US as most US airports (as discussed later) do not participate in the standard international allocation process.

The allocation of slots at Level 3 airports is dealt with at IATA Scheduling Committees and Slot Conferences which take place twice a year for the summer and winter seasons. This is an administrative process with a set of guidelines (Table 10.2). The most important principle is historic precedence (or so-called 'grandfather rights'), which means that if an airline operated a slot in the previous season it has the right to operate it again. This is as long as it meets the slot retention requirements of using the slots for 80 per cent of the time (the so-called 'use-it-or-lose-it' rule). Slots not allocated by historic precedence or new slots are placed into a slot pool with the aim of half of these going to new entrants. There are a number of additional criteria that can be considered when allocating these pool slots.

Although the IATA co-ordination process is voluntary, it has been adopted in most parts of the world. The notable exception is the US where it would be in conflict with US antitrust laws, which prevent predatory acts and anti-competitive behaviour. In most cases here the system is designed instead around a 'first come, first served' basis with airlines planning their schedules independently to take account of any expected delays. Within the EU, slot allocation comes under the 1993 regulation EU/95/93 (EC, 1993). This regulation and subsequent revisions have adopted the main principles of the IATA system such as grandfather rights and the use-it-or-lose-it rule, although the latter was temporarily suspended in three exceptional circumstances, after 9/11 in 2001, the outbreak of SARS and the Iraq war in 2003 and the economic crisis in 2009. Over the years, the EU rules have been amended several times to clarify the process, ensure that the rules are

Table 10.2 Key features of the IATA slot allocation guidelines

Primary criteria	• First priority is historic precedence ('grandfather rights') • Remaining slots go into the slot pool • 50% of pool slots go to new entrants • Priority in the pool is given to year round operations and then the 'additional criteria' apply
Additional criteria	• Effective period of operation • Type of service and market • Competition • Curfews • Requirements of the travelling public and other users • Frequency of operation • Local guidelines
Slot retention rule ('Use-it or-lose-it')	The slot must be used for 80% of the season

Source: IATA (2015c).

better applied and enforced, and that the slot co-ordinators are fully impartial and financially independent.

Whilst the IATA systems (and EU regulation) have provided a relatively stable environment for airlines and other stakeholders, there has been growing concern as to whether it is the best way forward to cope with an increasingly congested situation at many airports. Critics have argued that it does not make the best use of the scarce capacity, nor does it encourage competition and it is burdensome to administer. It is also open to abuse when airlines may 'babysit' slots to ensure that they retain them and does not necessarily allocate slots to the airlines that value them the most.

10.7.2 Alternative slot allocation mechanisms

Two alternative mechanisms have generally been discussed (Czerny et al., 2008). The first would be an extension of the current administrative process but with different priority rules. For example the grandfather rights principle could be abandoned and the system could favour certain types of operation. This could be long-haul flights, which normally have less flexibility in scheduling, or new entrants. Lower priority could be given to flights which are already served by frequent services, or where there are surface transport alternatives. Alternatively slots could be allocated to achieve some economic, social or environmental objective, for instance favouring larger aircraft or those that have a smaller emissions or noise impact.

However, even such a revised process would still continue to be administratively burdensome and would not allocate the slots to those who value them the most. To achieve this latter aim, a market-based mechanism is needed, such as new pricing or other economic techniques to balance demand with the available supply. The current level of airport charges, and the existence of peak/off-peak differentials at a few airports, are not sufficient to be the market-clearing prices needed to achieve this rationing of demand. The general view is that charges would have to be raised significantly to have a major effect on the airlines' behaviour. An alternative mechanism for this primary allocation of slots would be to have a slot auction rather than raising charges. A major issue with both of these options is who (for example the airport operator or government) should benefit from the money generated. Also, whilst these options can theoretically provide for much better use of the runway, they may be detrimental to airline competition as they will tend to favour the financially strongest and largest airlines, and may do little to achieve any other wider objectives.

Within this market mechanism, in addition to this primary or initial allocation of slots, there could be an opportunity for further secondary allocation, when the airlines can trade slots amongst themselves. Whilst slot exchanges are allowed under current IATA guidelines and the EU regulation, slot trading is not specifically allowed or banned although the EC announced in a 2008 Communication that it would not pursue infringement proceedings against countries that allowed secondary trading in a transparent way (EC, 2008). Practice within Europe varies, with extensive secondary trading taking place at Heathrow and Gatwick. There is also evidence of some 'fake' exchanges, whereby a valueless slot is exchanged with money for a more attractive one, at other airports such as Düsseldorf, Frankfurt and Vienna. In 2010 it was estimated that at Heathrow Airport, over 400 weekly slots were being traded and that the value of a slot pair was £30–40 million for pre-0900 arrivals and £10 million for 0900–1300 arrivals (Steer Davies Gleave, 2011). The EC has proposed that it would like to allow airlines to trade slots with each other at airports anywhere in the EU in a transparent way, but this has yet to be incorporated into the regulation.

The only other significant experience of market-based slot mechanisms exists with the US. Whilst in general the airlines are not allowed to discuss schedule co-ordination, way back in 1969 exceptions were granted to the very congested so-called 'high density' airports of New York, Chicago O'Hare and Washington Reagan National and in 1985 permission was given to allow slot trading. However, there were very few outright sales of slots or new entrants slots, as well as a reduction in the level of regional services, and as a result the established airlines increased their dominance (Starkie, 1998). In 2002 the highdensity slot allocation rules were withdrawn at Chicago O'Hare (where there had been the addition of new capacity) and in 2007 the New York airports followed suit. However, because of congestion and delays, temporary slot control had to be introduced at these airports with permission to undertake secondary trading on a temporary basis through leasing, an 80 per cent use-it-or-lose-it rule and a cap on the number of slots available. It was planned that these temporary measures would be replaced in 2009 by the auctioning of 10 per cent of slots but this was abandoned due to fierce opposition from the airlines and other stakeholders. Instead the FAA is proposing a more permanent solution (the Slot Management and Transparency Rule) which would establish a secondary market for US and foreign airlines whilst still maintaining slot control (FAA, 2015c).

10.8 Summary

This chapter introduced the concept of economic regulation by exploring in general terms why this is often deemed necessary. In an airport context most regulatory control is at a national level, within the broad framework of ICAO's long-established charging principles, although there is also the Charges Directive which is applied to EU airports. The chapter has discussed why incentive or price cap regulation is much more popular than traditional rate of return or cost-based methods, and has presented the arguments for a more light-handed approach which already exists at some airports. Once the type of regulation is established there are many details that need to be considered such as the type of regulatory till, the definition of 'price' and the extent of pre-financing that should be allowed.

The regulation of slots or slot allocation has also been considered. Weaknesses with the current situation have been identified and alternative approaches explored. Options include the extension of the current administration system with different allocation priorities, or a market-based mechanism. There are some major advantages with market-based approaches but there are also significant obstacles to their implementation – perhaps with the exception of secondary slot trading which is becoming more acceptable in Europe. Arguments related to the best way forward as regards slot allocation, as well as economic regulation, are likely to continue well into the future.

Overall this chapter has complemented Chapter 8 on privatisation and Chapter 9 on competition by providing a detailed consideration of these important aspects of the airport operating environment. This is essential in order to fully appreciate the financial characteristics of airports, and how financial performance can be measured, which is discussed in the earlier chapters.

References

Abrate, G. and Erbetta, F. (2010), Efficiency and patterns of service mix in airport companies: An input distance function approach, *Transportation Research Part E*, 46(5), 693–708.

ACI (2006), *Airport Benchmarking to Maximize Efficiency*, Geneva: ACI.

ACI (2012), *Guide to Airport Performance Measures*, Montreal: ACI.

ACI (2013), *ACI Guide to Airport Economic Regulation*, Montreal: ACI.

ACI (2015a), *ACI releases 2014 world airport traffic report*, press release, 31 August.

ACI (2015b), *Airport Economics Survey 2014*, Montreal: ACI.

ACI Europe (2010), *The Ownership of Europe's Airports*, Brussels: ACI Europe.

ACI Europe (2011), *ACI Europe Position on Requirements for a Performing Ground Handling Market*, Brussels: ACI Europe.

ACI Europe (2013), *ACI Position on Aviation Security Technology Roadmap*, Brussels: ACI Europe.

ACI Europe (2014), *Competition in the European Aviation Sector*, Brussels: ACI Europe.

ACI Europe (2015a), *Airport Charges Survey 2014*, Brussels: ACI Europe.

ACI Europe (2015b), *ACI Europe Economics Report 2014*, Brussels: ACI Europe.

ACI Europe (2015c), *Performance Management at European Airports*, Brussels: ACI Europe.

ACI Europe (2015d), *Airport Industry Connectivity Report*, Brussels: ACI Europe.

ACI-North America (NA) (2014), *2014 ACI-NA Concessions Benchmarking Survey Results*, Washington, DC: ACI-NA.

Adler, N. and Liebert, V. (2014), Joint impact of competition, ownership form and economic regulation on airport performance and pricing, *Transportation Research Part A*, 64, 92–109.

Adler, A., Oum, T. and Yu, C. (2009), A response to 'Understanding the complexities and challenges of airport performance benchmarking', *Journal of Airport Management*, 3(2), 159–163.

AENA (2015), *Información Analítica de Cuenta de Resultados Ejercicio 2014 por Aeropuertos de Aena S.A. (Individual, según PGC)*, Madrid: AENA.

Aéroports de Paris (2015), *Annual Report and Financial Statements, year to end December 2014,* Paris: AdP.

Airline Business (2008), Airports global groupings, *Airline Business*, December, 52–54.

Airline Business (2015), Airport group financials, *Airline Business*, November, 40–41.

Airline Leader (2015), Low-cost airports and terminals are changing shape, *Airline Leader*, 26, 22–28.

Airport Research Center (2009), *Study on the Impact of Directive 96/67/EC on Ground Handling Services 1996–2007*, Aachen: Airport Research Center.

Airports Commission (2014), *The Inner Thames estuary airport proposal has not been shortlisted,* press release, 2 September.

Airport World (2012), Outlook 2013, *Airports World*, October–November, 52–53.

Arblaster, M. (2014), The design of light-handed regulation of airports: Lessons from experience in Australia and New Zealand, *Journal of Air Transport Management*, 38, 27–35.

Ashford, N. and Moore, C. (1999), *Airport Finance*, 2nd edition, Loughborough: The Loughborough Airport Consultancy.

Assaf, A. and Gillen, D. (2012), Measuring the joint impact of governance form and economic regulation on airport efficiency, *European Journal of Operational Research*, 220(1), 187–198.

ATAG (2014), *Aviation Benefits beyond Borders*, Geneva: ATAG.

ATRS (2015), *Global Airport Benchmarking Report*, Vancouver: ATRS.

Aviation Strategy (2006), Air Deccan: IPO struggle reflects Indian overcapacity worries, *Aviation Strategy*, June, 4–7.

Aviation Strategy (2015a), Airport valuations update, *Aviation Strategy*, March, 17–18.

Aviation Strategy (2015b), Airport valuations, *Aviation Strategy*, April, 11.

Aviation Strategy (2015c), Airport pipeline: A round-the-world tour, *Aviation Strategy*, December, 12–13.

Bel, G. and Fageda, X. (2010), Privatization, regulation, and airport pricing: An empirical analysis for Europe, *Journal of Regulatory Economics*, 37(2), 142–161.

Biggar, D. (2012), Why regulate airports? A re-examination of the rationale for airport regulation, *Journal of Transport Economics and Policy*, 46(3), 367–380.

Bilotkach, V., Clougherty, J., Mueller, J. and Zhang, A. (2012), Regulation, privatization and airport charges: Panel data evidence from European airports, *Economics of Transportation,* 42(1), 73–94.

Bilotkach, V. and Mueller, J. (2012), Supply side substitutability and potential market power of airports: Case of Amsterdam Schiphol, *Utilities Policy*, 23, 5–12.

Boeing (2015), *Current Market Outlook 2015–2034*, Seattle, WA: Boeing.

Bonnefoy, P., de Neufville, R. and Hansman, J. (2008), Evolution and development of multi-airport systems: A worldwide perspective, *Journal of Transport Engineering*, 136(11), 1021–1029.

Brutsch, U. (2013), International airport management: The government perspective, *Journal of Airport Management,* 8(2), 100–104.

Bush, H. and Starkie, D. (2014), Competitive drivers towards improved airport/airline relationships, *Journal of Air Transport Management*, 41, 45–49.

CAA (2007), *De-designation of Manchester and Stansted Airports for Price Control Regulation,* London: CAA.

CAA (2013), *Estimating the Cost of Capital: A Technical Appendix to the CAA's Final Proposal for Economic Regulation of Heathrow and Gatwick after April 2014*, CAP 1115, London: CAA.

CAA (2014a), *Estimating the Cost of Capital: A Technical Appendix for the Economic Regulation of Heathrow and Gatwick from 2014,* CAP 1140, London: CAA.

CAA (2014b), *Economic Regulation at Heathrow from April 2014: Notice of the Proposed Licence,* CAP 1138, London: CAA.

CAA (2014c), *Economic Regulation at Gatwick from April 2014: Notice of the Proposed Licence,* CAP 1139, London: CAA.

CAA (2014d), *Notice of Determination under Section 8 of the Civil Aviation Act 2012 – Stansted Airport,* CAP 1135, London: CAA.

CAA (2015), *Economic Regulation at New Runway Capacity*, CAP 1279, London: CAA.

CAPA (2015a), *The world's biggest airport construction projects 2015; total value over USD500 billion, Part 1,* 20 January, available from http://centreforaviation.com/analysis/the-worlds-biggest-airport-construction-projects-2015-total-value-over-usd500-billion-part-1-205200, accessed 1 November 2015.

CAPA (2015b), *Airport construction mid-year review 2015: USD441 billion in airport investment, 2,520 projects,* 21 July, available from http://centreforaviation.com/analysis/airport-construction-mid-year-review-2015-usd441-billion-in-airport-investment-2520-projects-235518, accessed 1 November 2015.

CAPA (2015c), *CAPA airport finance and privatisation review 2014/15; emerging markets attract investor interest,* 23 March, available from http://centreforaviation.com/analysis/capa-airport-finance-and-privatisation-review-201415-emerging-markets-attract-investor-interest-214953, accessed 2 December 2015.

CAPA (2015d), *The US airport system is lagging badly, but there is still little appetite for private investment,* 15 April, available from http://centreforaviation.com/analysis/the-us-airport-system-is-lagging-badly-but-there-is-still-little-appetite-for-private-investment-219308, accessed 2 December 2015.

CAPA (2015e), *Global airport finance and privatisation: CAPA review 2014. The big funds dominate transactions*, 5 June, available from http://centreforaviation.com/analysis/global-airport-finance-and-privatisation-capa-review-2014-the-big-funds-dominate-transactions-202694, accessed 2 December 2015.

Castillo-Manzano, J. (2010), Determinants of commercial revenues at airports: Lessons learned from Spanish regional airports, *Tourism Management*, 31(6), 788–796.

Changi Airport Group (2015), *Reductions and rebates of aeronautical fees at Changi Airport*, press release, 24 April.

Charlton, A. (2009), Airport regulation: Does a mature industry have mature regulation? *Journal of Air Transport Management*, 15(3), 116–120.

Cheong, K. (2015), Aux armes, citoyens! A revolution in airport economic regulation: A regulator's perspective, *Journal of Airport Management*, 9(4), 338–346.

Competition Commission (2009), *BAA Airports Market Investigation*, London: Competition Commission.

Condie, S. (2016), Airport ownership trends in Europe, *Journal of Airport Management*, 10(1), 14–23.

Copenhagen Airport (2015), *Annual Report 2014*, Copenhagen: Copenhagen Airport.

Copenhagen Economics (2012), *Airport Competition in Europe*, Copenhagen: Copenhagen Economics.

Czerny, A., Forsyth, P., Gillen, D. and Neimeier, H.-M. (2008), *Airport Slots: International Experiences and Options for Reform*, Farnham: Ashgate.

De Wit, J. G. (2013), Unlevel playing field? Ah yes, you mean protectionism, *Journal of Air Transport Management*, 41, 22–29.

Department for Transport (2008), *Decision on the Regulatory Status of Stansted Airport*, London: Department for Transport.

Department for Transport (2015), *New regional air routes offer fast journeys across UK and Europe*, press release, 2 December.

Department of Transport (2003), *Dublin Airport – Review of Expressions of Interest for an Independent Terminal – Panel Report to Minister for Transport*, Dublin: Department of Transport.

Doganis, R. (2010), *Flying Off Course: Airline Economics and Marketing*, 4th edition, London: Routledge.
Doganis, R. S. and Thompson, G. F. (1973), *The Economics of British airports*, Transport Studies Group Research Report 1, London: University of Westminster (formerly Polytechnic of Central London).
EC (1993), *Regulation (EEC) No 95/93 of European Parliament and of the Council of 18 January 1993 on Common Rules for the Allocation of Slots at Community Airports*, Official Journal L14, 22 January, Brussels: EC.
EC (1996), *Council Directive 96/67/EC of 15 October 1996 on Access to the Groundhandling Market at Community Airports*, Official Journal L272, 25 October.
EC (2004), *Commission's Decision of 12 February 2004 Concerning Advantages Granted by the Walloon Region and Brussels South Charleroi Airport to the Airline Ryanair in Connection with its Establishment at Charleroi*, Official Journal L137, 30 April.
EC (2005), *Community Guidelines on Financing of Airports and Start-Up Aid to Airlines Departing from Regional Airports*, Official Journal C312, 9 December.
EC (2008), *Communication from the Commission to the European Parliament, the Council, the European Economic and Social Committee and the Committee of the Regions on the Application of Regulation (EEC) No 95/93 on Common Rules for the Allocation of Slots at Community Airports, as Amended (COM(2008) 227 Final)*, Brussels: EC.
EC (2009), *Directive 2009/12/EC of the European Parliament and of the Council of 11 March 2009 on Airport Charges,* Official Journal L070, 14 March, Brussels: EC.
EC (2011), *State aid: Commission welcomes Court judgment in the Leipzig-Halle airport case,* press release, 23 March.
EC (2014a), *Communication from the Commission: Guidelines on State Aid to Airports and Airlines,* Official Journal C99, 4 April.
EC (2014b), *New State Aid Rules for a Competitive Aviation Industry*, Competition Policy Brief, Issue 2, Brussels: EC.
EC (2014c), *State aid: Commission adopts package of decisions regarding aid to airports and airlines in France and Germany; asks France to recover incompatible aid granted to airlines*, press release, 23 July.
EC (2014d), *Commission adopts package of decisions regarding support to airports and airlines in Belgium, Germany, Italy and Sweden*, press release, 1 October.
EIB (2015), Projects, available from http://www.eib.org/projects/, accessed 2 June 2015.
Enrico, S., Boudreau, B., Reimer, D. and Van Beek, S. (2012), *Considering and Evaluating Airport Privatisation,* ACRP Report 66, Washington, DC: Transportation Research Board.
Eurocontrol (2013), *Challenges of Growth 2013*, Brussels: Eurocontrol.
FAA (2010), *Air Carrier Incentive Program Guidebook: A Reference for Airport Sponsors*, Washington, DC: FAA.
FAA. (2013), *Fact sheet – What is the Airport Privatisation Pilot Program?*, available from http://www.faa.gov/news/fact_sheets/news_story.cfm?newsId=14174, accessed 15 December 2015.
FAA (2015a), *Passenger Facility Charge (PFC) Program*, available from http://www.faa.gov/airports/pfc/, accessed 1 October 2015.
FAA (2015b), *Airport Improvement Program (AIP)*, available from http://www.faa.gov/airports/aip/, accessed 1 October 2015.
FAA (2015c), *Fact sheet – Notice of proposed rulemaking: Slot management and transparency for LaGuardia Airport (LGA), John F. Kennedy International Airport (JFK), and Newark*

Liberty International Airport (EWR), available from https://www.faa.gov/news/fact_sheets/news_story.cfm?newsId=18054, accessed 6 June 2015.

Faulhaber, J., Schulthess, J., Eastmond, A., Lewis, S. and Block, R. (2010), *Airport/Airline Agreements—Practices and Characteristics*, ACRP Report 36, Washington, DC: Transportation Research Board.

Feldman, D. (2008), Making airport privatisation consortia work, *Journal of Airport Management*, 3(1), 48–53.

Feldman, D. (2009), Thinking outside the box, *Airport World*, 15 November.

Forsyth, P., Gillen, D., Knorr, A., Mayer, O., Niemeier, H. and Starkie, D. (eds) (2004), *The Economic Regulation of Airports*, Farnham: Ashgate.

Forsyth, P., Gillen, D., Mueller, J. and Niemeier, H.-M. (eds) (2010), *Airport Competition*, Farnham: Ashgate.

Francis, G., Fidato, A. and Humphreys, I. (2003). Airport–airline interaction: The impact of low-cost carriers on two European airports, *Journal of Air Transport Management*, 9(4), 267–273.

Fraport (2015), *Visual fact book full year 2014*, available from http://www.fraport.de/content/fraport/de/misc/binaer/investor-relations/visual_fact_book/visual-fact-book-2014/jcr:content.file/fraport-visual-fact-book-april2015.pdf, accessed 26 June 2015.

Freathy, F. and O'Connell, F. (1998), *European Airport Retailing*, Basingstoke: Macmillan.

GAO (2015), *Airport Finance: Information on Funding Sources and Planned Capital Development*, GAO-15-306, Washington, DC: GAO.

Gillen, D. and Lall, A. (2004), Competitive advantage of low-cost carriers: Some implications for airports, *Journal of Air Transport Management*, 10(1), 41–50.

Gillen, D. (2011), The evolution of airport ownership and governance, *Journal of Air Transport Management*, 17(1), 3–13.

Graham, A. (2005), Airport benchmarking: A review of the current situation, *Benchmarking: An International Journal*, 12(2), 99–111.

Graham, A. (2009), How important are commercial revenues to today's airports? *Journal of Air Transport Management*, 15(3), 106–111.

Graham, A. (2011), The objectives and outcomes of airport privatisation, *Research in Transportation Business and Management*, 1(1), 3–14.

Graham, A. (2013), Understanding the low cost carrier and airport relationship: A critical analysis of the salient issues, *Tourism Management*, 36, 66–76.

Graham, A. (2014), *Managing Airports: An International Perspective*, 4th edition, London: Routledge.

Graham, A., Saito, S. and Nomura, M. (2014), Airport management in Japan: Any lessons learnt from the UK?, *Journal of Airport Management*, 8(3), 244–263.

Halpern, N. and Graham, A. (2013), *Airport Marketing*, London: Routledge.

Hazel, R., Blais, J., Browne, T. and Benzon, D. (2011), *Resource Guide to Airport Performance Indicators*, ACRP Report 19A, Washington, DC: Transportation Research Board.

Heathrow Airport Holdings (2013), *Annual Report and Financial Statements to End December 2012*, London: HAH.

Heathrow Airport Holdings (2015), *Annual Report and Financial Statements for the Year Ended 31 December 2014*, London: HAH.

Humphreys, B. (2015), Davies Commission exposes pre-funding dilemma, *Aviation Strategy*, July/August, 4–9. IATA (2013), *Airport Competition*, IATA Economics Briefing No. 11, Geneva: IATA.

IATA (2015a), *IATA air passenger forecast shores dip in long term demand*, press release, 26 November.

IATA (2015b), *Economic Performance of the Industry End Year 2015*, Geneva: IATA.

IATA (2015c), *Worldwide Slot Guidelines*, 6th edition, Geneva: IATA.

ICAO (2012a), *ICAO's Policies on Charges for Airports and Air Navigation Services*, Doc. 9082, 9th edition, Montreal: ICAO.

ICAO (2012b), *Manual on Privatisation in the Provision of Airports and Air Navigation Services,* Montreal: ICAO.

ICAO (2013), *Airport Economics Manual*, Doc. 9562, 3rd edition, Montreal: ICAO.

ITF (2015), *Liberalisation of Air Transport, Summary: Policy Insights and Recommendations*, Paris: ITF.

Jones, O., Budd, L. and Pitfield, D. (2013), Aeronautical charging policy incentive schemes for airlines at European airports, *Journal of Air Transport Management*, 33, 43–59.

Jorge-Calderon, D. (2013), Airport valuation: Using passenger generalised cost to measure competitive advantage and pricing power, *Journal of Airport Management*, 7(3), 255–264.

Jorge-Calderon, D. (2014), *Aviation Investment*, Farnham: Ashgate.

Kalakou, S. and Macario, R. (2013), An innovative framework for the study and structure of airport business models, *Case Studies on Transport Policy*, 1(1–2), 2–17.

Kamp, V., Niemeier, H.-M. and Mueller, J. (2007), What can be learned from benchmarking studies? Examining the apparent poor performance of German airports, *Journal of Airport Management*, 1(3), 294–308.

Kasarda, J. (2013), Airport cities: The evolution, *Airport World*, 21 April.

Kim, H.-B. and Shin, J.-H. (2001), A contextual investigation of the operation and management of airport concessions, *Tourism Management*, 22(2), 149–155.

Lei, Z. and Papatheodorou, A. (2010), Measuring the effect of low-cost carriers on regional airports' commercial revenue, *Research in Transportation Economics*, 26(1), 37–43.

LeighFisher (2011), *Resource Manual for Airport In-Terminal Concessions*, ACRP Report 54, Washington, DC: Transportation Research Board.

LeighFisher (2012), Brazil: The waking giant seeks a private pilot, in *Finding the Opportunity in Change*, available from https://www.leighfisher.com/sites/default/files/free_files/compendium_opportunity-in-change-march-2012.pdf, accessed 3 June 2016.

LeighFisher (2014), *Airport Performance Indicators 2014*, London: LeighFisher.

Levine, M. (1969), Landing fees and the airport congestion problem, *Journal of Law and Economics*, 12(1), 79–108.

Liebert, V. and Niemeier, H.-M. (2013), A survey of empirical research on the productivity and efficiency measurement of airports, *Journal of Transport Economics and Policy*, 47(2), 157–189.

Lin, Z., Choo, Y. Y. and Oum, T. H. (2013), Efficiency benchmarking of North American airports: Comparative results of productivity index, data envelopment analysis and stochastic frontier analysis, *Journal of the Transportation Research Forum*, 52(1), 47–68.

Littlechild, S. C. (2012), German airport regulation: Framework agreements, civil law and the EU Directive, *Journal of Air Transport Management*, 21, 63–75.

Lobbenberg, A. (2010), *Fraport: would be advancing but for ash*, Equity Note, Royal Bank of Scotland, 19 May.

Lobbenberg, A. (2014a), *Airports: Let me play among the stars*, HSBC Global Research, 19 May.

Lobbenberg, A. (2014b), *Fraport: Momentum ahead but we do not see value*, Equity Note, HSBC, 12 November.

Lobbenberg, A. (2015a), *Company Report: AENA*, HSBC Global Research, 22 April.

Lobbenberg, A. (2015b), *Fraport: Company Report*, HSBC Global Research, 6 November.

Maertens, S. (2012), Estimating the market power of airports in their catchment areas – a Europe-wide approach, *Journal of Transport Geography*, 22, 10–18.

Malina, R., Albers, S. and Kroll, N. (2012), Airport incentive programmes: A European perspective, *Transport Reviews*, 32(4), 435–453.

Martín, J. and Voltes-Dorta, A. (2011), Scale economies in marginal costs in Spanish airports, *Transportation Research E*, 47(2), 238–248.

McLay, P. and Reynolds-Feighan, A. (2006), Competition between airport terminals: The issues facing Dublin airport, *Transportation Research Part A*, 40(2), 181–203.

Merkert, R., Odeck, J., Brathen, S. and Pagliari, R. (2012), A review of different benchmarking methods in the context of regional airports, *Transport Reviews*, 32(3), 379–395.

Miyoshi, C. (2015), Airport privatisation in Japan: Unleashing air transport liberalisation, *Journal of Airport Management*, 9(3), 210–222.

Mohammed, A. and Roisman, R. (2014), *2013 Washington-Baltimore Regional Air Passenger Survey*, Washington, DC: Metropolitan Washington Council of Governments.

Moodie International and the SAP Group (2014), *The Airport Commercial Revenues Study 2014*, Brentford: Moodie International and the SAP Group.

Moody's (2007), *Financial Metrics Key Ratios by Rating and Industry for Global Non-Financial Corporations*, New York: Moody's.

Morrell, P. (2007), *Airline Finance*, 3rd edition, Farnham: Ashgate.

Morrell, P. (2010), Airport competition and network access: A European analysis, in Forsyth, P., Gillen, D., Mueller, J. and Niemeier, H.-M. (eds), *Airport Competition*, Farnham: Ashgate.

Morrell, P. and Turner, S. (2003), An evaluation of airline beta values and their application in calculating the cost of equity capital, *Journal of Air Transport Management*, 9(4), 201–209.

Morrison, S. and Winston, C. (2007), Another look at airport congestion pricing, *American Economic Review*, 97(5), 1970–1977.

Morrison, W. (2009), Understanding the complexities and challenges of airport performance benchmarking, *Journal of Airport Management*, 3(2), 145–158.

Mott MacDonald (2015), *Annual Analyses of the EU Air Transport Market 2013*, Brussels: EC.

Niemeier, H.-M. (2009), Regulation of large airports: Status quo and options for reform, *International Transport Forum – Airport Regulation Investment and Development of Aviation*, Paris: ITF.

Njoya, E. and Niemeier, H.-M. (2011), Do dedicated low cost passenger terminals create competitive advantages for airports? *Research in Transportation Business and Management*, 1(1), 55–61.

Oum, T., Adler, N. and Yu, C. (2006), Privatisation, corporatisation, ownership forms and their effects on the performance of the world's major airports, *Journal of Air Transport Management*, 12(3), 109–121.

Oum, T., Yan, J. and Yu, C. (2008), Ownership forms matter for airport efficiency: A stochastic frontier investigation of worldwide airports, *Journal of Urban Economics*, 64(2), 422–435.

Oum, T., Yu, C. and Fu, X. (2003), A comparative analysis of productivity performance of the world's major airports: Summary report of the ATRS global airport benchmarking research report – 2002, *Journal of Air Transport Management*, 9(5), 285–297.

Oum, T. and Yu, C. (2004), Measuring airports' operating efficiency: A summary of the 2003 ATRS global airport benchmarking report, *Transportation Research Part E*, 40(6), 515–532.

Oum, T., Zhang, A. and Zhang, Y. (2004), Alternative forms of economic regulation and their efficiency implications for airports, *Journal of Transport Economics and Policy*, 38(2), 217–246.

Oxera (2010), *Valuation of airport assets*, Expert Report prepared at the request of the New Zealand Airports Association, July 12.

Oxera (2013), *Regulatory Regimes at Airports: An International Comparison*, Gatwick: Gatwick Airport.

Parker, D. (2011), Valuation of airports for financial reporting: Fair value? *Journal of Property Investment and Finance*, 29(6), 677–692.

Pels, E., Nijkamp, P. and Rietveld, P. (2003), Inefficiencies and scale economies of European airport operations, *Transportation Research Part E*, 39(5), 341–361.

Peters, T. J. and Waterman, R. H. Jr. (1982), *In Search of Excellence*, London: Harper & Row.

Polk, A. and Bilotkach, V. (2013), The assessment of market power of hub airports, *Transport Policy*, 29, 29–37.

Poole, R. (2015), *Annual Privatization Report 2015: Air Transportation*, Los Angeles, CA: Reason Foundation.

Productivity Commission (2011), *Economic Regulation of Airport Services*, No. 57, Canberra: Productivity Commission.

Redondi, R., Malighetti, P. and Paleri, P. (2012), De-hubbing of airports and their recovery patterns, *Journal of Air Transport Management*, 18(1), 1–4.

Reinhold, A., Niemeier, H.-M., Kamp, V. and Mueller, J. (2010), An evaluation of yardstick regulation for European airports, *Journal of Air Transport Management*, 16(2), 74–80.

Richardson, C., Budd, L. and Pitfield, D. (2014), The impact of airline lease agreements on the financial performance of US hub airports, *Journal of Air Transport Management*, 40, 1–15.

Rikhy, H., Roberts, J. and Cheung, S. (2014), Global airport privatisation: Trends, recent developments and challenges ahead, *Journal of Airport Management*, 8(4), 300–304.

Salazar de la Cruz, F. (1999), A DEA approach to the airport production function, *International Journal of Transport Economics*, 26(2), 255–270.

Sevcik, T. (2014), The end of retail, the future of retail, *Journal of Airport Management*, 8(4), 308–311.

Sharp, R. (2012), In praise of hybrids, *Journal of Airport Management*, 7(1), 36–44.

SH&E (2006), *Capital Needs and Regulatory Oversight Arrangement: A Survey of European Airports*, London: SH&E.

SITA (2015), *Airport IT Trends Survey 2015*, Geneva: SITA/ACI.

Starkie, D. (1998), Allocating airport slots: A role for the market? *Journal of Air Transport Management*, 4(2), 111–116.

Starkie, D. (2001), Reforming UK airport regulation, *Journal of Transport Economics and Policy*, 35(1), 119–135.

Starkie, D. (2006), Investment incentives and airport regulation, *Utilities Policy*, 14(4), 262–265.

Starkie, D. (2008a), *The Airport Industry in a Competitive Environment: A United Kingdom Perspective*, Discussion paper no. 2008–15, Paris: ITF.

Starkie, D. (2008b), A critique of the single-till, in Starkie, D., *Aviation Markets*, Aldershot: Ashgate.

Starkie, D. (2012), European airports and airlines: Evolving relationships and the regulatory implications, *Journal of Air Transport Management*, 21, 40–49.

Steer Davies Gleave (2010), *Possible Revision of Directive 96/67/EC on Access to the Ground Handling Market at Community Airports*, London: SDG.

Steer Davies Gleave (2011), *Impact Assessment of Revisions to Regulation 95/93*, London: SDG.

Steer Davies Gleave (2012), *Review of Operating Expenditure and Investment*, London: SDG.

Steer Davies Gleave (2013), *Evaluation of Directive 2009/12/EC on Airport Charges*, London: SDG.

The Economist (2015), Flying high: Why buying airports has taken off, *The Economist*, 6 June, 64.

Thomas, J., Lobbenberg, A., Winarso, J. and Khoja, M. (2013), *After the storm: Back to port*, HSBC Global Research, 3 April.

Tovar, B. and Martin-Cejas, R. (2009), Are outsourcing and non-aeronautical revenues important drivers in the efficiency of Spanish airports? *Journal of Air Transport Management*, 15(5), 217–220.

Tretheway, M. and Markhvida, K. (2013), *Airports in the Aviation Value Chain*, Discussion paper no. 2013–15, Paris: ITF.

Vasigh, B., Erfani, G. and Sherman, B. (2014), Airport performance and ownership structure: Evidence from the United Kingdom, United States, and Latin America, *Journal of Aviation Technology and Engineering*, 4(1), 40–49.

Vasigh, B. and Gorjidooz, J. (2006), Productivity analysis of public and private airports: A causal investigation, *Journal of Air Transportation*, 11(3), 144–163.

Vogel, H.-A. (2006), Impact of privatisation on the financial and economic performance of European airports, *The Aeronautical Journal*, 110(1106), 197–213.

Vogel, H.-A. and Graham, A. (2010), Driver based approach to airport valuation, *Journal of Air Transport Studies*, 1(1), 20–47.

Vogel, H.-A. and Graham, A. (2013), Devising airport groupings for financial benchmarking, *Journal of Air Transport Management*, 30, 32–38.

World Bank (2015), *Private participation in infrastructure database*, available from http://ppi.worldbank.org/snapshots/sector/airports, accessed 2 December 2015.

Wright, S., Mason, R. and Miles, D. (2003). *A Study into Certain Aspects of the Cost of Capital for Certain Regulated Industries in the UK*, a report for UK economic regulators and the UK Office of Fair Trading, February 13.

Index

Please note that page numbers relating to Figures will be in italics followed by the letter 'f', while numbers indicating Tables will be in the same format but contain the letter 't'. Any references to Notes will contain the letter 'n', followed by the relevant Note number.

Printed in the United States
by Baker & Taylor Publisher Services